"Every preacher wants the sermon to not only say something but also do something. This book will tell you how! Two consummate performers of the Word themselves, Clayton Schmit and Jana Childers have assembled the leading figures in the field of performance studies—ranging from theology to dramaturgy to musicology—and have produced a book like no other. It will bless preachers and those who listen to preaching for a long time to come."

—**Richard Lischer**, James T. and Alice Mead Cleland
Professor of Preaching, Duke Divinity School

"Mention the words 'preaching' and 'performance' in the same sentence and some in the church get nervous. This helpful volume proves that such nervousness is unwarranted. Yes, preaching must be sincere, free of forced theatrics or any whiff of the pastor's merely 'putting on a show.' But these essays remind us that pastors must bring the Word to life by paying attention to their delivery of that Word as the Holy Spirit uses vocal chords, cadences, rhythms, and the preacher's entire body to help the Word of God become flesh and blood Sunday after Sunday. Preachers take note: God has called the entirety of your being into the service of proclaiming the Word, and this fine book will challenge you to remember that each and every Sunday!"

—**Scott Hoezee**, director, Center for Excellence in Preaching,
Calvin Theological Seminary

engaging
worship

series editors
Todd E. Johnson
Clayton J. Schmit

Engaging Worship, a Brehm Center series, is designed to promote reflection on the practice of Christian worship by scholars, artists, and practitioners, often in conversation with each other. Each volume addresses a particular liturgical issue from one or multiple academic disciplines, while exploring ways in which worship practice and leadership can be renewed. Volumes in this series include monographs and edited collections from authors of diverse theological and ecclesial communities. The goal of this series is to bring scholars, students, artists, and church leaders into conversation around vital issues of theology and worship.

The Brehm Center for Worship, Theology, and the Arts is an innovative space for the creative integration of worship, theology, and arts in culture. It is located at Fuller Theological Seminary in Pasadena, California.

Performance
in
Preaching

BRINGING THE SERMON TO LIFE

EDITED BY JANA CHILDERS AND
CLAYTON J. SCHMIT

Baker Academic
a division of Baker Publishing Group
Grand Rapids, Michigan

Published by Baker Academic
a division of Baker Publishing Group
P.O. Box 6287, Grand Rapids, MI 49516-6287
www.bakeracademic.com

Printed in the United States of America

Library of Congress Cataloging-in-Publication Data
Performance in preaching : bringing the sermon to life / edited by Jana Childers and Clayton J. Schmit.
     p. cm. — (Engaging worship)
    Includes bibliographical references and index.
    ISBN 978-0-8010-3613-2 (pbk.)
    1. Preaching. 2. Performance. I. Childers, Jana. II. Schmit, Clayton J.
  BV4211.3P47 2008
  251—dc22   2008019338

This book is dedicated to Charles L. Bartow.
The trajectory of his thought and theology has plotted a path that we,
with gratitude and humility,
have been blessed to follow.

Contents

    Clayton J. Schmit
11. The Musicality of Black Preaching: Performing the Word   191
    William C. Turner Jr.
12. Performance Study in Service to the Spoken Word in Worship   211
    Charles L. Bartow

    Bibliography   225
    Index   243

Contributors

Ronald J. Allen
Nettie Sweeney and Hugh Th. Miller Professor of Preaching and New Testament
Christian Theological Seminary
Indianapolis, Indiana

Charles L. Bartow
Carl and Helen Egner Professor of Speech Communication in Ministry
Princeton Theological Seminary
Princeton, New Jersey

Jana Childers
Dean of the Seminary and Professor of Homiletics
San Francisco Theological Seminary
San Anselmo, California

Todd Farley
Associate Professor of Speech and Drama
Calvin College
Grand Rapids, Michigan

Alyce M. McKenzie
Associate Professor of Homiletics
Perkins School of Theology, Southern Methodist University
Dallas, Texas

John M. Rottman
Associate Professor of Preaching
Calvin Theological Seminary
Grand Rapids, Michigan

Clayton J. Schmit
Arthur DeKruyter/Christ Church Oak Brook Associate Professor of Preaching

Academic Director for the Brehm Center for Worship, Theology, and the Arts
Fuller Theological Seminary
Pasadena, California

Marguerite Shuster
Harold John Ockenga Professor of Preaching and Theology
Fuller Theological Seminary
Pasadena, California

Mary Donovan Turner
Vice President for Academic Affairs and Dean of the Faculty
Carl Patton Professor of Preaching
Pacific School of Religion
Berkeley, California

William C. Turner Jr.
Associate Professor of the Practice of Preaching
Duke Divinity School, Duke University
Durham, North Carolina

Richard F. Ward
Associate Professor of Preaching and Performance Studies
Iliff School of Theology
Denver, Colorado

Paul Scott Wilson
Professor of Homiletics
Emmanuel College, University of Toronto
Toronto, Canada

Acknowledgments

This project follows the trajectory of a small set of key figures whose work in the areas of homiletics and performance studies has been seminal. They include William Brower, W. J. Beeners, and most recently Charles L. Bartow. These three "Bs," like Bach, Brahms, and Beethoven, are the guiding lights of their art. Bartow is dean of the school of performance studies in preaching, and has tutored and mentored several of the authors in this volume. All of us have learned from his deep understanding of the intersection between God's Word and our human necessity to use every means at our disposal to bring this Word to life in the hearing of God's people. He is both the author of the concluding chapter in this volume and the friend and teacher to whom this book is dedicated.

We are grateful to two organizations for the generous support that brought this project to life: Director John Witvliet and the Calvin Institute of Christian Worship, and Executive Director Fred Davison and the Brehm Center for Worship, Theology, and the Arts at Fuller Seminary. We are also grateful to Bob Hosack and Jeremy Cunningham of Baker Academic; Bob shared the vision for such a volume, encouraged its development, and brought it to production, and Jeremy paid scrupulous attention to editorial details in the preparation of this book for print. Thanks go, as well, to a dedicated group of doctoral students whose administrative skills and assistance helped the book along in many ways: Ron Rienstra, Lisa Lamb, and Jeff Frymire. Finally, and as always, we thank our spouses and families (Tom, Carol, Kyrie, and Jacob) whose love and support for our academic work make it joyfully possible.

Introduction

JANA CHILDERS
AND CLAYTON J. SCHMIT

Preaching is a big tent with nearly as many kinds of preachers as there are people. High-wire artists, lion tamers, sideshow barkers, and ringmasters are only the beginning. In preaching's tent there are acrobats and dancers, strongmen, sequined ladies, and, of course, several kinds of clowns. Many successful preachers are extemporaneous performers. For others the real work gets done behind the scenes—in the dead of night, hunkered down in a pool of light in the middle of a battered desk. There are even some who do their best work at the business end of a cannon or behind the proverbial elephant.

There are a million ways to be an effective preacher. Probably more. Often a preacher's style is more a matter of life experience and temperament than conscious choice. Personality shapes pulpit style, sometimes for good and sometimes for ill. The preaching styles of teachers, life coaches, text critics, and priests will be different, no matter their homiletical training. The pulpit voices of therapists, soothsayers, exegetes, father figures, motivational speakers, and raconteurs will be easy to distinguish. What resources does homiletics have for helping preachers sift out the idiosyncratic from the individual? How much of the preacher's performance should be "doing what comes naturally" and how much should be governed by principles?

Preachers come in so many different stripes and styles. There are preachers who think of themselves as gurus, and preachers who think of themselves as CEOs. There are preachers who aim to change minds, and preachers who mean to touch hearts. One big tribe of preachers looks forward to the preaching moment as an occasion for self-disclosure, and another would rather die than reveal a single square millimeter of their own souls. It goes without saying that this is a field where stand-up comedians and hams coexist with prophets and martyrs. How can homiletics help them all?

The questions of persona, performance style, and authenticity in preaching, always important, are particularly pressing in this age. Hypocrisy is the number one charge leveled at the churched by the unchurched these days, with preachers being caught in the hottest part of the spotlight. In the person-on-the-street's mental dictionary, the word "phony" is illustrated with a picture of a televangelist. At the same time, the need of congregations for powerful preachers has not changed. "Passionate" or "dynamic" preaching is at the top of every search committee's list of requirements, as it has been for decades.

What does passionate preaching look like in the diverse contexts of the twenty-first-century church? How can authentic, lively preaching be distinguished from schlocky, manipulative preaching? What makes the difference, anyway, between sermons that fly through the air and into the minds and hearts of the listeners and those that dribble down the front of the pulpit and out into the aisle? Is preaching's tent big enough to include new personalities, theories, and technology? These are the kinds of questions this volume addresses.

This book is intended for three audiences. First, it is for pastors and preachers who are interested in the question of how sermons get formed and embodied—and how they can be better formed and embodied. Second, it is for use in the seminary classroom where sermon skills are learned and reflected upon. Third, it is for those involved in the ongoing scholarly conversations about performance issues in preaching. While the chapters are written for a broad range of readers, we have also provided a bibliography particularly intended for those who are pursuing research in performance and related areas of inquiry.

The question of performance is often avoided relative to preaching. While every teacher of preaching knows she has to deal with teaching students how to perform the sermons they have crafted, it is usually handled quickly and in the most cursory manner. This book provides more than a passing look at a topic that is often treated as sub-theological, even sub-homiletical, not to mention antithetical to worship. The very word *performance* in relation to worship and preaching tends to make some people shiver with anxiety. The word (and the art) is, nonetheless, essential to preaching and other dimensions of worship leadership if preaching and prayer are to be lively means of communication. Performance does not have to mean "mere performance," or playacting. It is critical to the execution of things, in the way that a surgeon *performs* life and death medical procedures. Performance, here, is treated as a necessary element of sermon production, valued alongside the other aspects of sermon preparation and delivery.[1] To perform the sermon, however it is created, is to admit that God still uses a human person to proclaim God's message. Once, that person was Jesus "who came and dwelt among us, full of grace and truth" (John 1:14 RSV). Today, God's speech is incarnate in the lives, voices, and bodies of men and women who preach God's Word. It is, as Charles Bartow teaches us, God's human speech. To put it simply: to perform the sermon is to bring it to life.

In this volume, major scholarly voices from every area of homiletics are brought to bear on questions of performance. But this book is not simply a rehash of homiletical theories. Nor is it merely the product of twelve homileticians talking among themselves. Instead, we have sought to place homiletics in conversation with the academic field of performance studies. It is out of the confluence of these two fields of research that the large questions of the age are addressed.

Performance studies is the academic field that provides critical analysis of performance and performances, broadly understood.[2] It incorporates the insights of such disciplines as anthropology, sociology, and philosophy as well as the performance arts. Homiletics has been in dialogue with performance studies for some time; however, this is the first volume to undertake a comprehensive approach to the conversation.

A relatively new field among the formal disciplines of the academy, performance studies is comprised of several schools. Two approaches have been of particular interest to contemporary homileticians:

1. The school of thought represented by Richard Schechner and Victor Turner combines the research insights of theater and anthropology in order to describe and evaluate performance events. Intercultural performance, ritual studies, and social drama offer related methods.
2. The speech act theory, associated with philosopher J. L. Austin, is concerned with the performative function of words. Austin and other proponents of this theory have shown that some words do more than describe or state facts, they perform actions.

Methods of each of these are represented in the chapters that follow.

1. For more on useful and congenial descriptions of the performance aspects of preaching, see books by Charles L. Bartow, Jana Childers, Clayton J. Schmit, and Richard F. Ward noted in the bibliography.
2. For more information, see Richard Schechner, *Performance Studies: An Introduction* (London and New York: Routledge, 2002).

The homileticians whose essays appear in this volume represent various corners of the academic field of homiletics. All are seminary or college professors. All are prominent preachers. The work of some focuses on theological reflection, some on biblical studies, and some on performance arts. Some write from a progressive theological perspective, others are more evangelical, but all are committed to the lively execution of the preached Word. Each of the contributors has applied his or her particular subfield of expertise to a performance question relating to preaching.

Marguerite Shuster gets us started in chapter 1 with a word of caution, pursuing a theological question about the legitimacy of performance in preaching. In chapter 2, Paul Scott Wilson explores the temporal element of performance and shows the theological implications of preaching's "now." In chapter 3, Alyce M. McKenzie shows how a performance-sensitive approach to reading Scripture can produce a genre-sensitive approach to preaching. John M. Rottman uses theological tools to critique speech act theory in chapter 4. Chapters 5 and 6 bring together biblical studies and performance issues. Mary Donovan Turner focuses on Miriam's song in Exodus 15 in order to explore the role of ritual performance and to discover the effects of putting performance theory and prophecy in conversation. Ronald J. Allen examines the oral aspects of the New (what he calls the Second) Testament and shows how a performance perspective can be useful to contemporary interpreters of these texts.

In the second half of the volume, various performance methods, theories, and arts are brought to bear on preaching. As a teacher of mime and communication, Todd Farley gets to the core of the issue in chapter 7, showing how the hands and body can be trained to be responsive and articulate tools for communicating a sermon's message. In chapter 8, Richard F. Ward mines the metaphorical and physical meaning of the preacher's "voice." In chapter 9, Jana Childers applies the insights of artists and creativity theorists to the preacher's experience. Clayton J. Schmit explores the intersection of music performance and preaching in chapter 10, and William C. Turner Jr. considers the musicality of African American preaching in chapter 11. Finally, in chapter 12, Charles L. Bartow presents a thorough study of performance issues seen within the broader scope of worship.

Along the way, it became clear that a book on performance in preaching ought to include a means by which to demonstrate some of its teaching. Given that among our team of scholars are some of the most able teachers of the performance aspects of preaching currently available, it seemed wise to share some of their practical performance exercises and techniques so that they could be used by those who are not performance specialists. Accordingly, we have created a DVD that brings to life much of the teaching explored or implied in the written material.

In an initial planning meeting for this project, Professor Bartow encouraged the participants to think afresh what performance could mean for the discipline of homiletics. He invited the writers to be creative in rethinking performance for preaching because contemporary performance studies have moved in recent years away from areas most fruitful for preaching. Two meetings and twelve chapters later, the results of this rethinking have been surprising. The conversation between homiletics and performance studies has raised questions and provided a number of tantalizing insights. Most of all, it has opened a promising avenue for further research and reflection. In an age that has been more interested in and cynical about the performance aspects of preaching, the twelve homileticians whose work comprises this book show that there is more fruitful ground to till than we previously imagined, and that twenty-first-century homiletics is well positioned for the task.

1

The Truth and Truthfulness

Theological Reflections on Preaching and Performance

M A R G U E R I T E   S H U S T E R

In a postmodern, pluralistic age, titles beginning with "the truth," as if one could actually speak of "truth" in the singular and preceded by a definite article, must immediately come under suspicion, and the problem is only compounded if the further term *truthfulness* should end up being construed to entail something more than the sincerity and authenticity that have become the all-purpose characterological honorifics of our day. Be, then, forewarned! For I do indeed propose to say that every time a preacher enters the pulpit, he or she is called to speak as accurately and faithfully as possible of the One who unequivocally spoke of himself as the Truth (John 14:6); and I further propose to say that having good intentions, however fervent, is no guarantee of speaking in a way that is genuinely truthful.

The subtitle adds its own set of pressing problems, for many—and I include myself high on the list among them—will have a powerful and negative visceral reaction against construing proclamation of God's Word as a sort of "performance." Emphasis on the importance of *delivery* is of course ancient and commonplace. The sticking point with *performance* would seem to be the way the term brings to the fore connotations of self-conscious intentionality and artifice and perhaps emotional manipulation of hearers that mere talk of delivery may conceal. Pulpit "performers" may readily be seen as distancing themselves from both their sacred subject matter and their congregations, while aiming at effect and at the sort of excellence to which applause is a suitable response. Presumably they do not have to be doing these things. But they could be. And those of us who retain a view of preaching as, properly, a holy mystery not in any human being's full control can only cringe at every tendency to turn the service of Christian worship into theater, with its leader a well-tooled actor. We cannot banish all that smacks of self-display, falseness, manipulation, or the mere pursuit of audience approval from the deliverances of those of us who mount pulpits (or, equally, those of us who would never dream of preaching from behind a pulpit, but who nonetheless preach), for we are every last one of us sinners; but we can at least avoid baptizing such things.

I count it entirely proper, then, to wrap any discussion of performance aspects of preaching in cautions, for it is all too easy to forget the nature and dignity of one's task and aim, when one is focusing primary attention on oneself as one undertakes the task. After all, as Augustine, and Luther following him, observed, the essence of sinfulness is to be curved in on oneself. That the preacher should hope to disappear behind the proclaimed Word—that the test of a good sermon is that hearers should remark not on how wonderful the preacher is but on how wonderful the Lord is—is a classic and, I believe, correct view. Similarly, the old inscription on the interior of pulpits or on the door from the sacristy to the chancel reminding the preacher, "Sir, we would see Jesus" (John 12:21 KJV), is good advice even if terrible exegesis. It would seem that such concerns can hardly be overemphasized at a time when all manner of self-revelation, however tawdry, is lauded as key to the authenticity people say they desire in a preacher, and when members of an entertainment-oriented society instinctively apply criteria derived from secular media when attending church.

The trouble is that we do not get rid of sin by failing or refusing to notice what we actually do in the pulpit.[1] Indeed, we may simply be engaging in self-deception. Or we may be lazy, a laziness with respect to presentation no more defensible than the laziness teachers of preaching have traditionally declined to tolerate when it comes to exegesis. Or—and this aspect may be as

---

1. See my *The Fall and Sin: What We Have Become as Sinners* (Grand Rapids: Eerdmans, 2004) for extended discussion of the doctrine of sin as it affects all of our faculties, including our use of language.

troubling as any—we may be so deeply imbued with our age's deep suspicion of rhetorical excellence that it infects every aspect of our presentation of our materials.[2] Doing a poor job in the pulpit at the level of presentation cannot be defended as a proper way of honoring God, any more than one can defend refusing to prepare one's sermon at the level of content on the grounds that one wants to leave the Spirit free to work (as if the Lord were more likely to redeem and use our slovenliness than our honest effort).

Performance and Truth in Preaching

Making an argument for the legitimate importance of the performance aspect of preaching involves taking account of the sort of thing "preaching" is and the sort of truth it purports to convey. No one seriously denies that preaching is fundamentally an oral (or, as is often said by other contributors to this volume, oral-aural) activity involving speaking to a particular group of people.[3] While it may be unfair to count all printed sermons as mere corpses—many of us will have been deeply moved by classic sermons we have read—it still holds that many gripping proclamations of God's Word for a particular time and place translate badly if at all into written form. We also know that preaching has traditionally been understood specifically to involve proclamation of the truth of the gospel, truth of life-and-death importance both for coming to faith in Christ in the first place and for growing in grace. One doesn't stand in a pulpit and just say whatever comes to mind; one is responsible for a fundamental sort of content that may be truly or falsely conceived and well or badly communicated. Furthermore, however much we may already know of this gospel truth, many of us can testify that at critical points we have found ourselves unable effectively to tell *ourselves* the truth that we "know" in our heads, but

2. See, for example, the extended argument of John McWhorter, *Doing Our Own Thing: The Degradation of Language and Music and Why We Should, Like, Care* (New York: Gotham Books, 2003). Similarly John Dillenberger: "Language forms and transforms, and its many styles and powers could enrich us more than they do. The so-called decline of preaching, or the demise in our time of oratory—so prominent a part of nineteenth-century life—means that the widening, disciplined, imaginative use of language is in short supply," *A Theology of Artistic Sensibilities: The Visual Arts and the Church* (New York: Crossroad, 1986), 232. As something of an aside, I might note the distinction that Donald Davis makes between "presentation" and "communication," the latter suggesting a relational quality that the former lacks. Donald Davis, *Writing as a Second Language* (Little Rock: August House, 2000), chap. 3. It will be obvious from what follows that I consider attentiveness to one's relationship to one's hearers essential to faithful preaching; mere "presentation" of some material will not do. Nonetheless, I am also arguing that presentational flaws can seriously limit communication.

3. The very lack of particularity of broadcast media as preaching venues constitutes a limitation of these media: what one may gain in scope, one loses in immediacy and specificity.

have needed to hear it from another (the old gospel hymn by Katherine Hankey puts it, "Tell me the old, old story, / For those who know it best / Are hungering and thirsting / To hear it like the rest"). As a kindergartner torn between divorcing parents begged as she climbed into her teacher's lap, "Tell me again that Jesus loves me. I keep forgetting."[4] Faith comes by hearing, said the apostle Paul (Rom. 10:17). The spoken word has power to enter into us in a peculiarly pressing way. All of this is surely related to the fact that the truth conveyed by proclamation is not a merely propositional matter, as if one could enshrine a series of life-giving principles far above the vicissitudes of time and space and culture and present crises. Rather, the mysterious importance of hearing has to do both with the nature of sound itself and with fitting personal address in what may at least sometimes be a highly particular context.

Precisely because of the Incarnate One who identified himself as the Truth, Dietrich Bonhoeffer, in a provocative essay unfinished at the time of his death, argued that truth and truth-telling are relational in their essence, part of a total reality seeking expression, and that for a word to be "true," it must first of all fit the relational requirements of a particular encounter.[5] One might think here of certain biblical propositions, such as those commanding slaves to be subject to their masters, that are true when they are addressed to slaves as a way of affirming their full human agency in a constraining situation, but false when used as a tool by masters to deny that same full human agency: to whom or by whom the statement is made is critical to its truth-value (this is my example, not Bonhoeffer's). Emil Brunner makes a similar point when he says that "the truth of which the Bible speaks is always a happening."[6] Again, "what God wills to give us cannot really be given in words, but only in manifestation: Jesus Christ, God Himself *in persona* is the real gift. The Word of God in its ultimate meaning is thus precisely not 'a word from,' but God in person, God Himself speaking, Himself present, Immanuel."[7] He makes the application to preaching specific by saying, "When we consider the Biblical

---

4. Story told by the teacher, Marlene Linthicum, in my presence.

5. Dietrich Bonhoeffer, *Ethics*, trans. Neville Horton Smith (New York: Macmillan, 1955): "'Telling the truth' means something different according to the particular situation in which one stands. Account must be taken of one's relationships at each particular time" (363). "The lie is a contradiction of the word of God, which God has spoken in Christ, and upon which creation is founded. Consequently the lie is the denial, the negation and the conscious and deliberate destruction of the reality which is created by God and which consists in God, no matter whether this purpose is achieved by speech or by silence" (369).

6. Emil Brunner, *The Divine-Human Encounter*, trans. Amandus W. Loos (Philadelphia: Westminster, 1943), 201. One should note that the original German title, *Wahrheit als Begegnung*, means "truth as encounter." Martin Buber's seminal volume *I and Thou*, 2nd ed. (New York: Scribner, 1958), is also highly relevant here.

7. Brunner, *Divine-Human Encounter*, 109.

understanding of proclamation, we observe that it means an event entirely personal, in the nature of a personal meeting."[8]

An argument of this kind—which implies that propositions not only fail fully to capture the essence of the truth but may also sometimes in the most important senses falsify it even if making factually accurate claims—must not be confused with a sort of postmodern affirmation that "true" means "true for me, from my perspective." The point is a quite different one, namely, that we rightly speak of truth only when the whole context is properly taken into account and ordered, including, in Bonhoeffer's analysis, what entitles or causes one to speak, one's own location, and that about which one makes some assertion (this last component makes clear that one cannot claim truthfulness if one has lied merely to smooth over a difficult situation or to make someone feel good).[9] For the preacher, these elements involve at the very least: (1) the authority of the God to whom one must first and foremost seek to be rightly related, (2) who one is as a person related to other persons in a particular cultural setting, and (3) the biblical text as one interprets and applies it. This, then, is a very demanding requirement for truth. And it is important to note that it implicitly requires including whatever bears on our interpersonal relationships, including the formal and presentational shape of our sermons.

But—even granting that matters involving presentation are intrinsic to our actual experience of what someone says—is there something about deliberate attention to performance that *essentially* betrays the truth, perhaps by shaping a purpose that substitutes the workings of human psychology for the work of the Holy Spirit? Or is there a fatally compromising loss of immediacy, as if one were thinking merely of the excellence of one's technique instead of one's beloved while making love? More about the immediacy question below. For now, I simply note that the question of thinking about technique is a form of the old question of the use of means in the proclamation of the gospel.[10] An entirely traditional

8. Ibid., 176.

9. Bonhoeffer, *Ethics*, 370.

10. Debates about the use of means are old, and they contributed to the divide between "Old School" and "New School" Presbyterians. Charles Finney was a leading advocate of applying what he considered to be appropriate means in the seeking of conversions, though he was often accused of emotional manipulation. Evangelicals as a whole have been particularly eager to use whatever methodologies have promoted success (leading to a good deal of sometimes well-founded criticism by those who have doubted the integrity of the methods), but, as always, misapplication of a principle is not a proper argument against its legitimate use. Augustine's oft-quoted words from *On Christian Doctrine* bear repeating yet again:

> Now, the art of rhetoric being available for the enforcing either of truth or falsehood, who will dare to say that truth in the person of its defenders is to take its stand unarmed against falsehood? For example, that those who are trying to persuade men of what is false are to know how to introduce their subject, so as to put the hearer into a friendly, or

view is that God in his providence ordains the means along with the end. Thus, while we know that God knows our needs fully, he nonetheless invites us to bring them to him in prayer (e.g., Matt. 6:8–13). That God gives the increase does not mean that it is unnecessary that one plant and another water (1 Cor. 3:6–8), and so on. Preaching is itself a means: we are informed that "God decided, through the foolishness of our proclamation, to save those who believe" (1 Cor. 1:21). He could have accomplished his ends another way, perhaps without making use of us at all. The proper question, then, is not whether means are used, but whether the means have integrity and are suitable to the ends.

The Truth, Beauty, and Language

Performance in preaching may be taken to include both the verbal shape and the physical embodiment we give to what we have to say, and either or both of these may betray the truth by incompetence or ugliness. The God who is spoken of as beautiful (Ps. 27:4) is not rightly represented by the ugly, the vulgar, or the careless, or by a form that generates merely ennui and boredom—a point to which a significant proportion of today's students seem curiously insensible. It is not just that they lack the sort of liberal education that would give them power to make clear and accurate distinctions with a measure of articulate grace, but that they are suspicious of the whole enterprise, as if whatever is done carefully or whatever is lovely thereby establishes itself as false.[11] One

---

attentive, or teachable frame of mind, while the defenders of the truth shall be ignorant of that art? That the former are to tell their falsehoods briefly, clearly, and plausibly, while the latter shall tell the truth in such a way that it is tedious to listen to, hard to understand, and, in fine, not easy to believe it? . . . Since, then, the faculty of eloquence is available for both sides, and is of very great service in the enforcing either of wrong or right, why do not good men study to engage it on the side of truth, when bad men use it to obtain the triumph of wicked and worthless causes, and to further injustice and error? (4.3)

And:

It is the duty, then, of the interpreter and teacher of Holy Scripture, the defender of the true faith and the opponent of error, both to teach what is right and to refute what is wrong, and in the performance of this task to conciliate the hostile, to rouse the careless, and to tell the ignorant both what is occurring at present and what is probable in the future. But once that his hearers are friendly, attentive, and ready to hear, whether he has found them so or has himself made them so, the remaining objects are to be carried out in whatever way the case requires. (4.6)

Nicene and Post-Nicene Fathers, First Series, ed. P. Schaff, vol. 2 (1887; repr., Peabody, MA: Hendrickson, 1994). I am obviously taking a positive view of Augustine's points here; but see below for McKenzie's worries about the "Aristotelian captivity of the sermon."

11. See, again, the whole of McWhorter, *Doing Our Own Thing*. He comments on the common perception that Al Gore lost the presidency to George W. Bush in part because he was too articulate (xxi).

can only grieve a generation so much of which seems to suppose that only the utterly unstudied, the broken, and the misshapen are true—most particularly when that same generation is quite allergic to the sort of doctrine of sin that would put pervasive misshapenness in its proper context as a violation of God's will.

Of course artistic and Christian truth cannot simply be identified, as if the ineffability of beauty and of the holy were simply different aspects of the same thing.[12] Not only do emotional and evocative aspects of art have a slippery relationship to truth—equally stirring appeals can be made on both sides of many questions—but also, imaginative and intuitive perceptions, however compelling, do not in themselves have quite the status of divine revelation.[13] Furthermore, as the Thomist theologian Jacques Maritain notes, art in itself is not properly judged by moral criteria, nor does art as such have anything to say about the good of human life. But he continues,

> Yet human life is in need of that very Beauty and intellectual creativity, where art has the last word; and art exercises itself in the midst of that very human life, those human needs and human ends, where morality has the last word. In other words it is true that Art and Morality are two autonomous worlds, each sovereign in its own sphere, but they cannot ignore or disregard one another.[14]

I have already affirmed that, in a sense, human needs and ends are the least of it: at stake is how we learn, consciously or unconsciously, to conceive of God himself. If, as George MacDonald commented, we would view God quite differently if we lived our whole lives under a flat white ceiling instead of

12. Pelikan warns against this danger as especially prominent when religion has been put in an emotional framework (Jaroslav Jan Pelikan, *Fools for Christ: Essays on the True, the Good, and the Beautiful* [Philadelphia: Muhlenberg, 1955], 121). He later continues, "To a greater extent than either intellectualism or moralism, aestheticism has been able to satisfy yearnings deep within the human breast. For that reason, those who had possessed the Beautiful could very easily be deluded into supposing that they had taken hold of the Holy itself" (124); "it [is] more comfortable to live with an art form than with God, and this has been the fundamental temptation of the identification of the Holy and the Beautiful—that in aesthetic rapture I had enough commitment to satisfy me, yet not so much that I lost my self-respect" (133): surely these dangers are ones to which the contemporary worship and the arts movement needs particularly to pay heed.

13. See John Hospers, *Meaning and Truth in the Arts* (Chapel Hill: University of North Carolina Press, 1974), esp. 215; also Bernard C. Heyl, *New Bearings in Esthetics and Art Criticism: A Study in Semantics and Evaluation* (New Haven: Yale University Press, 1943), 85–86. The former speaks of art as the sort of truth that is "true to" its subject rather than conveying "truth about" the universe (162–207).

14. Jacques Maritain, *The Responsibility of the Artist* (New York: Scribner, 1960), 41.

under the starry heavens,[15] so also would we view God differently if we heard of him only in ways that convey nothing of grandeur, beauty, design, power, or purpose. That is, those who preach in a way that is careless, sloppy, and unskilled, perhaps thinking that they are thus being "authentic," may fail to recognize that they are communicating something else as well. Humans have a perfectly natural and unselfconscious response to real beauty and power of expression whether visual or verbal or characterological: we need to regain candor about our almost instinctive appreciation of these sorts of excellence and about how excellence is achieved—not, surely, apart from God's good gifts, but not without effort, either. The needed skills do not just fall on our heads (note 2 Tim. 2:15, as well as Paul's pervasive metaphors involving athletic training: plain laziness is not a Christian virtue!). Form and content cannot be torn apart in these matters or in any others.

Even apart from questions of beauty, we get many hints that the relationship of language to truth is not simply a matter of propositions that may stay lodged neatly in our brains. It is not just the words used but their intonation that conveys the meaning of the sentence, as can be seen in those sentences in which one has a choice of which word to emphasize, and each choice conveys distinctly different meaning.[16] In fact, it has been shown that in situations that are even slightly ambiguous, intonation will trump literal meaning.[17] What is more, literal meaning itself is often best conveyed to the ear. Thus biblical scholars often recommend that, in particular, the book of Revelation be read

15. C. S. Lewis, *George MacDonald: 365 Readings* (New York: Macmillan, 1947), 66.

16. For a particularly engaging example, consider the sentence and interpretations offered by Leo Rosten, *The Joys of Yiddish* (New York: Pocket Books, 1968), xvi: "Problem: Whether to attend a concert to be given by a neighbor, niece, or friend of your wife. The same sentence may be put through maneuvers of matchless versatility:

"(1) '*Two* tickets for her concert I should buy?' (Meaning: 'I'm having enough trouble deciding if it's worth one.')

"(2) 'Two *tickets* for her concert I should buy?' ('You mean to say she isn't distributing free passes? The hall will be empty!')

"(3) 'Two tickets for *her* concert I should buy?' ('Did she buy tickets to *my* daughter's recital?')

"(4) 'Two tickets for her *concert* I should buy?' ('You mean to say they call what she does a "concert"?!')

"(5) 'Two tickets for her concert *I* should buy?' ('After what she did to me?')

"(6) 'Two tickets for her concert I *should* buy?' ('Are you giving me lessons in ethics?')

"(7) 'Two tickets for her concert I should *buy*?' ('I wouldn't go even if she gave me a complimentary!')"

An extended treatment of these matters is given by Stephen H. Webb, *The Divine Voice: Christian Proclamation and the Theology of Sound* (Grand Rapids: Brazos, 2004).

17. For demonstration of how nonverbal cues may actually reverse the meaning of the explicit message, see Albert Mehrabian, *Silent Messages: Implicit Communication of Emotions and Attitudes*, 2nd ed. (Belmont, CA: Wadsworth, 1981).

aloud if one wishes rightly to interpret it: one's understanding changes as one speaks and hears the words. The converse can also be true: if, in the presence of smoke and flames one has just noticed, one says, "fire," without any suggestion of capitals and an exclamation point, one presumably has not understood one's situation, and one's hearers will not rightly perceive their danger.[18]

One wonders whether this phenomenon of the importance of tone (and, as we will remark later, bodily involvement as a whole) rests in significant part on our bodily experience being embedded from the beginning in our language. As Mark Johnson argues in a provocative volume,

> understanding is never merely a matter of holding beliefs, either consciously or unconsciously. More basically, one's understanding is one's way of being in, or having, a world. This is very much a matter of one's embodiment, that is, of perceptual mechanisms, patterns of discrimination, motor programs, and various bodily skills. And it is equally a matter of our embeddedness within culture, language, institutions, and historical traditions.[19]

In Johnson's view, not just our metaphors and ways of expressing ourselves, but everything about our reasoning and our attribution of meaning, depends heavily on our relationship to our physical world. This relationship has both the particularity of our own experience and the universality provided by the uniform laws and aspects of our physical reality; but no human being thinks or speaks or hears or reads without a body and a world. One is not, in thinking, simply manipulating logical symbols or making abstract statements; even in abstract statements—as, say, when one refers to "higher" values—physical realities lurk behind the scenes. Insofar as what Johnson says is accurate, we cannot escape our bodies even when reading in private. How much less, then, when we are speaking in public and are ourselves being both observed and heard. (The highly visual character of many mathematical insights suggests that Johnson's point may hold even in what may appear to be a supremely abstract arena.)[20]

18. "Contemporary research in cognitive science makes it clear that content cannot be separated from form, abstract thought from bodily function, or intellectual grasp from emotional commitment. Theology, art, and technique thus converge in any human performative enterprise." Charles L. Bartow, *God's Human Speech: A Practical Theology of Proclamation* (Grand Rapids: Eerdmans, 1997), 3.

19. Mark Johnson, *The Body in the Mind* (Chicago: University of Chicago Press, 1987), 137. This philosophical view may have a concrete physiological representation, as manifested by the fact that, at least in males, whether one is right- or left-handed appears to bear importantly on whether language is processed primarily in, respectively, the left or the right hemisphere of the brain.

20. There may be parallels to be explored between Bonhoeffer's view of truth as entailing right interpersonal relationships and Johnson's view of truth as relative to standards of

The Truth and Truthful Presence

That conveying and receiving truthful communication involve our bodies in a fundamental way, even at the level of our thinking and the level of meaning, should not make anxious those Christians who are convinced that God likes physical stuff, since he made it and did not scorn becoming incarnate. Without engaging the currently popular but largely fruitless and inconclusive debates between monists and dualists on the ontological constituents of persons, one can surely affirm that in human life as we normally experience it, human bodies and souls or spirits cannot be disentangled, and both are involved in all normal communication. In the lovely tones of a theologian of an earlier century, J. R. Illingworth remarks that "thought and will and love must needs communicate themselves to others; spirit craves intercourse with spirit; and here again we depend on matter. . . . To give expression to a thing is to realize it, in the sense of making it more real; and hence matter, as being the language of spirit, is also the medium of its realization." He continues, "good intentions are of no avail, till they have faced the resistance of the outer world, and in overcoming its opposition become moral acts; and love can never rest, till it has proved its own intensity by a thousand tender, thoughtful, self-sacrificing deeds. In every case contact with matter strengthens the spiritual fibre, forcing vagueness into outline, confusion into clearness, doubt into decision, hesitation into act."[21]

So, indeed, we might agree, it should be; but the question comes when we wonder whether, so to speak, the inside actually matches the outside, whether there is a wholeness and integrity in the act or whether what we perceive on the surface is designed in some sense to deceive, manipulate, or otherwise take advantage of us. That is the question that plagues focus on "performance."

Our doubts can scarcely be wondered at. On the one hand, we are bombarded by the productions of a slick and highly sophisticated commercial advertising industry, whose concern for our well-being we have every reason to doubt. This industry very much wants us to believe what it says, but it solicits our trust in order to enhance self-interested aims (and thus there is a certain credibility gap when churches or public service agencies use these same techniques: those who are at all self-reflective will be likely to generalize the assumption that their good is *not* the primary goal of such appeals). On the

---

adequacy with respect to our purposes and our interactions with our environment (Johnson, *Body in the Mind*, 211), though Bonhoeffer intends theological claims that Johnson would plainly reject.

21. J. R. Illingworth, *Divine Immanence: An Essay on the Spiritual Significance of Matter* (New York: Macmillan, 1898; repr., Kessinger, date unknown), 11–13.

other hand, the ability to enjoy the contemporary crop of movies and video games involves being told and believing that, however realistic they appear, they are *not* in fact real. One may safely (?) be deeply engrossed and emotionally engaged only by discounting the correspondence of these depictions to one's behavior in the world in which one lives. How the act of preaching and the preacher will be perceived in such a cultural setting can hardly be anything but very, very tricky. And the complexity is surely increased to the extent that the preacher seems to be engaged essentially in either advertising or acting. In fact, one wonders to what extent the current attraction to plain sloppiness in preaching manifests a confusion of skill with artifice and an instinctive desire for distance from polished cultural forms that we define as involving some intrinsic measure of falseness.

In any case, one cannot *not* present oneself. Whatever one does or fails to do will communicate something; we make choices in these matters.[22] Even if one is dissimulating, it is not unimportant that one chooses this mask rather than that one. I can always get a laugh from my homiletics class when, in discussing such questions, I ask them to contemplate how differently they would have regarded me on the first day of class had I come in attired in spike heels and a micro-miniskirt, with spiky, multicolored hair, and liberally adorned with piercings and tattoos, instead of appearing in tailored garb and looking utterly conventional.

Enter, here, the old emphasis on "ethos" and credibility, or what has traditionally been called the importance of the person of the preacher, if the message is to be believed. Richard Lischer has noted that the question of holiness in the one proclaiming the gospel, once considered so important, has garnered little attention in recent days.[23] No doubt that is attributable at least in part to the perception that the alleged "holiness" of too many preachers was itself a charade, so that only confessions from the pulpit of the less-redeemed aspects of one's humanity have come to be seen as authentic.[24] It is not difficult to discern that we have a double downward spiral here if believability becomes linked to presentations of poor quality and manifesting flawed character:

22. See here the old sociological classic of Erving Goffman, *The Presentation of Self in Everyday Life* (Garden City, NY: Doubleday, 1959).

23. Richard Lischer, *Theories of Preaching: Selected Readings in the Homiletical Tradition* (Durham, NC: Labyrinth, 1987), 3.

24. In a fascinating volume, Lionel Trilling comments that "much that culture traditionally condemned and sought to exclude is accorded a considerable moral authority by reason of the authenticity claimed for it, for example, disorder, violence, unreason" (11); and, "that the word [authenticity] has become part of the moral slang of our day points to the peculiar nature of our fallen condition, our anxiety over the credibility of existence and of individual existences" (93). *Sincerity and Authenticity* (Cambridge, MA: Harvard University Press, 1972).

soon there is nothing that seems *worth* listening to or believing. It would seem that higher aspirations on both fronts can hardly be misplaced. Meanwhile, we are faced with the conflicting facts that in important respects we become what we do, and hence rightly reach beyond where we currently are, and that every gap between what we do and what we now are may be perceived as a manifestation of hypocrisy.

So how can one attend to "performance" in preaching without violating the truthfulness of one's presence? (When one speaks of "presence" in preaching, one normally intends to refer to a particular magnetism felt in fine speakers, usually linked to an intensity that is not fully unleashed, which virtually compels attention from listeners. Here, I intend only the weaker meaning of the way one presents oneself and is perceived, with the physical aspects particularly in view.) Does not attention to methodology create, at the very least, a sort of distance from oneself and one's hearers that is every bit as serious as the distance created by reading, or even memorizing, a manuscript?[25]

One answer to that question is perfectly straightforward and uncomplicated: namely, that one practices technique while one is out of the pulpit precisely so that one will not need to pay attention to it while one is in the pulpit, so that one will in fact be free to be fully present to one's material and one's hearers. An athletic analogy is as good as any here. If the tennis pro tells her charge to change his grip, for a time he will be able to think of nothing else, and his game will suffer. Only when the grip becomes natural will it serve him well; only then will his game improve. Or imagine telling a soccer player that she shouldn't work out in the weight room or run to increase her wind or practice kicking the ball because it would spoil her "natural" style: obviously, that would be ridiculous, for playing a sport well involves practice and training and development of skill. One's freedom in the game is enhanced by the discipline outside of it; one can do all sorts of things that would otherwise be impossible, and do them without thinking about them. Presumably the correspondence to training in the proper use of voice and body for the preacher is transparent. One does not thereby become false, any more than one becomes false by learning Greek and Hebrew and sound exegetical method; one simply gains needed skills.

Still, might there not be a difference, for the preacher, between getting exegetical and theological training and getting training in presentation of self? In the former case, one focuses on something other than oneself that has its

25. Note well that preachers whose concern for as perfect as possible a form of words, which keeps them anchored to a written text, do not escape the problem of sinful self-absorption of which "performers" are readily accused; they simply manifest a different form of it (*mea maxima culpa!*).

own integrity and makes its own demands; in the latter, a certain solipsism may threaten. True, yet preachers should recognize that many actors and those who write about acting are keenly aware of this danger; they are very solicitous that the text retain its own integrity and not be twisted and swallowed up by the performer, who thereby makes all pieces she performs sound pretty much alike[26]—not unlike the preachers whose own experience so dominates what they say that they make all biblical texts sound alike.

The following words of secular writer Wallace Bacon—who notes that it is the speaker who is "sure, controlled, attentive to the text" who disappears or becomes transparent[27]—might well be taken to heart by preachers trying to meet the broad requirements of their task in the pulpit (reading "biblical text" where the writer has "poem," which latter means in the context any work of literary art, and making other necessary translations):

> Perfect congruence is not possible, nor even to be hoped for, since there are in fact two different bodies involved. But it is best for the interpreter to seek to match his body with that of the poem, since the interpreter exists (in terms of the art form) to perform the poem. (Bacon, 38)

> The performer who cares more about pleasing an audience than about enactment of the poem will endanger the whole poetic experience, both for the performer and for the audience. The interpreter needs always to remember that reader and audience must be brought together to the act of communion with the poem; if the reader communes with the audience but not with the poem, the audience is likely to come away with spirits unfed. (Bacon, 69)

> The more passionately a reader *cares* about literature, the more devoted will be the search into its nature. The caring must come first; no amount of cold critical analysis will itself lead to genuine literary life. Nevertheless, such critical analysis can stimulate the reader who already feels the life of literature. The capable reader draws on reservoirs of knowledge and feeling. One cannot simply wait until there is a specific need for knowledge; one must seek it constantly, ingest it, be nourished by it. We do not suddenly develop strength; we grow to it. (Bacon, 195)

> It is to the process of matching—of bringing one's own life form for the moment into congruence with the life form of the poem—that the interpreter first and foremost devotes attention. The process of matching is also a process of

---

26. Wallace A. Bacon, *The Art of Interpretation*, 3rd ed. (New York: Holt, Rinehart & Winston, 1979), 38. Note also Alla Renée Bozarth, *The Word's Body: An Incarnational Aesthetic of Interpretation* (Tuscaloosa: University of Alabama Press, 1979).

27. Bacon, *Art of Interpretation*, 10. Cited in text in following paragraphs.

maturation; one grows by giving in to the otherness of the life of the text by
extending oneself, by reaching out, by loving. (Bacon, 511)

The argument "from the lesser to the greater" surely applies here: if secular
performers are enjoined to give such care to the whole of their task, how much
more ought the preacher to do so. The aim is not falseness or dissimulation
of any kind, but rather the fullest possible faithfulness to both the text and
the congregation, which latter, as we have noted, will always and inevitably
respond to the whole of what the preacher does in (and, of course, also outside
of) the pulpit, not just to the bare words of the sermon.

While faithfulness to the text is a sine qua non of preaching, since the
preacher does not speak out of his or her independent authority, faithfulness
to one's congregation in the sense of attending to what enables them to hear
accurately (not to be construed as necessarily involving their liking what they
hear) is of comparable significance, insofar as one holds a relational view of
truth. Speaking Dutch to Koreans obviously won't work. But neither will a
certain sort of stiffness with most young people, or a certain sort of sloppiness
with most high-church Episcopalians. A volume and level of personal expan-
siveness appropriate in a living room won't work in the open air; norms of
eye contact befitting white American contexts may be rude in many African or
Asian ones. To care about these matters is not to become captive to technique
but simply to respect and care about other people and to try to speak in a way
that makes it possible for what one says to be heard by those whom one is
actually addressing. As Augustine put it, "what advantage is there in purity of
speech which does not lead to understanding in the hearer, seeing that there
is no use at all in speaking, if they do not understand us for whose sake we
speak?"[28] Yes, there are temptations here, most especially along the lines of
confusing approval with understanding, but to ignore how one is actually being
perceived is to fail to consider the relational character of telling the truth. If
one is to be rejected, one should hope that it will be for the right reasons.

Caveats

In the preceding pages, I have intended to argue that because "truth" is not
merely a matter of accurate propositions but has an intrinsically personal,
relational character, and because human beings are so constituted that how they
use their bodies cannot be separated from what they say when they speak in
public, it follows that proper attention to "performance" aspects of preaching

28. Augustine, *On Christian Doctrine* 4.24.

is highly important to its truthfulness. "Highly important": should I not have written, "essential"? That I did not do so suggests that I think that despite the importance of what one *does* as well as *says* (and the importance of *how* one says what one says at the level of use of language), this importance is not absolute. And the first and foremost reason it is not absolute is because of God's freedom to accomplish his ends as he chooses, through the weakest and most inadequate means as well as through the most skillful. That God is not in any absolute sense limited by our failures may be all that enables some of us to step into a pulpit at all. Many of us can, in any case, recall life-changing sermons that were technically flawed—even seriously so—and impressive ones that made no lasting difference.

If the Spirit does not work through what the preacher does, nothing else ultimately matters, and anything—most explicitly including a cultivated talent for highly skilled performance garnering enthusiastic response—that seduces the preacher or the congregation away from recognition of that fact is a positive hazard. Surely the extreme dangers of prideful self-reliance here constitute at least one of the reasons Paul said so sharply in 1 Corinthians 1:17 that he was sent to proclaim the gospel precisely *not* "with eloquent wisdom, so that the cross of Christ might not be emptied of its power." When a powerful effect occurs, the humble and even cracked vessel will better reveal that the power is God's than will the elegant and admirable one that calls attention to itself (2 Cor. 4:7). There is a corresponding temptation on the side of the hearer who may come to church with much the same attitude with which she attends a movie—wanting, perhaps, to be moved; taking the posture of an observer; freely evaluating style as much as substance; and in general having an attitude far removed from active worship that attends first and foremost to God. That the better the performance, the more acute these dangers, does not constitute an argument for clumsiness in the pulpit; it simply provokes a warning that here as elsewhere, the greater the power, the more the risk of grave harm accompanies it. Effective hypocrites can do more spiritual harm than ineffective ones. But even by hypocrites, God's hands are not tied: Paul rejoiced that the gospel was being proclaimed whatever the motives of the proclaimer (Phil. 1:15–18). I myself had a student, the fruitfulness of whose ministry I had no reason to doubt, who was converted under the preaching of the infamous Jim Jones, destroyer of hundreds of lives at Jonestown in Guyana (which I take to be an argument for the power of the sheer content of the gospel, not an evidence that character and mental health do not matter).

Unfortunately, much as we rightly fear hypocrisy and dissimulation, simply "being ourselves" will not do, either, in a fallen world; supposing that it will is a sort of romantic delusion, similar to the sentimental supposition that every voice has something equally worthwhile to say, provided it is the genuine voice of the speaker.[29] No, we need something to rely on much steadier than our sinful selves. As Bonhoeffer acutely observed, God made clothes to cover humankind after the fall: not everything ought now to be revealed. It is cynical to assume that evil that cannot be eradicated should be exposed (an important warning for preachers too attached to self-display in the pulpit).[30]

One should also be aware that although it is desirable that all the aspects of one's preaching be aligned with and supportive of one another, many forms of excellence cannot be reduced to cookie-cutter rules. Certain skills will be more important to some hearers than to others; certain faults will distress some hearers more than others. Some faults can be compensated for by strengths; some faults are fatal; and the lapses in performance are rarely fatal if the preacher is a person of conviction and character. (I, for instance, though I inevitably notice and am greatly distracted by poor grammar, sexism, poor sermon design, faulty inflection, and so on, will and do put up with them all; but if I distrust a preacher's character, I will never return, no matter how great his or her skills.)

Other important warnings might include the commonly made observation that adequacy and truthfulness of proclamation do not correlate in any precise way with positive reception of what one says; if they did, the ministry of Jesus would condemn itself. Yes, for a time, large crowds may have listened with delight (Mark 12:37); but in the end, most of them demonstrated the legendary fickleness of crowds and left. And those whom Jesus confronted most directly were as likely to want to kill him as to follow him. He seemed not to have had the slightest inclination to make hearing and following him pleasant and easy, as if one could get people through the door and then get to work on them. Truthfulness, in other words, is not determined by customer satisfaction surveys. And it is not enhanced by the rapport one may achieve by dealing only with sins and evils committed by people half a world away.

Nor is the kind of beauty that Scripture reveals the Savior to have the innocuous sort that fits in well with elevator music (see, e.g., Isa. 52:14–53:5), or the sort of physical decorativeness that our society seems to hold in such high esteem. The "pretty" and sentimental are as offensive in the pulpit as they are in the visual and literary arts, and for more important reasons. Beauty of character and the beauty of holiness may terrify as readily as console. The

29. See Bartow, chap. 12, and (more extensively and from a more positive angle) Ward, chap. 8, below, on aspects of this point.
30. Bonhoeffer, *Ethics*, 372.

content of the gospel must govern the form of expression. Never must this order be reversed, least of all for aesthetic reasons.

And preachers must, perhaps supremely, guard against the temptation to think that if they have developed the proper performance skills, they may simply "present" something, as if it were an object, without first being addressed by it and without ever seriously addressing the living persons in front of them.[31] Not that we are always, or even usually, fully "present" to God and ourselves and others when we preach: everything from the complaint of the parishioner at the door, to a toothache, to serious illness, or another real calamity pulls us away and may leave us mechanically intoning what we have, one hopes, prepared. But something of character will still come through to those who have anything of an instinct for perceiving it, and if it is lacking, nothing whatever can substitute for it. The point is seeking a certain wholeness in what we do, never forgetting that we are doing it, first and foremost, before the God who cannot be deceived and who will not be mocked.

31. "Our Christian orator, while he says what is just, and holy, and good (and he ought never to say anything else), does all he can to be heard with intelligence, with pleasure, and with obedience; . . . and so far as he succeeds, he will succeed more by piety in prayer than by gifts of oratory. . . . He ought, before he opens his mouth, to lift up his thirsty soul to God, to drink in what he is about to pour forth, and to be himself filled with what he is about to distribute. . . . And who can make us say what we ought, and in the way we ought, except Him in whose hand both we and our speeches are?" (Augustine, *On Christian Doctrine* 4.32).

2

Preaching, Performance, and the Life and Death of "Now"

PAUL SCOTT WILSON

Performance is a temporal phenomenon, an act located in time. Preaching as performance normally focuses on the present moment, on orality and aurality, memory, delivery, bodily enactment, and articulation of meaning in the "now" before a congregation. Performance is a more robust word than delivery and may be better able to account for both divine and human activity in preaching. Performance is in a moment: until the notes of the musical score have been sounded, there is no music. Less noticed, performance is not easily confined to the small moment of the now. In fact, performance illuminates important dimensions of the preacher's task, and attempts to confine performance to a living instant may need to be balanced by an alternative vision. Both say something important. Here I explore four perspectives on now: the now that is oriented to the past, present, and future, as well as to the death of now and of the self that is needed for performance. In such death, preaching participates in the new life of Christ.

To people outside of performance studies, the word *performance* often implies something negative in preaching, such as focusing mainly on the preacher, or on theatricality, or on entertainment, on things that distract from the Word, and this danger is genuine and pervasive. Still, one does not condemn money because it can be used to ill purposes. The nature of the Word is itself eventful and performative. One recalls God speaking in Isaiah 55:11, "so shall my word be that goes out from my mouth; it shall not return to me empty, but it shall accomplish that which I purpose, and succeed in the thing for which I sent it." God's Word, like God's will, is God's action. God's thoughts are events. The expression of God's will is the promise and assurance of its fulfillment and completion. God thus provides the ultimate paradigm of performance: thoughts and words become action and event. God's Word does what it expresses. God's role in preaching (*actio divina*) tends to get lost in many discussions of performance and preaching (*homo performans*).[1] By contrast, when now is viewed as having past, present, and future perspectives, theological implications are enhanced.

Picturing Time

Time is often pictured in one dimension as a straight line, and the present is a tiny dot along that line. Past and future are separated on that line only by the infinitesimal moment of now. Any attempt to picture time is inescapably flawed, though greater richness is possible now in science where time is often pictured as being like a fishing net cast in space in embedding diagrams that depict space-time multidimensionally in the general theory of relativity. For preaching purposes, greater texture is given to now even if we think in a more limited way of time as a large wave in the open ocean approaching land.[2] It moves from an initial event or cause, such as the wind, in the same way that time moves forward from creation. The wave itself is the ever-changing present. It has a trough in front and behind, rising angled surfaces and a rounded crest at its highest point. Much of a wave cannot be seen beneath the surface of the water, and only when these lower depths meet increasing shallows does the wave begin to curl and break. Just as the end point of time is what God ultimately has planned, the end point of the wave is finally the shore.

1. Victor Turner, *The Anthropology of Performance* (New York: PAJ, 1988), 81, cited in Charles L. Bartow, *God's Human Speech: A Practical Theology of Proclamation* (Grand Rapids: Eerdmans, 1997), 60.

2. Another water image is that of time as a river. See Hans von Baeyer, "Gravity," in *Rainbows, Snowflakes, and Quarks: Physics and the World around Us* (New York: McGraw-Hill, 1984), 9–31. He speaks of space-time as being like an invisible stream that bends in response to objects and that carries all things along on its winding path.

The chief advantage in thinking of time in dimensional ways for preaching is that it allows us to think of now not statically but as motion, and to distinguish between different aspects of now. Instead of conceiving now as a fixed dot in a one-dimensional line, the present moment as a wave has a front sloped in the direction it is moving, a curl or breaking crest, and a backside. The present moment thus becomes three-dimensional. The backside of the wave looks to the past, the front side looks to the future, and the break is the event of oral delivery, the part of the wave that normally gets most attention in performance studies.

Performance at the Backside of Now

As a discipline, performance studies is richer for its orientation toward texts, literature, or what Ronald J. Pelias and James VanOosting call "aesthetic communication": "performance studies derives from the interpretation of literature and focuses on the performative and aesthetic nature of human discourse."[3] Preachers are trained primarily to work on texts and the meaning of those texts for today; thus they are trained to work mainly with the past and present—on the backside of the wave—and of course there is an enormous amount there to work on. Most of what normally is considered as exegesis, hermeneutics, and homiletics happens on that backside, studying biblical and other texts, anticipating and listening for God's Word for the contemporary community. An important part of performance happens looking back.

When Karl Barth refers to God speaking in proclamation as being "like a king through the mouth of his herald," he means that the herald is the conduit of the message that comes from God to the hearers.[4] Thomas G. Long has done as fine a job as anyone in exploring the metaphor of herald for preaching.[5] As he says, "Herald preachers, then, do not strive to create more beautiful and more excellent sermons; they seek to be more faithful to the message they receive in scripture."[6] We normally think of the herald predominantly in terms of past and present: the Bible as the Word of God (past) becomes the Word of God (present) in and through the process of scholarly engagement and prayerful discernment led, as Calvin stressed, by the Holy Spirit.

3. Ronald J. Pelias and James VanOosting, "A Paradigm for Performance Studies," *Quarterly Journal of Speech* 73 (1987): 219; see also 220–21.
4. Karl Barth, *Church Dogmatics* (Edinburgh: T&T Clark, 1936), I/1:57; cited by Thomas G. Long, *The Witness of Preaching* (Louisville: Westminster John Knox, 1989), 25.
5. Long, *Witness of Preaching*, esp. 24–30.
6. Ibid., 25.

Nicholas Lash and Performance

Nicholas Lash is one of a few writers who have brought fresh thinking to performance of Scripture. His notion of performance seems to draw more on J. L. Austin than on stage theory, and it seems unfettered by temporal constraint. He claims that every time a biblical text is properly interpreted, it is performed: "There is a creativity in interpretation which . . . is connected in some way with the fidelity, the 'truthfulness' of [the] performance."[7] In other words, to enact the New Testament texts as though Jesus did not historically live, or without concern for accuracy, or without correspondence to the truth of his life or the truth of God, would be to perform a different story. There needs to be no question that the text being performed is the text in its meaning as it was "originally intended."[8]

Lash also means performance in a second sense: every time a biblical text is lived as it is intended to be lived (i.e., as the church understands that intention), it is performed. He conceives of this interpretative activity as a full-time vocation, something larger than individual performance of a specific text: "The fundamental form of the Christian interpretation of scripture is the life, activity and organization of the believing community. The performance of scripture *is* the life of the church. It is no more possible for an isolated individual to perform these texts than it is for him to perform a Beethoven quartet or a Shakespeare tragedy."[9] For Lash, community life is to be construed as performance of the biblical text, and biblical interpretation is incomplete without it. Each text calls for its own distinct performance of particular human actions. Biblical texts cannot be performance in Lash's second sense if they are not first proclaimed and performed as specific texts in specific acts of proclamation: the congregation receives the Word for its own performance and enactment through reception of Word and sacrament.

Now as the Crest of a Wave

However we picture now, our means are inadequate. Now has no duration. We try to extend and give it thickness when we say, for example, "She is with us now," meaning the weeks while we are visiting at the farm, or "George Bush is president now," referring to a four-year term of office. Viewers of television willingly

7. Nicholas Lash, *Theology on the Way to Emmaus* (London: SCM, 1986), 40.
8. Ibid., 44.
9. Ibid., 43.

engage in an imaginative exercise with space and time when they view pictures taken in the past (when the program was made) as though they are real events happening here and now. Any illusion that now has duration is provided by the consistency of experience from one now to the next. Now is of course a largely human construct, the product of how we are conditioned to think, and every now is composed of many other nows—not just the nows we recall: the starlight we see is a now from millions of years ago; the now of thunder comes to us seconds after the now of the lightning; the texts that we plan to read originate in a former now and will be encountered in a future now. A. R. Ammons describes his experience of walking on a beach and seeing hundreds of birds arise and move as though with one mind, "the 'field' of action / with moving, incalculable center: / in the smaller view, order tight with shape."[10] The one potentially chaotic now of the flock was made up of the many nows of each individual bird. For preaching, unity in the now may describe a proleptic reality that has already been fulfilled in Christ. Now has many layers, and to think of now as a one-dimensional dot on a line is too restrictive. Now also has many performances: biblical text, sermon, preacher, congregation, God, and perhaps more.

Most of what has been published about preaching and performance has been said about preaching in the now, with good reason. As Charles L. Bartow says, the act of performance is the time of "turning ink into blood."[11] In the now of preaching the *actio divina* encounters the *homo performans*, or as Jana Childers says, "preachers hold one large mirror up to nature and a foggy, little pocket-sized one off at another angle, hoping for a glimpse of something Else."[12]

The Problem of Confining Performance to a One-Dimensional Now

Preaching brings forward to the present something that happened in the past, be it a biblical text, history about that text, the author/Author, Christian traditions, the sermon manuscript, stories of past events that have occurred in the contemporary world, or whatever. As long as a preacher in the moment of preaching is working to recapture a prior exegetical understanding of a biblical text or a rehearsed understanding of the text of a composed sermon, he or she looks to the past and uses memory as an essential part of any performance. Much that happens in preaching is looking back.

10. A. R. Ammons, "Corsons Inlet," http://boppin.com/poets/ammons.htm. I am grateful to Charles L. Bartow for pointing me to this poem.
11. Bartow, *God's Human Speech*, 53.
12. Jana Childers, *Performing the Word: Preaching as Theatre* (Nashville: Abingdon, 1998), 44.

By contrast, performance studies commonly limit performance to bodily or voice enactment of a text in the present before a live audience. The crest of the wave is the place of focus because it is most obvious and interesting and the visible action seems to happen there. Here we begin to see the limitation of confining understandings of performance to a traditional one-dimensional now. If Lash is right in saying that interpretation is performance, at what point does interpretation become performance? If the measurement is when a text becomes bodily action, might a text not be performed when someone thinks about it and neurons in the brain start firing, for then the text has become embodied and the text may be said to be directing the neuron action? Might a text not be performed when thought about a text is converted to action in the form of writing about it, the hand moving in distinctive patterns on page or a computer keyboard in ways prompted by the text? Is a text performed when it is silently read with comprehension;[13] when memory brings to mind what is prepared for delivery; when writing is converted to speech and action; or when the historical import of the text as the Word of God is properly understood and implemented in one's life with the help of the Holy Spirit? When does performance begin? How one frames performance becomes key. What aspects of performance events will be considered? In what sense is something a beginning, middle, or end?

Much of what happens in the now is oriented toward the past, as is plain in pulpit activities of recalling, rereading, reciting, reenacting, reminding, repeating, reemphasizing, and recapitulating. If all of the above may be considered as dimensions of performance, then performance is not restricted to the now of the "preaching moment," but extends to the past, even to matters we might otherwise consider as merely preparatory of performance.

Theological Problems with the Instant of Now

Attempts to limit performance in preaching to the present now also run into theological difficulties: too much emphasis is put on the performance of the preacher and not enough on the performance of God. The encounter of the *actio divina* with the *homo performans* has its primary location in the now, yet in fact it may happen as much along the way to the pulpit in sermon preparation as it does in the pulpit when performance is public. Does God start speaking in the moment of delivery or has God been working, perform-

---

13. In Lash's Roman Catholic tradition, the reading of Scripture is considered proclamation as well as the homily; reading can be proclamation even without preaching. In the Reformed understanding, proclamation is the reading and correct interpretation of Scripture, taken together.

ing, throughout the preparation process properly understood as prayerful and scholarly encounter with the biblical text and our world?

Preachers are unlike many actors who fully depend on someone else's script. Thus for the preacher, the actual scripting of the sermon is a dimension of the performance, both human and divine. To exclude that earlier dimension of performance is to privilege human performance over the divine. The preacher is in a sense the initial audience of God's performance and brings forward to the congregation what has been revealed through the week. If the Holy Spirit has not been performing the text in and through the preacher's daily meditations and labors, the preacher has no Word to perform on Sunday; only if the word on Sunday is the Word can the Holy Spirit be claimed to deliver that message as God's speech to the gathered community.

Performance as Process

An alternative way to consider performance in preaching is not as an incarnational *moment* of giving birth but as an incarnational *process* of the Word becoming flesh. In other words, performance moves through time. The incarnation for Mary does not suddenly happen at Christmas; it begins with conception by the Spirit.[14] From the first idea of a sermon, the Word is in a process of becoming. One could say that the Word has already become flesh for the preacher before Sunday, for one cannot preach what one has not received, and this is not without what we would call performance or enactment. Preachers mentally picture the text; compose their sermons by speaking them internally or out loud; test for suitable sound; listen for the voice of God through prayer and study; bring the voices of faith ancestors and the present congregation into conversation; and listen for what is not said that needs to be said to make the sermon more complete. Ideally the preacher rehearses the sermon out loud and has performed the text of the sermon prior to Sunday. Such prior performance, in its various degrees and stages, lacks the finality of performance in the pulpit when the congregation is present, but it nonetheless marks performance as a process that includes the backside of now extending into the past and that cannot easily be limited to the now.

We have been saying three things: (1) much of what happens in the pulpit happens on the backside of now, bringing the biblical text forward to the present;

---

14. Incarnational emphasis may be present when some homiletics books refer to the period of time necessary for creative reflection as gestation; also in Jana Childers, ed., *Birthing the Sermon: Women Preachers on the Creative Process* (St. Louis: Chalice, 2001). See also Childers, *Performing the Word*, 53–55.

(2) much of what happens in the now (such as remembering, repeating, and re-viewing) is oriented toward the past; and (3) performance in the now needs to be extended to the past. We now turn to the role of the future in performance.

The Front Side of Now

Performance takes on additional richness if one considers, in addition to the backside and the crest of now, also the front side of now, where anticipation and hope are instrumental. When now is pictured as a wave, the lead surface of the wave faces the future; it is here that the wave will first become what it will become, whether it meets a current, a wave from another direction, or the shore. Apart from when the crest curls and breaks, a wave is not water moving forward; it is energy moving through the water. The water molecules stay roughly in the same area, though they move up and down with each wave. Heraclitus said that one cannot step into the same river twice, and a wave is similarly new each moment. The water that constitutes a particular wave is continually changing because the wave moves through water. In the same way each new now contains new possibility. Jesus recognized this in preaching the radical in-breaking of the kingdom/realm of God: every moment announces the transforming presence of God. The preacher also proclaims the arrival of God's future, and in so doing performs that future in Christ's name.

The preaching process inevitably though unintentionally suppresses the future. The front side of now is normally obscured as a place of performance in homiletics because it is normally considered as delivery, a subject on which even most classical rhetoric had relatively little to record in writing. Exegetical and hermeneutical processes that preachers follow tend to be back and forth between exegesis and application, then and now, past and present, and the method affects the outcome. As a result, how the future impacts preaching performance receives relatively little discussion. In preaching, as at the table, we encounter the future present.[15]

Performance at the Front Side of Now

Performance at the front side of now looks to the future and involves antici-pation and hope. When classical rhetoric is the norm for preaching, its five canons each contain some future orientation: invention looks to what might

15. See Marianne H. Micks, *The Future Present: The Phenomenon of Christian Worship* (New York: Seabury, 1970).

be said; arrangement and style conceive how it will best be communicated; memory designs what is said so that it will be remembered by the performer and the listeners; and delivery always anticipates what comes next. Most of these canons function of course prior to delivery in the lead-up to the moment of presentation (though they are nonetheless performative).

When applied to preaching, delivery has obvious orientation to the lead edge of now, and relatively little attention is given to it in most preaching manuals. It is difficult to write about because it begs for one-on-one coaching, not abstract discussion. As Jana Childers says, the pulpit provides a measure of distance from the speaker that is essential—good communication depends on the listener having a choice to close the emotional or spiritual gap with the preacher. She identifies three stages in the creative process: voicing and hearing the text, even before exegesis; acting the text through physical movement in order to discover words to say; and filling the gap between preacher and hearer (and leaving others for the listener to fill) in a transformative experience of the Spirit.[16] The latter of these happens on the front side of now as the speaker anticipates the development of the sermon to discover what it will be and awaits a Word of encounter for all.

One might be tempted to limit the forward-moving aspect of preaching to the word or image of the sermon as it unfolds. However, congregational needs and nonverbal clues from the listeners in delivery also have a future component, even though they initially sound more like the preacher is responding rather than leading. The role of the congregation in the delivery is important, and without it, the preacher is given too central a role. The Word is most surely the Word when it is a community event. Delivery at the front side of now is not just a matter of the preacher performing, albeit with God's help; it is a process of the congregation receiving the Word through lively encounter with what is said and not said. In other words, the preacher and the congregation, together with the Holy Spirit, give birth to the sermon; they work together in a dance that is reminiscent of the trinitarian concept of *perichoresis* in which the persons of the Trinity demonstrate incomparable hospitality to one another.[17]

Much anticipation of the future, for instance in terms of congregational need, is already built into a composed sermon, but both the preacher and the congregation need to be responsive in the moment to the nudging of the Holy Spirit. The congregation expresses itself in the act of preaching, not just through the representative function of the office of the preacher. In churches

16. Childers, *Performing the Word*, 54–55.
17. Daniel Migliore, *Faith Seeking Understanding* (Grand Rapids: Eerdmans, 1991), 70.

where there is call and response, the elders and members of the congregation respond with various calls of encouragement and direction (e.g., "Make it plain") in the course of the sermon. In lesser degrees that require greater subtlety of interpretation, every congregation gives feedback through expressions, laughter, attention, posture, and so forth. In performing a sermon, preacher and congregation anticipate each other from the signals they offer one another. The preacher looks for connection, understanding, willingness to hear new ideas, and so forth, even as the congregation signals the need for explanation, qualification, repetition, or change of pace. All of this comes as a signal about the future that is the unfolding sermon.

The future affects the present in another way in addition to delivery that has to do with social justice. Ronald J. Allen and Joseph R. Jeter Jr. have used the notion of *perichoresis* to describe a circular dance that needs to take place within a sermon such that it demonstrates an awareness of many congregational perspectives, not just one: "people move around the circle in a way that implies intimacy, equality, unity yet distinction, and love."[18] Pelias and VanOosting speak of the performer as a social activist who gives voice to those silenced by culture.[19] In effect what happens in the sermon is that the preacher and the congregation participate in the new creation promised by Christ and realized even in the moment. God inaugurates in the now a new realm of the future in which justice, kindness, and humility reign (Mic. 6:8).

Performance and Manuscript

Attention to the front side of now opens new perspectives on performance. Most discussions of theater performance do not presume the actor to have a manuscript, whereas a manuscript is presumed in most discussions of pulpit performance. An effective preacher does not simply read a prepared manuscript but uses it as a prompt. The preacher tries to avoid looking at the manuscript more than necessary, and therefore must anticipate what comes next. Much is remembered and much needs a cue—at least it otherwise cannot be recalled immediately. Experienced preachers build into a manuscript or outline certain memory devices, key words, sensory details, images, linked thoughts, rhetorical structures, and stories. Because these proceed in a certain sequence and designate certain chunks of material, their effect is to lead the preacher's

---

18. Ronald J. Allen and Joseph R. Jeter Jr., *One Gospel, Many Ears: Preaching for Different Listeners in the Congregation* (St. Louis: Chalice, 2002), 121; see also 128.

19. Pelias and VanOosting, "A Paradigm for Performance Studies," 225.

thought and feelings during the performance. The preacher discovers what comes next in part by following a marked path.

The preacher brings past preparation forward into the present and is thus most attentive to the rehearsed items that come next in delivery. The preacher also tries to reach into the future, to anticipate what comes next by emotional tone and gesture, and to appropriate anew the gospel message that he or she is given to utter. Insofar as preaching consists in part of proclamation, of speaking words of liberation and forgiveness on God's behalf, the preacher stands as a kind of sentinel looking ahead for the first signs of God's in-breaking realm, a herald in a prophetic sense, anticipating God's mercy even now. Of course in this the preacher is no more at the forefront of now than anyone else, and the wave of God's future does not break first over the pulpit.

The Death of Now and Performance as Death

Performance involves not only the backside, crest, and front side of now, it also involves the death of now. Performance requires death. The most significant performance of preaching is God's act, the *actio divina*. The preacher, like any performer, gives over himself or herself to the performance, that is, to God. The proclamation of the gospel is the goal that overtakes all other performance goals. This giving over is often a formalized action in a dedicatory prayer preceding the sermon, using such words as Psalm 19:14, "Let the words of my mouth and the meditation of my heart be acceptable to you, O LORD, my rock and my redeemer." The faithful preacher approaches the pulpit with humility, hoping that God's Word will be heard through what is said and done, sometimes even in spite of what is said and done.

Part of giving oneself over to God in the preaching act is letting go of the sermon as an act of one's own love and labor. The words of the sermon are uttered and the moment they are offered they are gone; in the giving of them they recede into the past. Silence now swallows the spoken words. As acoustic images they die. The performance of them is a kind of death. During all of the stages of preparation for performance, the preacher of necessity pours oneself into it. Yet in performing the sermon, the preacher must let go. To replay the performance in one's mind may be of benefit if one is learning from mistakes, but otherwise to hang on to it can be vain or unfaithful. The preacher gives the sermon as an offering, lets it go, and leaves not empty-handed, but with the experience of having received the Word even through the giving of it. Still, in letting go, the preacher acknowledges what has been true all along: that it never was the preacher's and the preacher never was in control. There is no return to it, and already the next Sunday approaches.

Dying to Self

In Romans, Paul declares that "there is now no condemnation for those who are in Christ Jesus" for they are "free from the law of sin and death" (8:1–2 NIV); our old self has already been crucified with Christ (6:6) and death has no dominion over him or us (6:9, 14). According to the majority of New Testament references to death, Christians have already died the most significant death in Christ, and the death that lies ahead is but a shadow. On the front side of the wave new life is given, and no act of will on the part of the individual can negate this reality. This life is *actio divina* given in Christ, once and for all.

Still, as humans, we experience something like death, for instance, each time we sin; we need to keep coming to the Word and table to be restored again. For the preacher, giving oneself to God in preaching means dying to self to live for God. A preacher cannot remain aloof from the people or deaf to their concerns but must rather enter their pain and speak it for them, in a sense appropriate for community. As in the psalms of lament, one must bring the people's cries before God. One can do so only if one is in touch with one's own brokenness and pain as well as theirs. At the same time one must dare to speak words of correction and comfort on behalf of God, and venture in faith to say what God has done and is doing about the pain of the world. The words proclaimed on behalf of God (I love you. I forgive you. I will never let you go.) are the most intimate and loving words one can ever utter, and of course to speak in this way is costly; it was costly for God and it is costly for us. No one can speak these words and hold on to his or her own notions of life apart from Christ.

No wonder preachers often speak of feeling vulnerable and exposed after preaching. It involves a Christlike self-emptying (*kenosis*) as in the words of Philippians 2:5–7, "Let the same mind be in you that was in Christ Jesus, who, though he was in the form of God, did not regard equality with God as something to be exploited, but emptied himself, taking the form of a slave." Each of us humans has a misguided sense of being the center of the universe; the performance of a sermon reinforces this illusion of being at the center, and it is this illusion also that necessarily dies. In acknowledging that the role of herald is a role in service of One greater, the power of the Word is acknowledged. The Word does not die at the end of the sermon (though words as acoustic images die); the preacher's role dies as the deliverer of that Word. Already in the now of preaching the moment of death looms ahead, just as it has every Sunday.

The idea of death to self can be negative in these days, especially for women who have been taught to be invisible, and to be told to die to self can seem oppressive. Some women say that when they perform, they are most fully who they are; God is using them most fully. Alla Renée Bozarth speaks of *kenosis* as a necessary part of performance: "The self-aware ego places us in a subject-object relationship not only to others but to ourselves. . . . The way out of the ego is through attention toward others, especially through intense concentration on an *Other*."[20] She pairs *kenosis* with *plerosis*, or being filled, as two aspects of a single process: "But the interpreter never ceases to remain a person. There is no loss of consciousness or self in interpretation, but only of self-consciousness and ego-centric self, in order to reveal the true self so that it can become engaged with the poem. Kenosis for the interpreter is a loving attitude of humility and nonresistance toward the text."[21]

Bozarth implies that preaching as dying is only a part of the story in that new identity is received. If the *actio divina* is the gift of new life, the *homo performans* in part is the willingness to conform to that identity again and again as in repentance and coming to the table. Christians die to self to live for Christ such that it is not they who live but Christ who lives in them. They willingly allow their lives to take the shape of the cross and enter Christ's death in order that they may more fully conform to God's will. Death is part of the significance of baptism, dying to the old self to be born again; sanctification is an ongoing process of dying to old ways of being to become who the Holy Spirit empowers us to be.

The preacher must enter death through performance: the performance ends, the ideas, emotions, and gestures are released, and for the preacher the sermon is over. Our lives are hidden with Christ in God and so too our sermons. In faith these words of testimony to the cross and resurrection now become resurrection words. They take on new life, Spirit-given life, as the listeners receive and in turn perform the living Word. Thus the preacher, with a view beyond the self and beyond this moment, continues to entrust the sermon to God for life.

20. Alla Renée Bozarth, *The Word's Body: An Incarnational Aesthetic of Interpretation* (1979; repr., Lanham, MD: University Press of America, 1997), 86.
21. Ibid., 90.

Performance as Hope

More happens on the front side of now that has to do with a prevailing attitude of hope in performance. Long before a wave reaches its end point on the beach, the land mass affects it by making the water shallow. So too in preaching, the end that God has in store affects the performance long before that end point is reached. The end is larger than the important particular goal that Henry Mitchell calls the sermon's "behavioral purpose"—the end of the sermon is the end of all time, when all of God's salvation promises will be fulfilled and God's victory over principalities and powers is complete and all things are made new in Christ.[22]

Of course we are already affected by that ending; we already taste that victory in the resurrection and ascension of Jesus Christ and in the receipt of his Spirit in the church. Said another way, the character of the eschaton is already known in Jesus Christ who meets us in the now. He is God's eschaton. A sermon performed in the light of the end times necessarily demonstrates this hope in the performance of the preacher.

Indeed the preacher at the front side of now performs a practice of time different from what is available in strictly linear progression. Linear time keeps past, present, and future in sequence, and is something of a human construct. For God, past, present, and future are all in view at once. Jesus expresses this understanding when he reminds the Sadducees that Moses "speaks of the Lord as the God of Abraham, the God of Isaac, and the God of Jacob. Now he is God not of the dead but of the living; for to him all are alive" (Luke 20:37–38). We express this understanding of time at the communion table, when we affirm in faith that we are gathered with all Christians everywhere, past, present, and future, the communion of saints.

Time in the Sermon

We have been speaking of various dimensions of now including the death of now and of the self in the performance of preaching. There is one further aspect of time to be considered, namely, notions of time represented in the sermon itself, in aid of God's performance. Preachers typically are advised to speak of the biblical text in the present tense. The common explanation for this is in terms of communication theory; it makes the performance more engaging.

22. Henry H. Mitchell, *Celebration and Experience in Preaching* (Nashville: Abingdon, 1990), 52.

There is an important theological reason as well: easy division of past and present is practiced by much of our society, and says in effect that the past is past, live in the now. Such societal wisdom diminishes God's concern for justice, for past injustice is not dealt with until the guilty have been brought to account and the victims are vindicated. If the past is already taken care of, there is no reason to erase the burden of the past from the suffering or guilty soul.

By bringing the past into the present in the sermon, all of the forces of history are left in play along with God's dominion over them; our language does not bring premature closure. Moreover the future is also engaged: in faith we affirm the final outcome is known now, may be received now, may be trusted fully in the person of Jesus Christ. In other words there is both a present realization of eschatological hopes and a future realization (e.g., a final resurrection of the dead, John 6:39–40, 44). The preacher speaks of a past that is present and of a future that is here now. This present-tense affirmation of a hope that is here now, spoken on behalf of God, is genuine proclamation and takes the form of words such as, "You are mine. I love you. I forgive you. I will never let you go." Sermons that proclaim the gospel necessarily arrive at this place. Performance is done as an action of hope. How we picture time in the sermon itself needs to be done in such a way that it contrasts what society does, saying "the past is past, leave it behind." We need to bring the past into the present, to where healing is needed, and claim the proleptic reality already fulfilled in Christ.

The Preacher as Herald

It is precisely this attentiveness to the in-breaking of the future now that underlies the biblical notion of the preacher as herald. The preacher on the front side of now performs on the cusp of time and stands therefore also in the position of a sentinel, someone chosen to keep watch. There is biblical precedent for this in the appointment of a watchman for the king (1 Sam. 14:16; 2 Sam. 18:24–27; 2 Kings 9:17–20), in the prophet Ezekiel's appointment as a watchman over Israel, and in Psalm 127:1b, "Unless the LORD guards the city, the guard keeps watch in vain." Yet the preacher's role is so much more than keeping watch for trouble. The preacher is also like Daniel in Daniel 5, who reads signs, but in the case of the modern preacher the signs are of the reign of God breaking into the present in acts of justice, mercy, and love. The preacher's role is also like that of the angel proclaiming to the shepherds, "Do not be afraid; for see—I am bringing you good news of great joy for all the people" (Luke 2:10).

All of this simply underlines that there is urgency to performance within the sermon. Elizabeth Achtemeier said as much when speaking about the importance of clarity in preaching, "The eternal life or death of our people may depend on their knowing what we mean."[23] The future, in short, is more than the sum of all past and present causes and effects; it is also what God wills. In faith, the sermon puts listeners in the presence of Jesus Christ, and in such relationship, the future is present now. Charles Bartow comments, "We are eschatologically, not ontologically, determined. The future, our future, is fixed in Christ. . . . In him God is present for us, and in him we are present for God."[24] The preacher enacts this role of sentinel by performing God's Word.

Conclusion

This chapter has argued that the notion of time as the moment in front of hearers that normally governs performance studies is too limited for preaching. Preaching in the now is in fact a multilayered concept, and many notions of now make up our now. When does performance begin? Four particular notions are helpful to consider if one moves away from thinking of now as a dot in a line. If one thinks of time in three dimensions as being like a wave, one can speak in preaching of the backside of now, the crest of the wave, the front side of now, and the death of now and the self. Even this death is an act of conforming one's life to the cross so that one participates in new life in Christ. How the preacher speaks of time within the sermon is an aspect of God's performance. The advantage of rethinking time in this way is to bring to greater fullness various performative dimensions of the preaching task and to help remove notions of excessive theatricality from the idea of performance in preaching.

23. Elizabeth Achtemeier, *Creative Preaching: Finding the Words* (Nashville: Abingdon, 1980), 31.

24. Charles L. Bartow, *The Preaching Moment: A Guide to Sermon Delivery* (Nashville: Abingdon, 1980), 50.

3

At the Intersection of *Actio Divina* and *Homo Performans*

Embodiment and Evocation

A L Y C E M . M C K E N Z I E

In the fall of 1971 in a classroom at Cedar Cliff High School in Camp Hill, Pennsylvania, I sat morosely in the opening session of Mr. Vogelsong's required Speech 101 class. My stomach was knotted with dread at the prospect that one day soon I would be the one standing in front of the class. Apart from the butterflies, there was the practical question of how to organize the content of my address. By the end of the first class, I knew how to organize my material, and my dread had dissipated somewhat. All I had to do was tell them what I was going to tell them, tell them, and then tell them what I had told them.

As I was learning how to "spill the beans, gather the beans, and count the beans," a new approach to preaching was being launched that has come to be called "the New Homiletic." The immediate instigation was the publication of Fred Craddock's book, *As One without Authority*, in 1973. Other voices would soon enter the conversation.

The New Homiletic viewed much traditional preaching as cerebral monologues based on the reduction of texts to ideas and congregations to recipients of ideas. It insisted on the inseparability of form and content in sermons. It did not, however, address a related and crucial issue: the inseparability of delivery from form and content.

The New Homiletic highlighted the importance of poetic, often metaphorical language. It held out the goal of preaching as evoking experience rather than explaining and describing the character of God and the propositions inhering in texts.

It has been a long time since my high school speech class. Now, as a teacher of preachers, I notice that some things never seem to change. In introductory preaching classes, the assignment for students to preach their first sermons functions like a tap to the knee with a doctor's mallet. Many students still reflexively preach a three-point sermon of concepts boiled down from a historical-critical approach to the text, or a two-part background-application sermon based on the same exegetical approach. By no coincidence, Charles Bartow will insist, their delivery often lacks animation. Rather, it bespeaks distance in vocal, physical, and facial expression.

A Historical Perspective

Traditional preaching was governed by Aristotelian rules of rhetorical persuasion. The method was deductive, moving from general principles to specific applications. The goal was logical persuasion. The sermonic form was an outline with its series of deductively presented points. Aristotle's *Rhetoric* (330 BCE) was a contribution to a conversation about persuasive public address that had been going on for at least two hundred years. Rhetoric arose because of the need for means of argumentation in contexts of persuasive public discourse. These contexts were situations in which "matters could be otherwise," such as the law court (forensic speech), the legislature (deliberate speech), and the state funeral (epideictic speech). In such situations, the speaker advanced his position in as persuasive a manner as possible over against the weaknesses of alternative possibilities.[1] While solidly rooted in the legal, economic, and political systems of its day, rhetoric evolved to provide the basis of education, forms of entertainment (debate), and social grace.[2]

---

1. Andre Resner Jr., *Preacher and Cross: Person and Message in Theology and Rhetoric* (Grand Rapids: Eerdmans, 1999), 10.
2. Paul Scott Wilson, *The Practice of Preaching* (Nashville: Abingdon, 1995), 197.

Whether or not one gained the audience's assent depended on how closely one followed the five canons or sets of rules for creating speeches. They were *invention* (discovery of potential arguments to use), *arrangement* (the order in which one developed one's arguments), *style* (the way the speaker uses words), *memory*, and *delivery*.[3]

In the fourth century, Augustine wrote *On Christian Doctrine*. In the fourth book of this work, which he devoted to homiletics, he gave permission for the critical appropriation of rhetorical strategies for Christian proclamation. The stage was set for the centuries-long "Aristotelian captivity of the sermon."

By the medieval period, the canon of invention was fading as the canon of style increased in importance. Rhetoric as a whole came to be identified with issues of style, word choices, and manner of expression. Its partnership with logic was largely ended by the 1500s. Humanist and logician Peter Ramus (1515–72) signed the divorce papers between rhetoric and logic, assigning to rhetoric all matters of style and dress and delivery, and to logic all matters of invention and arrangement.

This dichotomy between rhetoric and logic deepened into a divide between imagination and intellect. Enlightenment philosophy considered the human soul to possess a number of attributes in an ordered hierarchy. The faculties of imagination and reason were distinct, and imagination was regarded as inferior to reason. Rhetoric as ornament was clearly inferior to logic. (This is evident in contemporary statements such as: "It's just rhetoric." "Let's cut through the rhetoric and get to the substance.")

The three-point deductive sermon increased in prominence around 1200 with the recovery of Aristotle and thus of empirical evidence based in reason. The growth of urban centers, need for instruction in the church, and emphasis on a better-educated clergy contributed to its popularity.[4] The propositional sermon commonly exhibits an exegesis-application approach. This form dates back to first-century synagogue preaching, when the norm was to read Scripture and comment on it. The Puritan plain-style sermon (exposition, doctrine, application) was yet another modification in which brief exegesis led to a specific doctrine that then became the subject of the sermon applied to the life of the people. Another practice that had an impact was the medieval disputation followed by nearly all the great teachers of the period. Teachers

---

3. Paul Scott Wilson, "Beyond Narrative: Imagination in the Sermon," in *Listening to the Word: Studies in Honor of Fred B. Craddock*, ed. Gail R. O'Day and Thomas G. Long (Nashville: Abingdon, 1993), 132.

4. Wilson, *The Practice of Preaching*, 205.

such as Thomas Aquinas would begin with a question, move to arguments against the position, and then move to arguments for it.[5]

The New Homiletic was a critique of the hegemony of three-point, propositional preaching on the basis of its negative impact on the purpose of preaching and the roles of preacher, Scripture, and congregation. In the first place, propositional preaching tends to imply that preaching by definition is the imparting of information. In the second place, as a mainstay of the pulpit's fare from week to week, it has been accused of implying a style of ministry that confuses authority with authoritativeness, in which the preacher stands over the congregation rather than with them, lecturing rather than proclaiming. Third, it can lead to an exegetical process in which this outline format is imposed on texts, short-circuiting the polyvalence of the text and its formative impact on both preacher and people. When characterized by static unity, in which points do not grow one from the other, three-point sermons impose a predetermined structure on the text that is not inherent to the text and may not be pertinent to the congregational context. In the fourth place, it tends to foster passivity in the congregation, a definition of response as remembering logical propositions.[6]

A chorus of voices arose in the seventies through the nineties offering varying but interrelated challenges to traditional preaching. Fred Craddock pointed out that traditional preaching made the congregation passive recipients of ideas. Eugene Lowry, popularizer of Aristotelian poetics for preaching in the book *The Homiletical Plot*, demanded to know: where is the plot? Feminist and liberationist homileticians questioned the notion of logical persuasion as the purpose of preaching. They also challenged its dispassionate tone and the over-under notion of the authority of the preacher implied by its monological format. Henry Mitchell, African American homiletician, demanded: where is the emotional logic in traditional preaching? Charles Rice, a narrative homiletician who taught for many years at Drew University, lamented the lack of imagination in preaching. David Buttrick argued that sermons should involve a flow in consciousness that results in the engendering of transformed identity and behavior.

A Theological Framework

Charles Bartow, in his books *God's Human Speech: A Practical Theology of Proclamation*, *The Preaching Moment*, and *Effective Speech Communication*

5. Ibid., 206.
6. Ibid.

in Leading Worship, offers a unique and invaluable contribution to the ongoing homiletical conversation and to the teaching of preaching. It is the gift of a theological articulation of the unity of form, content, and delivery in preaching. Bartow's work in speech communication grounds the New Homiletic's advocacy of sermons that are participatory, imaginative, and evocative in what he calls a "practical theology of proclamation." He understands preaching as an instance of practical theology, theology that is local, performative, inductive, and interdisciplinary.[7]

His explication of preaching as performative is especially clarifying and crucial for the preacher's articulation of a theology of preaching. Preaching is not merely an act of public self-expression. It is a performative act (*homo performans*) as contrasted with a spontaneous act. Preaching has intentionality about it, both in its preparation and in its delivery. As such it is characterized by call, choice, commitment, calculation, and a common goal.

The divine self-disclosure of Jesus Christ is the primary locus of performative action for practical theology. God's self-disclosure in Jesus Christ is a performative event, and as such it is also characterized by call, choice, commitment, calculation, and a common goal. Preaching is an event of divine self-disclosure or *actio divina*. Preaching expresses and embodies God's claim on us. In the preaching moment, *actio divina* and *homo performans* meet in Christ as the worlds of text and preacher encounter one another.[8]

Someone once defined preaching as "a risk God takes." No one has stated more clearly or hopefully than Bartow the positive potential that motivates the gamble. Preaching issues a "claim, it directs us toward the future, and to Him to whom the future belongs. The referent of a sermon . . . is not something in the past, nor is it any individual, thing, or circumstance of the present. Instead, the referent of a sermon is what lies beyond. Preaching has to do with what yet may be."[9] As Bartow eloquently puts it, "In Christ Jesus, God takes us as we are and presses us into the service of what God would have us be."[10] Bartow's theological construal of the act of preaching has transformative energy. It offers preachers a dynamic context in which to preach sermons that move from talking about God to evoking God's new possibilities, from the delivery of concepts to the embodiment of divine presence.

7. Charles L. Bartow, *God's Human Speech: A Practical Theology of Proclamation* (Grand Rapids: Eerdmans, 1997), 1.

8. Ibid., 111.

9. Charles L. Bartow, *The Preaching Moment: A Guide to Sermon Delivery* (Nashville: Abingdon, 1980), 18.

10. Bartow, *God's Human Speech*, 53.

Bartow's approach to preaching as an oral-aural event advances three key convictions of the New Homiletic: preaching and worship are dialogical; the emotional investment of the preacher in both preparation and delivery is crucial to the preaching moment; and the imagination has a far more profound role in preaching than merely providing stories and images to illustrate each of our three points.

From Explanation to Evocation

We have seen how recent homiletical reflection has emphasized that the goal of preaching is not so much to explain God as to invite listeners into the divine presence and to evoke wonder and possibility. Easier said than done. The ever-practical Bartow offers several suggestions for how we might preach evocatively.

The first is that we attend to the movement of thought in preaching, remembering that preaching is not a static arrangement of ideas. Listeners do not listen for ideas, in Bartow's view. They listen to be changed. "You are listening for ideas, facts, opinions, feelings . . . that start somewhere and that are headed somewhere and that mean to have you go along with them . . . when you are listening to a sermon . . . you are listening with some expectation of being changed."[11] This has much in common with David Buttrick's "moves and structures," in which sermons form faith in human consciousness by inviting hearers along a dynamic journey of several "moves," a term he prefers to the traditional "points."

Second, Bartow suggests we attend to the specific contexts that give rise to the movement of thought and be aware of our personal involvement in them, remembering that, in preaching, ideas are never abstract. They are, rather, grounded in past, present, and emerging situations of human life.[12] In this insight Bartow honors the local nature of practical theology and the insights of postmodernism into the contextual nature of texts and contexts.

Third, we are to allow ourselves to hear the claim made on us when we are preaching. When a preacher has no investment in what is being said, we know by myriad features of face, voice, gesture, and posture. Bartow makes a crucial connection between the physical, spiritual, and emotional investment of the preacher in the preaching moment and the use of poetic, metaphorical language. He comments that "preaching, after all, makes use of religious/metaphoric language, which has the power to disclose new ways—perhaps

11. Bartow, *The Preaching Moment*, 15.
12. Ibid., 20.

challenging, or even uncomfortable, but responsible ways—of being and acting in the world."[13]

The last half of the twentieth century witnessed an increase in philosophical and linguistic interest in metaphor. Metaphor has been transformed from a specialized concern of rhetoricians and literary critics to a central concept in the study of human understanding.[14] Philosophical and linguistic reflection on metaphor has led to several conclusions of relevance to preachers. Metaphor is part of all disciplines in the sense that thought is metaphoric. It is best understood within the parameters of some kind of tension or interaction theory. Context is essential to any understanding of metaphor. Metaphor has the potential to redescribe our world, restructure our concepts and categories, and reshape our experience of reality.[15]

Aristotle viewed imaginative language as ornamental. He held a substitutionary view of metaphor. It was a trope, a figurative way to express a word's literal meaning. (Other tropes included synecdoche, metonymy, and simile.)[16] Similarly for traditional homiletics, imagery, synecdoche, metaphor, and simile were window dressings for concepts. They were the spoonful of sugar that made the medicine go down.

However, advocates of the New Homiletic pointed out that the story or the image is all many people remember about the sermon. They believed this suggests a more fundamental role for metaphor and story and imagery than ornamentation for concepts. Rather than illuminating the point, they may be the point!

Bartow could not agree more. For him the tropes of human language, so vividly embodied in Scripture, point toward both the presence and the mystery of God, evoking a world that may yet be, by the power of God. They include oxymorons, in which opposites make up a whole; metaphors, in which juxtaposition of the unexpected creates a new view of life; and metonymy, in which an attribute of something, or something associated with it, stands for the whole. For him they are no mere window dressing for concepts. Bartow builds his theology of proclamation on these tropes, deeply rooted, linguistic structures of poetic evocation. They point to both the transcendence and the immanence of the divine in human life. They express both the speech and the silence of the divine-human relationship. Because they express more than

13. Ibid.
14. See Sheldon Sachs, ed., *On Metaphor* (Chicago: University of Chicago Press, 1978).
15. Rodney Kennedy, *The Creative Power of Metaphor: A Rhetorical Homiletics* (Lanham, MD: University Press of America, 1993), 59–60.
16. Janice Martin Soskice, *Metaphor and Religious Language* (Oxford: Clarendon, 1985), 56–57.

words can convey, they point to the truth about preaching that "the talk is never all."[17]

From Delivery to Embodiment

Bartow is adamant that what we commonly call delivery is charged with theological meaning. There is no such thing as a great divide between substance and style. What we say (content), the way in which we shape what we say (form), and how we say what we say are interwoven.

Bartow sees that interweaving as a theological enterprise embodied at any given time in a human voice, body, and person. Scripture reading and proclamation of the gospel are acts of interpretive speech.[18] Thus Bartow honors the study of the reading of the Scriptures and the preaching of sermons with particular focus on the scriptural text as *spoken* text and the sermon as *spoken* word. Such a study, he insists, "takes us straight to the theological heart of the matter. It directs our attention to God's self-disclosure as performative event, and it prompts a careful review of our listening and of our speaking in the light of that event."[19]

It is imperative that we attend to that self-disclosure in all its aspects, including embodiment by means of face, gesture, and voice. Bartow's concrete guidelines in matters of the public reading of Scripture and worship leadership are all in service to his theological understanding of proclamation. He encourages the preacher to ask, "How does my embodiment of this sermon express the call, choice, commitment, calculation and common goal of this act of divine self-disclosure?" Bartow offers preachers a practical, theologically astute approach to what has traditionally been called sermon delivery as an integral part of the process of sermon preparation from initial reading of text to preaching the sermon in the midst of the congregation.

Citing the traditional steps of classical rhetoric (invention, arrangement, style, memory, and delivery), Bartow warns us of the danger of thinking of these five dimensions of rhetoric as separate steps. They are not separate.

> Since delivery of the text is crucial to experiencing the impact of the text as an event of God's self-disclosure, laden with intellectual and emotional content, delivery skills clearly play a role in invention. Also, since arrangement of sermonic material has to do with how one most clearly and winsomely may bear witness

17. See chap. 1 of Bartow's *God's Human Speech*. See also chap. 1 of his *Preaching Moment*, 13–20.

18. Bartow, *God's Human Speech*, 4.

19. Ibid., 3.

to what has been experienced as God's Word in a text of Scripture, skill in delivery has an impact on the ordering of the sermon. Further, if style has to do with a preacher's distinctive use of language in light of the demands of subject matter and setting, then questions about self-expression in body and voice must have stylistic import. Finally, one cannot very well keep in mind what one has to say without giving due consideration to how what is thought faithfully can be expressed. Thus sermon delivery skills play an important role in the homiletical process from beginning to end. They do not just enable preachers to say things well. They help preachers to determine what they are to say. Sermon delivery skills have epistemological and hermeneutical significance.[20]

It wouldn't be a bad idea for teachers of preaching to read this paragraph at the beginning of every homiletics class session. It would go a long way toward the prevention of the two extremes that often occur in student sermons. The first is the sermon that is really an exegetical lecture. The preacher reads it in a wooden manner, every now and then coming up for air and realizing that she is boring everyone. At those points, she throws in an impromptu (and not always relevant) personal story to liven things up. The second is the sermon that is largely extemporaneous in which the student relies on his natural charisma and comfort in standing before a group. He apparently assumes that these genetic attributes compensate for his lack of preparation.

Homiletical Implications

Bartow's bridgework between speech communication and practical theology has been invaluable in my teaching of homiletics in the seminary classroom. It has also given both warrant and inspiration to my pursuit of a specific scholarly interest: preaching the Wisdom forms of the Bible. Wisdom literature in the Bible appears primarily in the books of Proverbs, Ecclesiastes, and Job, and the aphorisms and parables of the synoptic Jesus. Its forms include the majestic poetic reflections on the identity of Wisdom (for example, Prov. 8:22–36) and the short wisdom sentences (proverbs) of Proverbs, Ecclesiastes, and the teachings of the synoptic Jesus. Its forms also include the poetry of the Song of Songs and several psalms that evince wisdom themes.[21] They also include the extended reflections of Ecclesiastes and Job.

20. Charles L. Bartow, "Sermon Delivery," unpublished paper for class distribution, 4.
21. Roland E. Murphy in *The Tree of Life: An Exploration of Biblical Wisdom Literature*, The Anchor Bible Reference Library (New York: Doubleday, 1990) lists Pss. 1; 32; 34; 37; 49; 112; and 128 as "wisdom psalms," 103.

The Wisdom literature is filled with the kind of poetic language that Bartow rightly suggests leads to the embodiment of presence, not mere delivery of ideas. My work in preaching the Wisdom literature has been energized by Bartow's passionate vision of practical, physical sermons in which the preacher has something—or, rather, someone—to see and hear and feel, and not just some things to talk about.

Bartow's insights give preachers the theological rationale to explore the topic of genre-sensitive preaching at a more general level than Wisdom forms. His understanding of preaching as an event in which *actio divina* (divine action, divine self-performance) meets *homo performans* (human performative act) promises a respect for the pluralism of the scriptural witness in preaching. Scripture from both the Old and the New Testaments is replete with a variety of literary forms. These forms include narrative, poetry, hymn, lament, prophetic oracles, letters, apocalyptic visions, proverbs, and parables. Sermons that are shaped by the form and rhetorical intentions of the texts out of which they grow encourage congregational participation and are directed toward the wide spectrum of listeners' faculties, not solely to their intellects. It seems likely that such sermons will embody and evoke rather than deliver and explain.

Genre-Sensitive Sermons

An emphasis on genre-sensitive preaching arose out of the influence of rhetorical criticism and speech act theory on biblical studies. Rhetorical criticism is a school of literary analysis that focuses on how the audience is influenced or "manipulated" by a text's rhetorical devices. Speech act theory analyzes the rhetorical intentions of oral communication on the assumption that it is performative, that is, the speech act seeks to do things, to have certain effects on its audience, and not just to say things. Speech act theory is applicable to literary, specifically biblical texts, since they are the result of the inscription of material that was originally conveyed in oral performance.[22] Over the past couple of decades, a number of homileticians have made the case that sermons based on texts from specific genres ought to be shaped by the forms and rhetorical devices of those genres.[23] They insist that the literary form of the text

22. Rhetorical criticism has deep roots in Aristotle and other classical rhetorical scholarship. Important twentieth-century contributors to this approach include Kenneth Burke and Wayne Booth. Speech act theory is associated with J. L. Austin and John Searle.

23. Relevant works include: David L. Bartlett, *The Shape of Scriptural Authority* (Philadelphia: Fortress, 1983); John C. Holbert, *Preaching Old Testament: Proclamation and Narrative in the Hebrew Bible* (Nashville: Abingdon, 1991); Mike Graves, *The Sermon as Symphony: Preaching the Literary Forms of the New Testament* (Valley Forge, PA: Judson, 1997); Thomas G.

is part and parcel of the meaning of the text. It follows that literary forms of texts ought to be allowed to influence not only readers of biblical texts but also hearers of sermons whose goal is the renewed orality of the biblical text. Not just what the text says, but how it says it, navigates the distance between text and sermon. The form of the text provides its shape and energy and yearns to offer that to the sermon, and thus to become itself a vital force in how a sermon makes meaning.[24] This allows the sermon, as the renewed orality of the text, to be faithful to its performative purpose, but in a new setting with a contemporary group of people.

Several assumptions underlie the claim that literary form ought to shape sermon form:

1. Preaching is biblical.
2. The authority of the Bible is construed in functional rather than primarily propositional terms; that is to say it is performative rather than solely informative.
3. The goal of biblical hermeneutics for preaching is to release the identity-forming power of texts. The locus of energy in interpreting the inspiration of Scripture is between text and reader.
4. The Bible can legitimately be read as literature.
5. Author and reader share innate linguistic and narrative capacities, even if cultural aspects of their mental systems are different.[25]
6. Form has a communal origin and destination. The form of the text implies insight into the author and community of origin and reaches forward to impact the present-day community of the congregation.[26]

Genre-sensitive preaching is not a comprehensive homiletical theory. It is one valid approach to preaching among many. While homileticians have explored its significance for sermonic shape and purpose, the next step is yet to

---

Long, *Preaching and the Literary Forms of the Bible* (Philadelphia: Fortress, 1988); Alyce M. McKenzie, *Preaching Proverbs: Wisdom for the Pulpit* (Louisville: Westminster John Knox, 1996); and Don M. Wardlaw, *Preaching Biblically: Creating Sermons in the Shape of Scripture* (Philadelphia: Westminster, 1983).

24. See Long, *Preaching and the Literary Forms of the Bible.*

25. Edgar V. McKnight, *The Postmodern Use of the Bible: The Emergence of Reader-Oriented Criticism* (Nashville: Abingdon, 1988), 134–61.

26. Tom Long deals with psalms, proverbs, narratives, parables, and epistles. Graves deals with parables, aphorisms, pronouncement stories, miracle stories, Johannine discourses, stories of the early church, vice and virtue lists, poetic exhortations, admonitions, poetry, hymns, and apocalyptic visions.

be taken, connecting the shape/purpose of the sermon with its embodiment, traditionally referred to as "delivery."

The varying genres of oral communication that are inscribed in scriptural texts called for a variety of emotional tones in their originative performative contexts. The contemporary pulpit performance of sermons that grow out of texts from various biblical genres ought to be congruent with those genres' varying purposes, moods, and tones. Contemporary preachers need to give some thought to how their modes of vocal, physical, and facial expression relate to the genre of the text from which their sermon grows. Just as texts and sermons have rhetorical forms and intentions, so does their performance by the preacher by means of face, gesture, and voice.

Taking this a step further, perhaps we should give some thought to our identity or role in the performance of sermons that grow out of various genres, using a seldom-asked question: does the role I am taking on in the community of faith in preaching this sermon correspond to the rhetorical intentions of sermon and text? Various genres are often thought of in connection with specific social and religious roles in the ancient Near East. The roles of sage, prophet, priest, and seer had significant overlap but also distinctive functions and genres of choice. The sage was the teacher of wisdom, practical guidance for daily living. His genre of choice was the proverb and, in Jesus's case, also the parable. The prophet was one who envisioned the alternative reality that could come to pass if the community would repent and live in keeping with God's will. The prophet's genre of choice was the dramatic prophetic oracle, which often involved symbolic action. The priest mediated between the divine and the human, offering up to God signs of human repentance and offering from God to humankind assurances of divine forgiveness. The priestly role relied on symbolic action as much or more than on words. The seer offered visions of a catastrophic end to human history and the in-breaking of God's reign on earth. The seer's genre of choice was the vivid apocalyptic vision.

Within any one genre and role, there are many rhetorical functions. Prophets can upbraid, envision, lament, and inspire hope. Seers can inspire either fright or relief in their listeners, depending on where they locate themselves in the end-time drama. Sages can challenge and undercut habitual assumptions as well as offer moral guidance and inspire confidence in God's trustworthiness. Priests, by mediating encounters between the divine and the human realms, can comfort or chill.

It is worth considering that in preaching from various genres of biblical literature, we preach not just texts, but also roles within the community of faith. As we respectfully approach texts for preaching, it is worth asking, what is the genre of this text? Within that genre, what is the form and rhetorical function of this particular text? As we shape our sermons out of the interchange we are having with a given text, our question becomes, how will the form and rhetorical function of this text shape those of my sermon? Taking it one step further, we ought to ask, what role or combination of roles in my contemporary faith community am I taking on in the performance of this sermon from this textual genre? How can my performance of this sermon, encompassing face, body, and voice, be faithful to the form and rhetorical function of the text, the sermon, and the role of the speaker?

Liturgical Implications

The New Homiletic's critique of traditional sermonic form parallels the liturgical renewal movement's critique of traditional worship forms. Charles Bartow's work in speech communication furthers the contributions of both movements to acts and services of worship that are participatory, biblically based, and multisensory.

In his discussion of "the dialogue of the sanctuary" in *Effective Speech Communication in Leading Worship*, Bartow makes a case for a dialogical relationship in worship between the corporate and the individual, between the traditional and the innovative, and between the discursive and the mysterious. A question we do not often ask ourselves is, does this sermon do justice to the liturgy of which it is an integral part? Bartow's work issues that challenging question without hesitation. The sermon's liturgical context calls preaching to be participatory rather than observed, collaborative rather than monological, evocative of divine presence rather than explanatory, and dialogical in its biblical hermeneutic rather than archaeological.

The Gift of Silence

One way to look at Charles Bartow's contribution to homiletics is to say that he has dealt eloquently with the subject of words and speech. And he certainly has. But at a more profound level, he has understood himself to be dealing with the subject of stillness and silence. All the phenomena with which this chapter has dealt—textual inscription, biblical interpretation, sermonic shaping, and performance—proceed from the practice of prayerfully, silently attending to *actio divina*, both in individual and in corporate listening.

Preaching as God's human speech involves pause, listening on God's part and on our part, and not just speech.

Preaching is a dialogue that requires not a multiplication of speakers, but a multiplication of listeners. Preaching involves prior listening. It is speaking whose purpose is to facilitate other people's listening. Preaching issues from deep silence, the silence of God. There and only there, in ineffable prayer, do we understand the insight of Pascal: "We would not seek thee, O God, if thou hadst not already found us."[27]

---

27. Bartow, *God's Human Speech*, 111–12.

4

Performative Language and the Limits of Performance in Preaching

JOHN M. ROTTMAN

In a project focusing primarily on performance and the preaching moment, it may seem strange to examine the sermon as a language event. The selection and shaping of sermonic words usually take place well before the sermon ever begins to happen in the pulpit. But sermon performance is intimately wrapped up with one's understanding of how the language of the sermon functions. In addition, what the preacher envisions himself or herself doing bears heavily on how he or she sets about enacting sermon performance. This contribution will explore the limits against which performance can expect to bump up in light of how sermonic language functions to communicate the Word of God.

Sometimes sermons that roar out of the pulpit and hold the congregation nearly spellbound fail to perform even half as well when we try to race them again. For instance, a sermon that I preached on a particular Sunday when I was a full-time pastor preached wonderfully that morning. It was almost one of those "every eye was upon him" (cf. Luke 4:20) sort of days. People listened attentively and spoke appreciatively. Several days later I decided to use the same sermon in my homiletics class at the seminary. I make a practice of preaching one of my sermons to my classes, even though in my heart of hearts I would prefer not to provide them with such live demonstrations. Still, with my sure winner from Sunday in hand, I felt an unusual level of confidence even facing the anxiety of preaching to students. And so I valiantly preached Sunday's sermon to Wednesday's homiletics class. It seemed to go reasonably well, but apparently it didn't go as swimmingly as I had supposed. The students seemed considerably more critical than I thought my gem from the previous Sunday warranted. What went wrong? What might account for the differences in the two performances?

John L. Austin's Speech Act Theory

The language analysis of philosopher John L. Austin provides a useful set of tools for evaluating sermon performance. Austin, along with his student John Searle, reflected deeply about how people use language not only to say things but to perform actions. Austin's theory, formulated during his years of teaching at Oxford, is most comprehensively set forth in the 1955 William James Lectures at Harvard, published in 1962 as *How to Do Things with Words*.[1] Austin's approach has come to be called speech act theory and focuses its attention on what is known more technically as perlocutionary language. In his work on perlocutionary language, Austin examined units of language much smaller than those ordinarily comprised by the typical sermon.[2] But even though sermons are more complex units of speech, they can be thought of as speech acts at least inasmuch as they aim not only to say something, but also to do something beyond merely communicating information. Consequently, Austin's analysis offers promise for exploring the relationship between words and performance and the limits of sermon performance.

1. John L. Austin, *How to Do Things with Words*, The William James Lectures delivered at Harvard University in 1955, ed. J. O. Urmson (Cambridge, MA: Harvard University Press, 1962).
2. Theoretically, viewing the sermon as a speech act seems to violate a strict application of Austin's criteria. Speech acts rely on conventional formula, and sermons are in their content neither conventional nor obviously formulaic. Sermons vary, sometimes wildly, from preacher to preacher, from Sunday to Sunday, and from congregation to congregation. On one level, there may be certain formal conventions that exemplify sermons of certain eras, but convention on the formal level is not sufficient for satisfying Austin's A.1 criterion. The modern trend toward narrative sermons seems to take the sermon even farther from any conventional execution. Undoubtedly certain parts or sentences of the sermon may qualify as speech acts, but the unconventional nature of the sermon as a whole cautions against identifying the sermon as a speech act without qualification. While holding out for the performative nature of the sermon is essential, the most that one can say is that the sermon is in important ways like what Austin calls a speech act.

Before applying Austin's criteria, it will be helpful to take a brief look at the rudiments of his analysis. Austin explains his understanding of a performative or speech act as speech in which "the issuing of the utterance is the performing of an action—it is not normally thought of as just saying something."[3] For example, by uttering the words, "I now pronounce you husband and wife," a pastor (or other official of the state) performs the action of marrying two people to one another. Or by cracking a bottle of champagne across the bow of a ship, and pronouncing the words, "I christen you the *Queen Mary*," a person may perform the action of naming a ship. Christening, ordering, glorifying, marrying, and the like can all be thought of as examples of perlocutionary language. In these ways and many others, people not only say things but do things with words.

Of course there is more to Austin's conception of performative language than simply uttering the words. Such words need to be uttered and received in a certain manner. Austin points to the necessity of certain contextual features in the use of speech acts: "It is always necessary that the *circumstances* in which the words are uttered should in some way, or ways, be *appropriate*, and it is very commonly necessary that either the speaker himself or other persons should *also* perform certain *other* actions, whether 'physical' or 'mental' actions or even acts of uttering further words."[4] Said another way, Austin incorporates rhetorical concerns into his approach.

Austin proposes a general schema for what he calls the happy or smooth functioning of performatives:

(A.1) There must exist an accepted conventional procedure having a certain conventional effect, that procedure to include the uttering of certain words by certain persons in certain circumstances, and further,

(A.2) the particular persons and circumstances in a given case must be appropriate for the invocation of the particular procedure invoked.

(B.1) The procedure must be executed by all participants both correctly and

(B.2) completely.

(C.1) Where, as often, the procedure is designed for use by persons having certain thoughts or feelings, or for the inauguration of certain consequential conduct on the part of any participant, then a person participating in and so invoking the procedure must in fact have those

3. Austin, *How to Do Things with Words*, 6.
4. Ibid., 8.

thoughts or feelings, and the participants must intend so to conduct themselves and, further,

(C.2)   must actually conduct themselves subsequently.[5]

To summarize, happy or smooth functioning speech acts must be conventional, suitable, correct, complete, and sincere.

In order to sharpen how a speech act might conform to Austin's criteria, consider the act of confession and absolution as a speech act. To satisfy Austin's conventionality criterion there must be a procedure, a liturgical formula, or specific words of Scripture conventionally used by the worshiping community in question for the purpose of pronouncing absolution. The confession must be enacted in the context of an authentic worship service, and not, for example, in a play or movie that uses a worship service as part of its set to satisfy the suitability criterion. With reference to correctness, performance of the absolution must be uttered after and not before the confession of sin by the congregation. To reverse their order would count as an incorrect performance of the speech act. To satisfy the completeness criterion, all the words of the conventional formula must be spoken. And finally, the people must have genuinely confessed their sins and not merely pretended to do so, or they will have violated the criterion of sincerity.

Keeping in mind that for Austin sermons would qualify as speech acts only in an extended way, one might nevertheless subject the sermon to Austin's criteria. Like any speech act, the happy or smooth functioning sermon might be thought of as conforming to similar standards of conventionality, suitability, correctness, completeness, and sincerity.

Since the rise of modern homiletics and the decline of the three-point sermon, identifying a conventional form of the sermon has become more elusive. Certainly within particular faith communities the Sunday sermon usually displays conventional features. In some of these communities, for instance, the three-point sermon still thrives. But even as sermon form may vary more than it did in past eras, several other conventional aspects still may be identified. Ordinarily, sermons are based on or make use of some biblical text or texts. The way that the text is used may vary, but the Bible typically comes into it. And further, the sermon attempts to relate the text or texts to the lives of the listeners. Most sermons are in some way, shape, or form biblically based addresses that attempt to engage the listeners' lives.

Further, within particular faith communities, sermon length is regularly conventional. For instance, within North American Roman Catholic communities

5. Ibid., 14–15.

in the American Midwest, a sermon length of not more than ten minutes is conventional. In many Pentecostal communities in the same geographic area, a verse by verse form is the accepted convention for sermon form, and a sermon of less than forty minutes would be considered falling woefully short of the mark.

Austin's suitability criterion comes into play in several ways with the sermon. Ordinarily, a sermon may be preached only by an authorized person. Sometimes this authorization takes the form of formal ordination. Other times authorization is less formal, resting with the leaders of the faith community or in some conventional procedure for choosing the preacher or recognizing the "anointing." In any case, not just anyone ordinarily can get up and preach. Further, the sermon must be preached in the context of a worship service or other authorized meeting of the faith community.[6] Whether explicitly stated or implicitly assumed, these meetings involve some sort of expected or invited encounter with God.

The sermon is like a speech act in that the criteria of correctness and completeness also come into play. To count as a correct homiletical rendering, the sermon must track the manuscript, outline, or sermon plan that gave rise to it.[7] The words of the sermon must be uttered correctly. For example, on one occasion in a sermon, instead of saying "a recent Peanuts comic" as I had planned, I said the words, "a recent penis comic." This pushed the sermon toward what Austin would have called an infelicitous or unhappy outcome (even though they struggled to suppress giggles, most of the congregation would have agreed).

Sermons meet the completeness criterion when they are preached not in part but in their entirety. While preaching half a sermon would not happen regularly, on occasion it does. On rare occasions, the preacher may sense that the sermon seems not to be working and simply give up before completing it. Or as happened when I was a child, one of our pastors dropped dead of a heart attack shortly after he had begun his sermon. Such a sermon would fail Austin's completeness criterion rather dramatically.

6. These are usually typical Sunday morning or Saturday evening services, but Wednesday evening prayer meetings or week-long revival services could also qualify.

7. The ontology of the sermon is perhaps best thought of as akin to a musical piece, a play, or some other piece of performance art. Just as the musical piece is not identical with the score, the sermon must not be identified with the manuscript. The manuscript is best seen as directions or an aid to performance. Sometimes these directions are not even written down, but reside in some way or other in the mind of the preacher. For the philosophical grounds for these ontological directions, see Nicholas Wolterstorff's *Works and Worlds of Art*, Clarendon Library of Logic and Philosophy (Oxford and New York: Oxford University Press, 1980).

Finally, Austin's sincerity criterion comes into play when one considers issues of authenticity. This is the area that in rhetoric centers on the preacher's ethos. For the sermon as a speech act to have a felicitous outcome, the preacher must preach the sermon sincerely. The features of his or her performance must be in congruity with his or her internal emotional states. If the preacher pretends to be excited, but is in reality bored to tears, the sermon risks infelicity. If the preacher pretends to believe some truth that the sermon propounds, but in reality doubts or disbelieves it, the sermon risks infelicity. This threat happens because the listener often seems to be attuned intuitively to identifying incongruities between what the preacher says and the way he or she says it.

Sermons, like speech acts, risk infelicities in numerous ways. Austin's criteria suggest why sermons preached in homiletics classes might be especially prone to infelicitous outcomes. In light of the breakdown of consensus within homiletics, what counts as conventional for the sermon may vary considerably in preaching classes. In the evangelical seminary in which I re-preached my Sunday morning sermon, quite a number of students thought that a twenty-minute sermon was about twenty or twenty-five minutes too short. Twenty minutes seemed like half a sermon to them. Students also found the sermon unconventional in that it seemed to them to be excessively imaginative in its treatment of the biblical text. Homiletics classes in seminaries that cross denominational lines may find that standards of convention vary especially widely.

Issues of suitability also come into play more problematically with sermons preached in homiletics classes. The student who preaches holds no office within the group to which he or she preaches. Since sermons are normally preached in worship services, preaching them in the classroom pushes them toward infelicity from the get-go. Issues of correctness and completeness tend to be less of a problem in the classroom, but the sincerity criterion looms large. In class, the preacher preaches her sermon "as if"—as if to proclaim the good news of the gospel and invite listeners into the presence of God. But classroom preaching on one level often aims primarily to demonstrate competence, invite criticism, and achieve a grade. Such mixed motivation invites insincerity into the performance. One might conclude that the classroom setting itself almost invariably pushes the sermon toward an unhappy outcome, something too often confirmed by experience.

When speech acts are conventional, suitable, correct, complete, and sincere, Austin speaks of them as smooth functioning, or having happy or felicitous outcomes. He also speaks of speech acts that violate his criteria to the extent that they fail to do what the speaker intended of them; they are defective. While only on rare occasions might a sermon be pegged as almost a complete failure, too often sermons fail to perform as the preacher intended or the congregation had hoped. Bad sermons perform badly.

But sometimes the opposite is true. Sermons that under the standards of speech act performance ought to be judged horribly infelicitous or almost completely defective sometimes seem to perform in spite of themselves. Charles Spurgeon cites an example that he heard one Sunday morning. On the morning in question, a freak snowstorm prompted Spurgeon to venture down a convenient side street to take refuge in a small Primitive Baptist church. There were no more than ten or fifteen people in attendance that day, and Spurgeon found a seat in back under the gallery. The regular preacher was snowed out and never showed up. In his place Spurgeon reports that "a very thin looking man, a shoemaker or tailor, or something of that sort went up into the pulpit to preach. Now it is well that preachers should be instructed; but this man was really stupid. He was obliged to stick to his text for the simple reason that he had little else to say. . . . He did not even pronounce the words rightly. . . . When he had gone to about that length, and managed to spin out about ten minutes or so, he was at the end of his tether."[8] He had taken his chosen text, a fragment of Isaiah 45:22, as far as he could.

As Spurgeon reports it, the sermon violated conventionality in that it was woefully short in its length and failed to show the relevance of the text for his listeners. The preacher's unauthorized ascent to the pulpit violates suitability. His mispronunciation of words abuses the criterion of correctness. His giving up after ten minutes counts as an infraction against completeness. And yet despite all these infelicities that pushed the sermon that day toward a completely defective performance, Spurgeon reports that the sermon worked. He says that God used the infelicities of that sermon enacted by that inept preacher to bring about his conversion.

A bad sermon that still performs should not come as a complete surprise. Preaching traditionally has laid claim to speaking the Word of God. God speaks in and through the sermon. But prior to the rise of the New Homiletic, certain factors worked to diminish any sense of God speaking in the sermon. It may be helpful to notice this decline in historical context.

Philosophical and Theological Influences in the Decline of Preaching as God Speaking

Prior to the rise of some of the new inductive or narrative approaches to preaching in the last fifty years, preachers especially in the mainline churches labored under the shadow of the Enlightenment and scientific empiricism.

8. *The Autobiography of Charles H. Spurgeon* (New York: Revell, 1898), 1:102–13.

They expended the lion's share of their effort explaining a biblical text, some doctrine of the church, or God as God appeared in the text or relative to that doctrine. This approach was not surprising since there was pressure to view language as the servant of scientific investigation. Here the descriptive function of language was seen as primary. Austin points to the roots of this trend in Kant.[9] In the course of his philosophical work, Kant identified certain statements that in his view, though normal in their grammatical form, upon analysis turned out to be something other than straightforward statements. For example, he thought that most statements about God were really imperative sentences about how one should behave morally. These suppositions take the language of preaching far away from any sense of sermons as God's speaking, since even statements about God were seen as non-referential.

The Logical Positivists of the Vienna Circle[10] carried one of the impulses of Kant's analysis to an extreme. In their view, only statements of fact that were evident to the senses, or statements derived from such by accepted rules of logic, could be accepted as a scientifically legitimate use of language. Their sustained attempt to formulate a verification principle for distinguishing between legitimate and illegitimate linguistic descriptions failed,[11] but the Logical Positivist project continued to exert influence on theology long after it had been discredited as a philosophical movement. Especially in North America,[12] long after Logical Positivism as a philosophical movement died, the idea lingered that only descriptive statements of the sort the Logical Positivists tried to delineate really had meaning or scientific respectability.[13] As a consequence,

9. Austin, *How to Do Things with Words*, 3.

10. For a history and assessment of Logical Positivism, see John Passmore, *A Hundred Years of Philosophy* (London: Gerald Duckworth, 1957), 369–93.

11. Every formulation of the verification principle turned out to be self-referentially incoherent in that the formulations themselves were neither evident to the senses nor logically derived from statements that were, and so every verification principle was itself unverifiable. See R. W. Ashby, "Verifiability Principle," in *The Encyclopedia of Philosophy*, ed. Paul Edwards (New York: Collier Macmillan, 1967), 8:240–47.

12. Perhaps because in North America where the population had not experienced the direct effects of the two world wars, an optimistic faith in science remained less chastened.

13. Passmore says that

Logical Positivism, then, is dead, or as dead as a philosophical movement ever becomes. But it has left a legacy behind. In the German-speaking countries, indeed, it wholly failed; German philosophy as exhibited in the work of Heidegger and his disciples represents everything to which the positivists were most bitterly opposed. In the United States, Great Britain, Australia, and the Scandinavian countries, and other countries where empiricism is widespread, it is often hard to distinguish the direct influence of the positivists from the influence of such allied philosophers as Russell, the Polish logicians, and the British 'analysts.' But insofar as it is widely agreed that transcendental metaphysics, if not

preachers, especially in mainline churches, tended to limit their use of language to language that paralleled that of scientific description. And instead of conceiving of themselves as speaking the words of a God who could not be measured or captured by scientific description, preachers tended to speak of more substantial subjects such as texts or doctrines.

The specter of Logical Positivism and scientific empiricism cast a long shadow. Its descriptive bias once appropriated by theology remained long after it died in philosophy and continued in indirect ways to influence sermon making even longer still. Fred Craddock, writing in 1971, says that "some pulpits have discovered that this very definition of words, that is, as signs to point to verifiable information, has made highly questionable the legitimacy of even using the word 'God.'"[14] Especially prior to the rise of modern homiletics, sermons tended to tackle either some truth of Scripture or some church doctrine ostensibly derived from it. Preachers conceived of what they were doing in the sermon as explication of one of those Scripture passages or church doctrines. The sermon was the Word of God in that it clarified for the congregation something that God had once said or has always been saying. The Word of God, like God, was seen to be universal and timeless, and so the immediate context that God's Word addressed required little attention. God played no direct role in sermon performance.

Sermons in turn were judged not by whether they carried the listener into the presence of God, but almost exclusively by how well they adhered to the truth by explaining the particular text or doctrine under consideration. The language these sermons employed was largely a flattened language of description of which one could sensibly ask, is this true or false?[15] The sermon focused primarily on speaking about God. These scientifically dominated conceptions of language placed overly restrictive strictures on sermon performance, and in theory muzzled even the possibility of God's speaking.

meaningless, is at least otiose, that philosophers ought to set an example of precision and clarity, that philosophy should make use of technical devices, deriving from logic, in order to solve problems relating to the philosophy of science, that philosophy is not about the 'world' but about the language which men speak about the world, we can detect in contemporary philosophy, at least, the persistence of the spirit that inspired the Vienna circle.

John Passmore, "Logical Positivism," in *The Encyclopedia of Philosophy*, ed. Edwards, 5:56. Cf. Alvin C. Plantinga, "A Christian Life Partly Lived," chap. 3 in *Philosophers Who Believe: The Spiritual Journeys of 11 Leading Thinkers*, ed. James Kelly Clark (Downers Grove, IL: InterVarsity, 1993), 62–63.

14. Fred B. Craddock, *As One without Authority* (Enid, OK: Phillips University Press, 1974), 8.

15. Craddock points to this influence of scientific language on the language of the pulpit in his *As One without Authority*, 7–8.

Barth, the New Hermeneutic, and a Renewed Sense of God Speaking in the Sermon

From just after World War I through the 1960s, several important develop-ments in theology worked to move preaching away from treating God merely as the topic of conversation in the sermon and toward recognizing the role of God in sermon performance. The theology of Karl Barth, particularly the appearance of his *The Word of God and the Word of Man*, translated into English in 1928,[16] had a formidable effect on preaching.[17] Barth emphasized the Word of God as active and alive. Along with Barth, a fresh approach to the New Testament in the sixties and early seventies seemed to offer exciting new possibilities for preaching.[18] This movement, also steeped to a certain degree in the theology of Barth, became associated most closely with the work of two German theologians, Ernst Fuchs and Gerhard Ebeling, and became known as the New Hermeneutic.[19]

These theological developments together exerted a formative impact on how preachers viewed the biblical text.[20] Barth, for instance, spoke about the Bible not as an inert object of interpretation, but almost as if it has the ability to act on its own: "If the congregation brings to church the great *question* of human life and *seeks* an *answer* for it, the Bible contrawise brings an *answer*, and *seeks* the *question* corresponding to this answer: it seeks questioning *people* who are eager to find and able to understand that its seeking of them is the very answer to their question."[21] Here already in Barth we see the sort of tendency to intentionalize the text that later characterizes modern homiletics and leaves questions of agency in preaching indeterminate.

Barth also speaks about preaching as an "event" prior to which the preacher submits "to God's *question* by asking the question about God, without which

16. Karl Barth, *The Word of God and the Word of Man*, trans. Douglas Horton (New York: Harper & Bros., 1928).

17. See H. Grady Davis, *Design for Preaching* (Philadelphia: Fortress, 1958), 105. Barth's impact was already felt with the publication of his Romans commentary (*der Römerbrief*) in 1919.

18. See, for instance, Richard C. White, "Preaching the New Hermeneutic," *Lexington Theological Quarterly* 9 (July 1974): 61–71; David James Randolph, *The Renewal of Preaching* (Philadelphia: Fortress, 1969).

19. James M. Robinson, "Hermeneutics Since Barth," in *The New Hermeneutic*, ed. James M. Robinson and John B. Cobb Jr., New Frontiers in Theology: Discussions among Continental and American Theologians 2 (New York: Harper & Row, 1964), 39.

20. This impact in most instances was probably not direct in the sense that vast numbers of preachers were avidly reading Barth, Fuchs, Ebeling, and others, but the insights of these theo-logians likely trickled down through the systematic theologians and New Testament scholars to those teaching and writing about preaching, and from there to preachers.

21. Barth, *The Word of God and the Word of Man*, 116.

God's answer cannot be given." The preacher then "answers the *people's question* but answers it as a man who has himself been *questioned by God*, then he speaks—the word of God; and this is what people seek in him and what God commissioned him to speak."[22] Here Barth seems to stop short of saying that when the preacher speaks, God speaks, but Barth, of course, affirms that the preacher does speak God's Word. Again, questions of agency arise that press those who wish to reflect on preaching as performance.

Questions of agency remain somewhat opaque in Barth, and this is understandable for one who conceives of God as wholly other and yet wishes to speak of God's speaking through the preaching of human beings. Barth affirms the paradox of the preaching event:

> The word of God on the lips of a man is impossibility; it does not happen: no one will ever accomplish it or see it accomplished. The event toward which the expectancy of heaven and earth is directed is none the less *God's* act. Nothing else can satisfy the waiting people and nothing else can be the will of God than that he himself should be revealed in the event. But the word of God is and will and must be and remain the word of *God*.[23]

Barth uses language that intentionalizes the text yet fosters a sense of preaching as an event in which God's Word is spoken and God is not merely spoken about. Here is the foundation for much thought that would follow him. Preaching for Barth is performative in the very basic sense that through preaching God acts to answer deep human questions. No doubt Barth's reluctance to relate the Word of God and the word of human beings too closely prevents him from being clearer about questions of agency in preaching, though he is to be honored for preserving an uncompromising sense of God's freedom in his homiletic. As one might expect, for Barth, God is in no way compelled to speak through human preaching, but his homiletic does not show how this is possible.

Ebeling and Fuchs, theologians of the New Hermeneutic, also fostered an appreciation of preaching as God's speaking in the present and not merely as speaking about God's action in the past or as a figure in some ancient text. Anthony Thiselton identifies the roots of this concern both in the theology of Rudolf Bultmann and in the pastoral sensitivities of Fuchs and Ebeling.[24] The

---

22. Ibid., 122–23.
23. Ibid., 124–25.
24. Anthony Thiselton, "The New Hermeneutic," in *New Testament Interpretation: Essays on Principles and Methods*, ed. I. Howard Marshall (Carlisle, UK: Paternoster, 1986), 308.

problem that the New Hermeneutic attempts to address is how the language of the ancient text can speak anew in the present preaching moment.

Fuchs uses the concept of *Einverständnis* or "common understanding" to underpin the possibility of the language of Jesus speaking in the present. Thiselton explains that "like Heidegger's category of 'world,' it is pre-conceptual. 'It is neither a subjective nor an objective phenomenon but both together, for world is prior to and encompasses both.'"[25] This "common understanding" is a linguistic phenomenon and, philosophically speaking, is the condition of the possibility of all human understanding, and so also of understanding the Word of the New Testament.[26]

Ebeling and Fuchs are also interested in some sense in the performative nature of language. Ebeling's concerns sound similar to J. L. Austin's when Ebeling says, "we do not get at the nature of words by asking what they contain, but by asking what they effect, what they set going."[27] The language of Jesus constitutes a call or a pledge. Especially in his parables, Jesus establishes a common understanding, an *Einverständnis*.[28] This preconceptual sense of language that conveys reality is what Ebeling calls a word event and Fuchs calls a language event. As James Robinson explains, "Fuchs and Ebeling would argue that Jesus' word—not just the Easter kerygma—happens as reoccurring word today and thus mediates an eschatological self-understanding to him who hears it; that Jesus' claim of authority heard as a word of love, reaches beyond the time of his earthly activity to speak to us today."[29]

Ebeling contends that "in the word of God we have a case of a word event that leads from the text of Holy Scripture to the proclamation."[30] The biblical text participates in such a language event (or word event). As such it can no longer be thought of merely as an object of investigation, but as Fuchs puts

25. Ibid., 311. "World" here is seen as a preconceptual linguistic reality.
26. Like Barth, Ebeling and Fuchs hold for the singular and undivided character of the Word.
27. Quoted in Thiselton, "The New Hermeneutic," 312. Thiselton also notes that in their efforts to highlight the performative character of language, Ebeling and Fuchs to their detriment underplay the descriptive nature of language. Anthony C. Thiselton, *The Two Horizons: New Testament Hermeneutics and Philosophical Description* (Grand Rapids: Eerdmans, 1980), 354–55. Cf. Sallie McFague, who claims that parables are not "primarily concerned with knowing, but with doing," in *Speaking in Parables: A Study in Metaphor and Theology* (Philadelphia: Fortress, 1975), 79.
28. Fuchs says, for example, that "what is decisive is not in the first place the content, but that Jesus spoke at all." Ernst Fuchs, "The New Testament and the Problem," in *The New Hermeneutic*, ed. Robinson and Cobb, 123.
29. Robinson, "Hermeneutics Since Barth," 62.
30. Gerhard Ebeling, "Word of God and Hermeneutic," in *The New Hermeneutic*, ed. Robinson and Cobb, 88.

it, it is "a master that directs us into the language-context of our existence."[31] According to Thiselton, "in common with Heidegger's philosophy in both the earlier and later periods, Fuchs believes that man stands within a linguistic world which is decisively shaped by his own place in history, i.e. by his 'historicality.' But together with Heidegger, Fuchs also looks for a new coming-to-speech in which the confines and conventions of the old everyday 'world' will be set aside and broken through."[32]

Fuchs and Ebeling's appropriation of Heidegger's theory of language makes the theological insights on which it is based appear in many ways to be turbid and opaque. Carl Bratten, no doubt tending toward hyperbole, expressed doubts about whether hermeneutical development would "proceed much further along the Fuchs-Ebeling line, if for no other reason than that Fuchs lacks clarity (no one understands him) and Ebeling lacks substance (the objective content of the faith is reduced to a bare minimum)."[33] Consequently, this assessment of the New Hermeneutic must be satisfied with pointing out some advantages of the New Hermeneutic for preaching as performance along with certain theoretical limitations. In so doing it does not pretend to have completely penetrated the philosophical problems with which it is so closely intertwined.

From the perspective of preaching, much appreciation must be expressed for a hermeneutical approach that concerns itself with the Word of God as an active principle in proclamation. The plea of the New Hermeneutic was that the text not be treated instrumentally as an object to serve the preacher's preestablished rhetorical ends. It should be allowed to speak for itself (as it were). This raises a valid concern. The preacher ought to respect the integrity of the text. One wonders if the concerns of the New Hermeneutic had been developed further by New Testament scholars, whether a more lively sense of the biblical text's place in the life of the church as a source and guide for preaching the faith might have been more fully developed.[34]

31. Quoted in Thiselton, "The New Hermeneutic," 312.
32. Ibid., 318.
33. Carl E. Bratten, "How New Is the New Hermeneutic?" *Theology Today* 22 (1965): 220.
34. It would be interesting to explore further why the initial excitement over the New Hermeneutic seemed to die so quickly. Perhaps the social-political turmoil of the sixties with the student movement and the end of the Vietnam War shifted the emphasis in hermeneutics away from post-Reformational concerns to questions of liberation and power illuminated by the hermeneutical theories of Habermas and Foucault. It might also be that the community of New Testament scholars was rather uneasy with a hermeneutical approach that demanded relevance, ceded a certain amount of control, and was closely related to the preaching activity of the church.

The tendency of the New Hermeneutic to vest power in the text apart from human agency raises problems similar to the ones encountered by those who intentionalize the text in contemporary homiletics. The language events of modern proclamation are set in motion by the preaching of the historical Jesus. However, it is not at all clear whether Jesus is involved in sermon performance as the living and risen Lord who still speaks his Word through the proclamation, or if so, how so. As Thiselton notes, in tying the word event to the preaching of Jesus, "Fuchs can find no place in his hermeneutic for tradition, the church, or history after the event of the cross."[35]

Thiselton also notes that the approach of the New Hermeneutic is much better at "facing the problem of how the interpreter may understand the text of the New Testament more deeply, and more creatively . . . and less concerned about how they may understand it correctly." As Weber sees, "if the criterion for truth is only in the language-event itself, how can the language-event be safeguarded against delusion, mockery, or utter triviality?"[36] Some way of understanding the performative nature of preaching the biblical text is needed that does not vitiate the freedom of God as in Ebeling and Fuchs, and become "close to what has been described as belief in 'word magic.'"[37] An acceptable sense of God speaking that fully maintains the radical freedom of God to speak or remain silent, even as the human preacher speaks the Word, is required both for understanding the power of sermon performance and exploring its limits.

Modern homiletical theorists show influences from Barth and the New Hermeneutic in their tendency to emphasize the event character of the sermon. Don Wardlaw speaks of preaching as "an enterprise characterized by wave upon wave of words, sermons that become Word-events."[38] Richard C. White contends with reference to the biblical text that "we are to experience that *same* event in our own time and circumstances."[39] James Cox points to Ebeling's injunction that the text be "executed" and insists that "it is not nearly so important that the text should get explained as that it should get carried out."[40] Eduard Riegert acknowledges that the text is event and "one can (and should) reflect upon that event and articulate something about it (doctrinal

35. Thiselton, "New Hermeneutic," 325. Cf. Fuchs, "The New Testament and the Problem," 132–45.
36. J. C. Weber, quoted in Thiselton, "New Hermeneutic," 325.
37. Ibid.
38. Don M. Wardlaw, "Preaching as the Interface of Two Social Worlds: The Congregation as Corporate Agent in the Act of Preaching," in *Preaching as a Social Act: Theology and Practice*, ed. Arthur Van Seters (Nashville: Abingdon, 1988), 65.
39. Richard C. White, *Biblical Preaching: How to Find and Remove the Barriers* (St. Louis: CBP, 1988), 112.
40. James William Cox, *Preaching* (San Francisco: Harper & Row, 1985), 68–69.

formulation), but one never dare lose its eventfulness."[41] Fred Craddock notes that "preaching both proclaims an event and participates in that event."[42] The language of Barth and the New Hermeneutic has filtered down into homiletic theory and notions of performance in the pulpit.

Thiselton notes that to a certain degree the concerns of the New Hermeneutic were picked up on by parable scholars in New Testament studies. Eta Linnemann, student of Fuchs, published her work on parables in 1960 (in German).[43] Robert Funk, who calls parables "language events," Dan O. Via, who speaks of their capacity to "operate at a pre-conceptual level," and John Dominic Crossan, who characterizes certain parables "that subvert the world of accepted convention," are scholars who exemplify influence from the New Hermeneutic.[44] Perhaps homiletics has imbibed a dilution of the New Hermeneutic also through these parable scholars.

This event language, which Barth and the New Hermeneutic introduced to homiletics, also tended to introduce problems of divine and human agency into sermon performance. An approach is needed that is able to avoid intentionalizing the text[45] and to speak meaningfully about the freedom of God's speech. Speech act theory is helpful at this juncture inasmuch as it points to

---

41. Eduard R. Riegert, *Imaginative Shock: Preaching and Metaphor* (Burlington, ON: Trinity Press, 1990), 122.

42. Fred B. Craddock, *Preaching* (Nashville: Abingdon, 1985), 47.

43. Eta Linnemann, *Jesus of the Parables*, trans. John Sturdy (New York: Harper & Row, 1966).

44. Thiselton, *Two Horizons*, 350–52.

45. One can identify a tendency in modern homiletics to speak as if the text had an energy and impulse of its own. Fred Craddock, for example, refers both to "what the text is saying" and to "what the text is doing," and to the text as "correcting, instructing, celebrating, or probing" (Craddock, *Preaching*, 123). The text is spoken of almost as if it performs on its own. This impulse to attribute intention to the text might be called intentionalizing the text.

In casual conversation it is quite understandable that writers might intentionalize the text, that is, speak of the text's doing or saying something. This can be seen as personification, a figure of speech. However, when one intentionalizes the text in homiletics, it often masks ambiguity about whose intentions are at issue. The danger is that God's work in and through the preaching may be obscured. Texts as words on a page cannot do or say anything. Authors say things using a text, and readers understand meanings using texts, but texts by themselves have no intention.

W. K. Wimsatt argued against the importance of author in evaluating lyric poetry. His insights were extended by others to what Annabel Patterson calls "a kind of general anti-intentionalism in literary studies," a position that she argues is far less plausible than Wimsatt's limited original contention. (Annabel Patterson, "Intention," in *Critical Terms for Literary Study*, ed. Frank Lentricchia and Thomas McLaughlin [Chicago: University of Chicago Press, 1990], 140–42). Homileticians may tend to be overly influenced by this general anti-intentionalism because of their frequent dependence on literary scholars who operate without consideration of such matters as the authority of Scripture or Scripture as God's Word.

the performative possibility of how the language of the sermon might rise above the level of mere description of God and God's world.

But how might one understand God's part in the sermon if the sermon is viewed as a speech act? It might be tempting to see the sermon as a speech act without qualification. The preacher, as one designated by the worshiping community and filled with the Spirit, uses a conventional form called a sermon to speak God's Word to an assembled congregation. But to suppose that the sermon is a speech act much like any other speech act described by Austin raises a besetting theological problem for sermons.[46]

Theological Problems with the Sermon as a Speech Act

Strictly identifying the sermon as a speech act seems to leave little or no room for God in preaching. Austin points out that speech acts work simply by the speaking of the conventional words by the designated person with the proper dispositions in the proper context. This presents problems for the sermon in light of the freedom of God. God speaks when God wishes to speak and remains silent when God wishes to remain silent. One would not wish to conceive of the sermon in such a way that impugns this freedom, as if God and God's Word were at the beck and call of the preacher. Quite the opposite seems to be the case. Traditionally, it is God, not the congregation or the preacher, who sets the agenda and takes the initiative in speaking God's Word through the performance of a sermon.

God and the preacher stand in what has traditionally been understood as a covenantal relationship. Further, this relationship stands not as an arrangement between equals, but with God as the senior partner and God's human creatures as junior partners. Any understanding of sermon performance as speech acts must be conceived within this covenantal relationship.

But note as well that God appears to perform speech acts quite apart from human agency.

> For as the rain and the snow come down from heaven, and do not return there until they have watered the earth, making it bring forth and sprout, giving seed to the sower and bread to the eater, so shall my word be that goes out from my mouth; it shall not return to me empty, but it shall accomplish that which I purpose, and succeed in the thing for which I sent it. (Isa. 55:10–11)

---

46. The same problem besets the sacraments when one is tempted to embrace an *ex opera, ex operata* understanding of the human role in their enactment.

God uses God's Word to do things in upholding his creation. God's Word is powerful and effective.[47] Psalm 33:6 makes God's modus operandi in his initial creative act explicit: "By the word of the Lord the heavens were made." According to the Bible, God uses words much like some other creature might use a hammer, shovel, or some other implement to execute a task. God creates; God reveals; God gives life; God saves; God issues commands. God does a great many things, all using God's Word. God is most accomplished when it comes to doing things with words—masterful, superb, without peer. Human speech acts mirror the actions of the one whose image human beings bear.

But the idea of God speaking through the words of the human preacher involves a speech act with a certain degree of complexity and mystery. Such a case must encompass the possibility of two actors acting through a single utterance. In one sense this complexity has some analogies in ordinary human life. We all know of instances when, for example, the president makes assertions through a press secretary. One might say that the assertion of the press secretary counts as an instance of the president speaking. And so with the single utterance, the secretary speaks (acts) and the president or prime minister speaks (acts).[48]

But in the case of God speaking via a sermon, the situation is rather different. Unlike human instances in which one person performs an action through another person speaking her words, the sermon seems to function as an instance of God and the human speaker acting not only through the same words, but at the same time.

Furthermore, few would claim that whenever the preacher speaks words that comprise the sermon, his or her speaking counts in every case as an instance of God speaking. Rather, when the preacher speaks the words of the sermon, one finds that God frequently acts via God's Spirit to cause those words at the same time to be the words of God. As God causes these human words to become God's words, human words count as the words of God. At the same time it is possible that God will cause the hearer to understand what God is saying in ways that differ from the speaker's actual words. Some ambiguity and acknowledgment of mystery is appropriate, not least to safeguard God's freedom.

The Covenantal Context of Preaching the Word of God

God's radical freedom places certain limits on sermon performance. God may on occasion choose not to speak, and no amount of human analysis may be

---

47. See also 1 Thess. 2:13, "God's word, which is also at work in you believers."

48. Wolterstorff calls these sorts of actions count-generated actions in that one act of speaking counts at the same time as an act of someone else speaking.

able to ferret out a reason. The preacher may look back at each and every component of the sermon and not find anything fatally defective, but still the sermon falls flat. The human performance seems to have been virtuoso, but the divine partner seems not to have acted. While this may always be distressing, it is not always possible to identify a reason. As the senior partner in this covenantal context, God calls the shots. Consequently, sometimes sermon performance runs up against these mysterious limits of the preached word rooted in the depths of divine mystery.

One of the roots of performance anxiety on the part of the preacher may very well stem from this realization that God is free not to show up as he or she preaches. The possibility always looms that God may choose not to act through the words spoken from the pulpit on any given occasion. The possibility generates a healthy anxiety and humility in the preacher as the preaching moment looms.

The covenantal context of preaching suggests additional limits to sermon performance. Ancient Middle Eastern suzerainty arrangements, which provide the background for understanding the biblical idea of covenant, suggest these limits.[49] In those ancient suzerainty human treaties, the conquering king would set up images of himself in the conquered territory, and the vassal would be expected to rule according to the wishes and decrees of the suzerain. Inasmuch as the vassal played his proper role, the words of the vassal counted as the words of the suzerain, the actions of the vassal as the actions of the suzerain.

Similarly, God might be thought of as setting up living, breathing images of himself in the persons of his human creatures. This reality gives the preacher warrant for being both particular and incarnational in preaching. Being a particular representative of the great King in a particular time and place does limit sermon performance in certain ways. The preaching performance is always a unique and temporal voicing of the Word of God. God is everlasting, but the sermon performance by contrast is fleeting, so the preacher need not worry about making something to last for posterity.

As his image bearers and covenant representatives, preachers are obligated to represent God appropriately, to speak of God faithfully, and to speak the words that God wishes spoken.[50] The preacher is free only within the covenantal context in which he or she operates. Preachers, for example, who attempt

49. For instance, see G. E. Mendenhall, *Law and Covenant in Israel and the Ancient Mideast* (Pittsburgh: The Biblical Colloquium, 1955) or M. G. Kline, *Treaty of the Great King* (Grand Rapids, Eerdmans, 1963).

50. Gordon Lathrop identifies this obligation as a crisis both of leadership and of preaching; too often the preacher preaches his or her own text mindful only of his or her own interest and not God's. Gordon W. Lathrop, *Holy Things* (Minneapolis: Fortress, 2003), 183.

to use the text of Scripture to preach racism, as sometimes happened in the United States in the 1950s, misrepresent the great King and commit acts of rebellion.

It is within this framework of preaching performance as a cooperative act between covenant partners that issues of the holiness or spiritual fitness of the preacher also arise. Earlier homiletics took a great deal of interest in the character of the preacher. Was the preacher godly? Did the preacher spend time with spiritual disciplines? Did she spend time studying the Scriptures that make a person "wise unto salvation" (2 Tim. 3:15 KJV)? Did he spend time in prayer and meditation, making space for God in his demanding schedule? God working with the preacher in the preaching moment was seen not only as an anointing of the moment, but as something growing out of intimacy with God rooted in what have come to be known as the traditional spiritual disciplines.

These issues must be explored while being mindful of the mystery and freedom of God. Ordinarily, God blesses the preacher who stands in intimate relationship with God via the Holy Spirit. One's close relationship with God is thought to impact the preaching in a positive way as covenant partners work together in the preaching moment. This is what Pentecostals call anointing. However, such anointing is not completely a function of the quality of the preacher's relationship with God.

God sometimes chooses to anoint a woefully broken and sinful preacher in spite of the preacher's inadequacies. This consequence of the freedom of God gives the preacher confidence, even as it also serves as reason for anxiety. Since God is merciful and mindful of our weakness, the preacher mounts the pulpit with hope stirring in her heart, knowing that none of her inadequacies or failures can defeat God's desire to speak God's Word through her should he choose to do so. Further, being mindful of the covenantal context in which and out of which preaching takes place helps to inoculate the preacher against perfectionism. The preacher need not read everything that has been written. The words chosen and later enacted need not be flawless, not that they ever could be. The preacher takes the gifts that he or she has been given and the time provided, prepares carefully, and then preaches what he or she has been given. Final responsibility as it were rests with the senior partner in this covenantal performance. Consequently the preacher always approaches sermon performance with an appropriate mixture of anxiety and hope stirring within, but predominantly hope.

A cautionary note needs to be sounded here. Whenever one speaks of the performative nature of God's speaking through human persons to speak God's Word, it is necessary to preserve the mysterious tension between human responsibility and divine initiative. The divine primacy of place in sermon performance must never be used as an excuse for an anti-intellectual attitude or for laziness on the part of the preacher. The preacher ought never to presume upon the power and grace of God as he or she approaches the moment of performance.

Given the covenantal context of preaching, the limits of preaching performance must always be assessed with this context in mind. The preacher's performance contributes to the sermon and presents a number of possibilities that may limit performance. But as the senior partner in preaching, God always has the final word. God may graciously choose for whatever reason to override sermonic infelicities. On other occasions, God may choose not to speak when there are few of these infelicities. Given these limits and the possibilities of God's gracious intervention, the preacher approaches the preaching moment with boldness, humility, and hope.

5

Reversal of Fortune

The Performance of a Prophet

MARY DONOVAN TURNER

The conversation between performance and Old Testament studies has forged new pathways of exploration, and consequently new knowledge. Inquiries into the worlds of the prophets and psalms alike have encouraged interpreters to consider the significance of the oral nature of both.[1] Studies have focused on dimensions of power, imagination, subversive potential, and implied narrative. Rather than review the work done on these larger bodies of the Old Testament corpus, this article will explore performance studies in conversation with a particular text, a poetic one, found at the conclusion of the account of the exodus narrative. What new paths of investigation will be discovered? What new interpretive questions will be broached? The text is Exodus 15:20–21, the Song of Miriam, sung after the Israelites successfully cross the Red Sea.

> Then the prophet Miriam, Aaron's sister, took a tambourine in her hand; and
> all the women went out after her with tambourines and with dancing. And

1. See, for instance, William Doan and Terry Giles, eds., *Prophets, Performance, and Power* (New York and London: T&T Clark, 2005); also Dave Bland and David Fleer, eds., *Performing the Psalms* (St. Louis: Chalice, 2005).

Miriam sang to them: "Sing to the Lord, for he has triumphed gloriously; horse
and rider he has thrown into the sea."

These two short verses from the book of Exodus have drawn the attention
of archaeologists, artists, and biblical scholars alike. The portrait of Miriam,
tambourine in hand, singing and dancing with the women in the community,
has brought brush to canvas and captivated the imagination of generations. As
part of the exodus narrative, the celebration of Miriam and the women holds a
place in one of the formative events for describing and understanding others in
the Old and New Testaments. In this chapter, I will describe some of the varied
fascinations with this text, explore the importance of the women's celebration
from the perspective of performance theory, and sketch some implications that
arise from putting performance in conversation with prophecy. In particular, this
text will help us to explore a key question: what is the relationship between ritual
performance and the quest for justice, the overthrowing of bondage, and God's
constant striving to reverse the fortunes of the poor and oppressed among us?

The Fascination with Miriam

The story of Miriam and the women dancing at the shore has captivated both
artist and archaeologist. Carol Meyers, for instance, discusses ancient terracotta figurines that depict women dancing, drums in hand. She also identifies
Exodus 15:20, Judges 11:34, 1 Samuel 18:6, and Jeremiah 31:4 as texts where
women are dancing while holding drums. She posits the possibility that there
was a "victory song" genre, a kind of song that celebrated God's deliverance
and was performed by female percussionists.[2] Textual evidence suggests that re-
turning warriors expected the drum/dance/song welcome by groups of women
performers who had prepared to respond. These roles transcend household
or domestic life and operate in the public sphere. Recognized gender-specific
women performers were able to exercise control of themselves and the world
and thus enjoyed some sense of power.[3] The emergence of feminist scholarship,
research that recognizes the validity of women's experience and investigates
aspects of gender cross-culturally and historically, provides new insights into
women's performance. Studies of women and music in various cultures are
few, but pioneering efforts have been made. Studies in ethnomusicology have

2. Carol Meyers, "A Terracotta at the Harvard Semitic Museum and Disc-holding Female
Figures Reconsidered," *Israel Exploration Journal* 37, nos. 2–3 (1987): 122.
3. Carol Meyers, "Miriam the Musician," in *A Feminist Companion to Exodus to Deuteronomy*, ed. Athalya Brenner (Sheffield: Sheffield Academic Press, 1994), 227–28.

recognized that music and society as cultural phenomena are complementary and interdependent; studying women's performance genres cannot be distinct from analyzing social structures and values. Feminist ethnomusicology thus investigates the relationship between music behavior and gender behavior. The nature of a society's gender structure impacts women's expressive forms; these in turn reflect and symbolize gender constructions. The relationship of performance, gender, social roles, and status is then analyzed.[4]

While archaeologists have studied material culture, paintings, and statues of the dancing women, artists throughout the centuries have painted their own renditions of Miriam and the women. There are many interesting paintings of Miriam, some on separate canvas, some as illustrations in Bibles. One example is *The Story of Moses (The Dance of Miriam)* by Lorenzo Costa (1460–1535), who depicts the women dancing and celebrating the Israelite escape; Moses is in the foreground to the right.

Critical Questions about Miriam and Her Song

In Exodus 15:20–21, Miriam is mentioned by name for the first time. She is called "prophet," making her the first woman in all Israel to be given this title.[5] The Song of Miriam (Exod. 15:21b) is one of the shortest pieces of ancient Israelite poetry and, at first glance, is overwhelmed by the much longer song of Moses (Exod. 15:1b–18).[6] Miriam's song echoes the first line of Moses's own, though not perfectly. The repetition has given rise to varied conjectures about the relationship between the two. Is Miriam's song derivative and deficient? Or does the simple remembrance of Miriam's song signal the antiquity and tenacious authority of the traditions of Miriam? Which one came first?[7] Were they dependent on a separate, but common source? Why did the editor preserve both songs for us? Is the narrative account of the exodus dependent on this

4. Ibid., 225–26. See also Carol Meyers, "Of Drums and Damsels: Women's Performance in Ancient Israel," *Biblical Archaeologist* 54, no. 1 (1991): 16–27.

5. Phyllis Trible, "Bringing Miriam out of the Shadows," in Brenner, *A Feminist Companion to Exodus to Deuteronomy*, 171.

6. See Frank M. Cross Jr. and David Noel Freedman, "The Song of Miriam," *Near Eastern Studies* 14, no. 4 (1955): 237. The authors designate the longer hymn in Exod. 15 as the "Song of Miriam." They distinguish it from the Song of Moses in Deut. 32 and suggest a superiority of the tradition that associates the song with Miriam rather than with Moses. It is easy, the authors say, to understand the ascription of the hymn to Moses and much more difficult to explain the association of Miriam.

7. For a historic summary of scholarly opinions regarding the relationship of the two songs in Exod. 15, see Fokkelien van Dijk-Hemmes, "Some Recent Views on the Presentation of the Song of Miriam," in Brenner, *A Feminist Companion to Exodus to Deuteronomy*, 200–206.

older poetic rendering? Or is the poem dependent on the accounts of the sea crossing? Does Moses's song include references to the wilderness wandering and the experiences of the people at Mount Sinai?[8] Why is Miriam identified as the sister of Aaron rather than the sister of Moses? At what stage in the tradition do the three become siblings who work together to bring about and celebrate liberation?[9] There are many questions.

Miriam's song begins with an imperative plural verb that summons the community to give praise to Yahweh. This invitation is followed by the reason for that praise: Yahweh is powerfully ascendant. Yahweh rose up as a power, and the horse and rider he hurled into the sea. The song celebrates a moment of liberation or redemption for a group of fugitives fleeing from a powerful enemy.[10]

The reader cannot ignore the fact that the primary metaphor in the story of the exodus is God as warrior. God's liberating action leads to the saving of one people and the downfall and death of another. Theologies must take this seriously, especially those that appeal to the exodus story as a paradigm for God's comprehensive justice. Martin Luther King Jr. once presented a sermon titled "The Death of Evil upon the Seashore." In this sermon he portrays the crossing of the slaves through the sea. "It was a joyous daybreak that had come to end the long night of their captivity. . . . The meaning of this story is not found in the drowning of the Egyptian soldiers, for no one should rejoice at the death or defeat of a human being. Rather, this story symbolizes the death of evil and of inhumane oppression and unjust exploitation."[11]

The Performance

The story of Miriam's song and dance comes at a pivotal point in the Israelite narrative. The Israelites led by Moses have crossed through the Red Sea

8. See David Noel Freedman, who advocates, with others, that the Song of Moses contains not only allusions to the crossing of the sea but also allusions to the wilderness journey and, in particular, the community's experience at Mt. Sinai. D. N. Freedman, "Moses and Miriam: The Song of the Sea," in *Realia Dei: Essays in Archaeology and Biblical Interpretation in Honor of Edward F. Campbell Jr.*, ed. Prescott H. Williams Jr. and Theodore Hiebert (Atlanta: Scholars Press, 1999), 73.

9. See an elaboration of the varied traditions related to Aaron, Moses, and Miriam in Martin Noth, *Exodus*, Old Testament Library (Philadelphia: Westminster), 122.

10. Bernhard W. Anderson compares Miriam's song with Ps. 117, which also begins with a plural imperative. He concludes that brevity of a poem does not provide certainty about the antiquity of the literary unit. Thus one cannot argue from observations of brevity that Miriam's song is older than that attributed to Moses. Nor, he says, is brevity a certain indication that the short hymn is a fragment and necessarily a part of a more extensive one. B. W. Anderson, "The Song of Miriam Poetically and Theologically Considered," in *Directions in Biblical Hebrew Poetry*, ed. Elaine R. Follis, JSOTSup 40 (Sheffield: JSOT Press, 1987).

11. Ibid., 293.

(Exod. 14). Moses sings a song of triumph wrought by the hand of God. Then after a brief recapitulation of the story (Exod. 15:19), Miriam sings. In the final, edited version of the exodus story it is *Miriam's voice we last hear*. Immediately following her singing, Moses moves the people away from the seashore and into the wilderness. Miriam's words provide the definitive closure to the exodus narrative. A new chapter in their life together begins.

Exodus may result from a decision to leave a place; hence, it may be voluntary. Exodus may occur when people are forced out involuntarily because of natural disaster such as drought or hurricane, or by political or economic instability. In the latter cases, a person's status changes from that of citizen to that of refugee or immigrant. Exodus has been carried out through kidnapping and slavery, the forced removal of persons from a homeland because of race or ethnicity or gender. Persons become displaced, landless. They may experience a loss of identity, powerlessness, political impotence, or alienation from others or from self. The consequences of exodus can be enormous, and sometimes the damage is irreversible.

How does one counter the negative effects of exodus? How does one halt deterioration and mount a response that might make one strong at the points where the individual and community have been broken? This is a question of resiliency and sense of moral agency. One needs resources (inner and outer). One needs memory, the presence of others who are able to share the experience and share a desire for recovery. One must have a song and a desire to create something new and better, hence a vision of what can be in the light of what is. One needs a ritual performance. The Israelites are on the threshold of wilderness. They have lost the only home they have known and are headed into the unknown. What can sustain them is the story of God's deliverance from the mighty Pharaoh.

The Israelites experienced oppression at the hand of Pharaoh, an experience that shaped them. Now in the midst of an exodus experience, they need a new language, a new epistemology, and a new or different way to understand and interpret themselves and their world. They need a "liberation historiography"[12] so that they do not repeat or reproduce themselves as they had been. If they allow that to happen, they are still slaves. Exodus, like slavery, is an external and an internal reality. The Israelites, perhaps, adapted to their oppression in order to survive. When adaptive responses become routine and internalized, they become an unreflected part of everyday life. They work. But once exodus happens, then adaptive patterns of behavior may not work. Exodus is an exter-

---

12. John Ernest, *Liberation Historiography: African American Writers and the Challenge of History, 1794–1861* (Chapel Hill: University of North Carolina Press, 2004).

nal moving away, but it also must be internal in order to experience freedom. H. Richard Niebuhr called this external history and internal history (in the former, the events, and in the latter, their meaning). The movement, perhaps, is from embeddedness to exodus to wilderness: from the routine and familiar to upheaval to the new. Those moving through these life stages must "perform" something new in acts of spontaneity or intentionality, surprise, serendipity, and artistic expression. Perhaps the wild and uncharted wilderness, with its unknown challenges, is just the place to try out these new performances and new definitions of a "becoming people."

The exodus account describes the event of liberation, a miracle, a crucial moment in time when God was present and acted in the people's history. The event was then expressed and given voice in a poetic language that communicated its saving power. It became a communal experience that was shared and celebrated. These two events, the miracle and the celebration of it, are inextricably related.

This intimate relationship between event and the proclamation of it could explain what has been identified as awkwardness in the text between the conclusion of Moses's song and the beginning of Miriam's song. When the first song ends, there is a narrative interlude. The text reads, "When the horses of Pharaoh with his chariots and his chariot drivers went into the sea, the Lord brought back the waters of the sea upon them; but the Israelites walked through the sea on dry ground. Then the prophet Miriam, Aaron's sister, took a tambourine in her hand; and all the women went out after her with tambourines and with dancing" (Exod. 15:19–20). The audience joins in the performance. The people's seeing and believing do not simply follow the sea crossing. The seeing is brought forth by Miriam's performance, her song.[13] The liturgical performance is so closely interwoven with the event that it cannot be separated from it.[14]

Scholars have long suspected that perhaps there was a longer Song of Miriam that was somehow suppressed through the centuries. A recently published Dead Sea Scrolls fragment suggests that Miriam did have her own song and that this tradition survived until the time of the scrolls (this scroll from about 75–50 BCE). This text can best be appreciated as a genre of women's songs that not only celebrate God's victories, but also recognize that these victories involve a particular kind of reversal. The victory is brought about through the weak and the downtrodden. God's victory is

13. J. Gerald Janzen, "The Song of Moses, Song of Miriam: Who Is Seconding Whom?" *Catholic Biblical Quarterly* 54, no. 1 (1992): 218–19.
14. Terrence E. Fretheim, *Exodus*, Interpretation (Louisville: John Knox, 1991), 133.

shame for the proud and arrogant, and the mighty victory belongs to the powerless.[15]

The Ritual

There are many kinds of performance; these sometimes are separate and sometimes overlap in our life situations. These are performances in everyday life, in the arts, in sports, in business, in technology, in sex, in ritual (both sacred and secular), and in play.[16] We are concerned here with sacred ritual. Rituals are performances that provide structure and continuity for our living. We perform rituals to mark the passage of time, to transform our social status, or to ensure good fortune. We employ them to deepen meaning or to pass on traditions so that they can be remembered. Rituals exemplify and reinforce the values and beliefs of the community that performs them. Communities are defined by the rituals they share. Rituals emphasize efficacy over entertainment. They express or enact belief, connecting the participants with a spiritual power.[17]

Ritual scholars have tried to delineate basic categories or genres of ritual action. On the one hand, Victor Turner suggests a simple system of classification. He delineates two categories: life crisis rituals and rituals of affliction. On the other hand, Ronald Grimes proposes a system of sixteen ritual categories. As a compromise, Catherine Bell proposes a schema of six basic categories of ritual; she does not claim these categories to be comprehensive or inclusive of all ritual practice in all cultures. Her categories are rites of passage; calendrical and commemorative rites; rites of exchange and communion; rites of affliction; rites of feasting, fasting, and festivals; and political rituals.[18]

Because of the variegated compositional layers of the biblical text, it is possible, and even necessary, to determine varied purposes for texts that describe ritual performances. There could be, for example, a purpose for a particular ritual at the time/place of its happening *and* a completely different purpose derived from its placement in the final edited version of the story. In this instance, the Song of Miriam functions on one level as something akin to a communal rite of affliction. Redress, correction, and healing are not being

---

15. George J. Brooke, "Power to the Powerless: A Long-Lost Song of Miriam," *Biblical Archaeology Review* 20, no. 3 (1994): 62–65.

16. Richard Schechner, *Performance Studies: An Introduction* (London and New York: Routledge, 2002), 25.

17. Henry Bial, ed., *The Performance Studies Reader* (London: Routledge, 2004), 77.

18. Catherine Bell, *Ritual: Perspectives and Dimensions* (New York: Oxford University Press, 1997), 93–135.

sought; rather, they are being celebrated. The imbalance and injustice that came through the slavery of the Israelites by the Egyptians has been ameliorated. So the community celebrates and gives thanks. The fortunes of the Israelites have been reversed. It is through the power of Yahweh that this redemptive act has been wrought. Miriam sings that the horse and rider have been thrown into the sea.

On another level, however, the performance of Miriam functions as a rite of passage. In the exodus narrative the people are enslaved in Egypt, oppressed, and treated harshly by their masters. Through the power of Yahweh they are brought through birth waters to new life. The community stands on the threshold of something new, unknown, perhaps exciting or terror filled. Miriam calls the community to sing, and then the community moves forward. Her words echo and reverberate as the Israelites take their first steps in the journey that awaits them.

Performance and Prophecy

It is not unusual for us to think about ritual action and performance in relation to the role of the priest or the pastor. The story of Miriam, who is identified as "prophet," however, invites us to think about different dimensions of ritual activity. While some consider the addition of the term *prophet* anachronistic, in the final version of the story, Miriam's rituals are seen in relation to her prophetic role. Surely this is consistent with the role of the prophet in the Old Testament as we have come to understand it. The term *prophet* comes from a word that means to "bubble up" or to summons, announce, and call. The prophet was the spokesperson from God to the community and from the community to God. She named the realities of life around her and theologically interpreted them. Miriam names the deliverance the Israelites have experienced; she attributes the deliverance to the mighty Yahweh; she calls the community to express gratitude to God by naming and then claiming their liberation. "Sing to the Lord, for he has triumphed gloriously."

The ritualizing of God's deliverance is necessary if the community is to create a liberation story to counter the oppression story (or stories) they have known for so long. They must mark a distinction between the story of liberation and the story of oppression and create a site of liberation through performance. In so doing, they are able to place their individual experiences of bitter oppression within the framework of communal understanding. This way, then, the individual members can counter experiences of spiritual isolation and alienation and increase their sense of personal agency by strengthening the collective self in a stable community of like-minded believers. They may be homeless, but not forsaken. In this light, Miriam was not only giving them focus in the present moment (consolidating and reconciling them with past experiences), but also preparing and strengthening them to face the unknown future. If they can see the providential hand of the divine at work in their human history, then they may find ritual ways to embody or perform that memory in the future. They may derive strength and solidarity through ritual enactments, and be stronger to face the unknown.

Miriam's prophetic role in leading the community in celebration invites interesting questions about the use of ritual in relation to the struggle for justice. How can reenactment of the story of oppression keep awareness of the dangers of the misuse and abuse of power alive in our world? How can performance help us never to forget the atrocities that are perpetrated against those who are "other"?

The Song of Miriam takes its place in the canon with the songs of Hannah, Deborah, and Mary, the mother of Jesus. Though the women's life circumstances vary, each song gives witness to the God who reverses the fortunes of the oppressed and the vulnerable. Miriam is part of a "female anthropology of liberation."[19] She, along with the midwives at the beginning of the exodus story, are the resisters, the ones who usher in God's redemptive work and make liberation possible among the people. She, along with the women by the edge of the sea at the conclusion of the exodus story, celebrate that liberation.

The Ethics of Performance

Like all human action, performance has ethical consequences. On the most basic level, one can consider whether a given performance event respects the rights of others. We can seek to understand how performances are political acts, endorsing certain values.[20] While the ethical questions related to performance are many, here we will focus on just one. Which performers or what speakers are privileged in the performance of particular rituals?

The exodus story belongs in its beginning and ending to the women; the stories find their continuity in the figure of Miriam. At the beginning, she

19. Ana Flora Anderson and Gilberto Da Silva Gorgulho, "Miriam and Her Companions," in *The Future of Liberation Theology: Essays in Honor of Gustavo Gutierrez*, ed. Marc H. Ellis and Otto Maduro (New York: Orbis, 1989), 211.

20. Ronald J. Pelias, *Performance Studies: The Interpretation of Aesthetic Texts* (New York: St. Martin's Press, 1992), 165–67.

stands on the bank of the river protecting her brother Moses.[21] Then, at the end, she is again on the shore. The story comes full circle and becomes complete. But Miriam's dancing by the seashore and proclaiming the good and salvific deeds of Yahweh is more. Miriam's being labeled a prophet is more. Miriam's being the performer is more. These enlarge the parameters of who can be the speaker, who can name the people's experience, and who can be a spokesperson to God. Miriam was all of these, and Miriam was a woman.

The singing of Miriam is as bold as her own later questioning in Numbers 12:2, "Has the LORD spoken only through Moses? Has he not spoken through us [Miriam and Aaron] also?" The editor of Exodus has already answered this question for us by providing a subversive answer, one that subtly provides a corrective to the leprous consequences that Miriam later experiences for asking such an audacious question. Is it only through Moses that God speaks? No. Miriam the prophet leads the women in speaking for and to their God.

The questions of who can be the preacher, the liturgist, the ritualist, the performer are ones that have plagued and continue to plague Christian communities. What does it mean for those who have been silenced and marginalized from the pulpit? By taking up her tambourine and singing and dancing, perhaps Miriam simply represents a community of women prepared and designated as the ones who sing songs of celebration just when they are needed. But to do so as a prophet is something more. To be called a prophet is to be affirmed as God's spokesperson. When a person who is oppressed and silenced stands and speaks, that person experiences redemption. It is a redemptive moment for individual and community because it relies on grace and moves toward wholeness. It is healing because it moves us toward our godlikeness. The internal movement is from fear to faith, shame to acceptance, guilt to forgiveness, denial to affirmation. It is a mysterious and sacramental moment. Moving from silence into speech for any oppressed, colonized, or exploited being is healing. The gesture of defiance makes new life possible. It is liberation.

21. Norman J. Cohen, "Miriam's Song: A Modern Midrashic Reading," *Judaism* 33, no. 2 (1984): 181. Cohen elaborates on the midrashic traditions related to Miriam. Symbolically, Miriam births Moses by drawing him out of the water and bringing him to life. The rabbis identify Miriam as one of the Hebrew midwives mentioned in the previous chapter in Exodus. According to the tradition, Miriam was actually Puah, and along with her mother, Jochabed (or Shiphrah), openly rebelled against Pharaoh and saved the lives of the Israelite male children who, by the king's decree, were to be killed. More than being pictured as an advocate for life, Miriam is a symbol of Israel's redemption from Egypt and salvation. Cohen further discusses the relationship between Miriam and water. She was at the river watching over her brother and at the seashore singing the song of deliverance. Immediately after the report of her death in Num. 20, the Torah says that a dearth of water set in. Miriam was related to water because she was the source of the people's redemption.

What does it mean for one who has been silenced and oppressed to speak from the pulpit, to speak of God? The performance is not only redemptive, but itself is prophetic. When Miriam breaks out into song, she embodies the inclusive spirit-filled nature of the Word. She fulfills her God-given nature to be created in the "sound" of one who brought the earth into being through speech, creating goodness. By her very presence a new world is drawn out of the old. The old is destroyed, plucked up, turned over. The new is built. It is a creative act of justice and inclusivity. It breaks barriers.[22]

That is the beauty of Exodus 15:20–21. The words are of redemption and liberation, the miracle of God bringing the Israelites through the sea, reversing their oppression. And *the performance itself* is an act of liberation and redemption because it is Miriam, the prophet, who sings. God puts the song into her mouth and she calls Israel to sing. The individual's song becomes communal. Her participation in the total event gives redemption its revelatory voice.[23]

The Echoes of Performance

Mary's song in Luke 1:46–55, commonly known as the Magnificat, has inspired composers throughout the centuries. In her hymn, Mary praises God for performing mighty deeds and for showing great mercy. God looked kindly on Mary, and all generations would call her blessed. Mary's song is more than an expression of gratitude; it functions to announce that Israel's ultimate eschatological deliverance was coming to fulfillment. Many interrelated themes are found there, and they include allusions to the exodus, David, and covenant. In the song, Mary speaks of reversal of fortune. God would overturn Israel's condition as foretold in the prophets, allowing it to become the means through which God would keep the covenant promise to Abraham to bless all the families of the earth. Mary's prayer stands in the line of Miriam's song performed by the sea. We find multiple points of similarity between Miriam and Mary—including their name. "Mary" (Maria) is the transliteration of the Hebrew "Miriam."

In the time of the second temple, the resurgence of traditional names was one way of asserting Jewish nationalism. In naming a child Miriam, or Mary, a Jewish family would have been announcing their hope that Yahweh would turn the tables and bring a reversal of fortune, just as Yahweh had done in ancient

22. Mary Donovan Turner and Mary Lin Hudson, *Saved from Silence* (St. Louis: Chalice, 1999), 93–94.
23. Janzen, "Song of Moses, Song of Miriam," 219.

times, and bring about a new exodus. By placing Mary's song at the opening of the book, Luke echoes Miriam's song of deliverance, signaling that the new exodus was about to happen. The placement of the Magnificat indicates that Mary is uttering a prophetic announcement predicting that God will deliver Israel through the child Mary is carrying. Mary's child would bring to Israel a greater freedom than Moses.

Miriam's voice, then, echoes and reverberates through the centuries. The sensuous, performed word names the community's experience, ushers the people forward, and empowers them to face the unknown. Centuries later, through those who come after Miriam, other communities find hope in their own place and time.[24] They are the oppressed, but oppression does not have final say. They sing the song, and they dance the dance. They believe liberation is possible.

The Essence of It All

Deliverance from oppression is the desire of nations and individuals. If we are created in the image of the divine, then there is buried deep within us the unquenchable desire to live up to our full stature, be free from oppression, and live in dignity. This idealized desire underlies the struggles of nations for self-determination, to be free from oppression. This never comes without a struggle, often long-term suffering and trauma. Thus it is important to mark such a deliverance when it happens and give thanks for it. This article is about marking the experience of deliverance. Reversal of fortune is a communal act of celebration that names God's agency in human experience. In liberation, a divine promise is being revealed. A divine promise is being fulfilled. Performed rituals can help reverse a collective sense of demoralization, stimulate hope, and empower a people to move ahead, even in the face of uncertainty.

24. For an interesting discussion on the intimate relationship between ritual and liturgy and the search for justice, see Anne Y. Koester, ed., *Liturgy and Justice: To Worship God in Spirit and Truth* (Collegeville, MN: Liturgical Press, 2002). Can liturgy be instrumental in reversing the social order?

6

Performance and the New Testament in Preaching

RONALD J. ALLEN

The preacher may casually assume that the New Testament is a collection of letters and books to be silently read and interpreted in the way that we do printed materials today. Choosing a text for a sermon, a minister usually opens the Bible (a book) and reads silently through passages. Surrounded by biblical commentaries, preachers often prepare messages in the form of a manuscript that looks like a term paper. Indeed, some preachers even speak of *writing the sermon*. "I must write my sermon today."

In seminary, students are socialized into a print world through daily focus on reading books and writing papers. Presenting the Scripture lesson in worship, a lector says, "Our *reading* today comes from the *book* of Matthew." Preaching classes emphasize lively delivery, but the very term *delivery* implies that the preacher is conveying information in the same way a driver for United Parcel Service delivers packages.

This constellation of factors may obscure the fact that the materials in the Second Testament arose in a culture in the first century CE that was oriented more toward the oral and aural than to print. Many scholars today think that virtually every part of the Second Testament was generated in and for communities centered in speaking and hearing. A performance approach to preaching helps recover these aspects of the Second Testament. As Charles L. Bartow says, "Performance is a way of coming to know and understand a biblical text and its persona in such a way that fresh insight is gained into what a text is, what it says (denotation) and what it signifies (connotation)."[1]

This chapter first reviews characteristics of the rhetorical world (with its oral-aural tone) of the Second Testament and explores how a performance approach can work with conventional methods of biblical interpretation to help preacher and congregation experience a text in an oral-aural medium.[2] After pausing over the importance of critical theological reflection on performance, we then take up how performance perspectives can help preachers with the letters, with the Gospels and Acts, and with Hebrews and Revelation.

The Rhetorical World of the First Century CE

Vernon Robbins, a scholar of the Second Testament, speaks of the first century as a "rhetorical culture" (rather than simply "an oral-aural culture"), since documents were entering that world.[3] David Cartlidge, another scholar, notes, "The evidence from late antiquity is that oral operations (presentation and hearing) were (1) inescapably interlocked, and (2) they were communal activities."[4] Writing, reading, and hearing took many of their cues from speech, while speaking and hearing were manifesting some characteristics of writing and reading.[5] While the first century was thus not a pristine oral-aural culture (that can be so easily romanticized), it was nevertheless a setting in which

1. Charles L. Bartow, "Who Says the Song? Practical Hermeneutics as Humble Performance," *Princeton Seminary Bulletin* 17, no. 2 (July 1996): 143; cf. Charles L. Bartow, *God's Human Speech: A Practical Theology of Proclamation* (Grand Rapids: Eerdmans, 1997), 70–93.

2. Throughout I am indebted to Holly E. Hearon, *The Mary Magdalene Tradition: Witness and Counter-Witness in Early Christian Communities* (Collegeville, MN: Liturgical Press, 2004), and to Bruce E. Shields, *From the Housetops: Preaching in the Early Church and Today* (St. Louis: Chalice, 2000).

3. Vernon K. Robbins discusses rhetorical culture in a number of places, e.g., "Progymnastic Rhetorical Composition and Pre-Gospel Traditions: A New Approach," in *The Synoptic Gospels: Source Criticism and the New Literary Criticism*, ed. Camille Focant (Leuven, Netherlands: Leuven University Press, 1993), 111–47. The work of Werner Kelber sparked the recent emphasis on orality in studies of the Second Testament.

4. David Cartlidge, "Combien d'unités avez-vous de trios à quatre? What Do We Mean by Intertextuality in Early Church Studies," in *Society of Biblical Literature Seminar Abstracts and Seminar Papers*, ed. David Lull (Atlanta: Scholars Press, 1990), 407.

5. Walter J. Ong, *Orality and Literacy: The Technologizing of the Word* (London: Methuen, 1982); cf. Walter J. Ong, *The Presence of the Word: Some Prolegomena for Cultural and Religious History* (New Haven: Yale University Press, 1967).

oral-aural patterns set the tone for written communication. Indeed, people often wrote to extend the spoken word.[6]

Estimates of literacy in antiquity range from 2 to 15 percent of the entire population.[7] The literate included some slaves who needed to read and write in connection with their work, people at the top of the social pyramid, professional scribes who made documents for people who were illiterate, and a few others (e.g., administrators and occasional religious leaders). Reading and writing played four main roles: (1) the Romans ruled the empire by means of administrative letters and public inscriptions; (2) records were kept in commercial life; (3) the upper classes enjoyed literature; (4) people wrote personal correspondence and made personal documents (such as wills). Literacy among women was lower than among men.[8]

Similar literacy phenomena prevailed in the Jewish community. The upper classes (e.g., priests and elders) could read and write. Many Pharisees (a small group) were literate because they tended to work in jobs needing scribal skills.[9] Although the Hebrew Bible was circulating in written form, the average person had access to these texts only through hearing. Memory was more highly developed in the ancient world than today, so people could carry the essence of such material with them even if they could not recall it word for word. Judaism honored "oral torah."[10]

When a document was read publicly, listeners experienced authors as present through the reading. The private reading of a document by an individual even partook of the oral-aural. People did not read silently as we do today. They moved their lips, in effect reading aloud to themselves.[11] An author often wrote a document by dictating it so that the scribe essentially wrote down a spoken word.[12]

The great philosopher A. N. Whitehead reminds us that speaking and hearing engage the whole self in deeper and more penetrating ways than silent reading often does: "In the production of sound, the lungs and throat are

---

6. Vernon K. Robbins, *The Tapestry of Early Christian Discourse: Rhetoric, Sociology and Ideology* (New York: Routledge, 1996), 57.

7. On the low end, see Bruce Malina and Richard Rohrbaugh, *A Social Science Commentary on the Synoptic Gospels* (Minneapolis: Fortress, 1992), 3; and on the high, William Harris, *Ancient Literacy* (Cambridge, MA: Harvard University Press, 1989), 267.

8. The foregoing description is drawn from Joanna Dewey, "Textuality in an Oral Culture: A Survey of the Pauline Traditions," *Semeia* 65 (1994): 39–43.

9. Ibid., 44.

10. Jacob Neusner, *The Oral Torah: The Sacred Books of Judaism* (Chicago: University of Chicago Press, 1986).

11. Paul J. Achtemeier, "*Omne verba sonat:* The New Testament and the Oral Environment of Late Western Antiquity," *Journal of Biblical Literature* 109 (1990): 17.

12. Ibid., 15.

brought into play. So that in speech, while a superficial manageable expression is diffused, yet the sense of the vague intimacies of organic existence are also excited. Thus, voice produced sound is a natural symbol for the deep experiences of organic existence."[13] The act of speaking can emanate from the deepest reaches of the self. Similarly, in the act of hearing, the entire self is stirred. Sound waves vibrate the eardrum and set the body itself into motion. The listener responds not only to the direct words of the speaker, but to the feelings and visceral qualities generated by the speaker's persona as well as by the communal settings in which such speaking and hearing take place. People are thus affected at multiple levels, but because some of these levels are sensorial and intuitive, we cannot always state in conventional propositional language what has been communicated.

Not every interaction of speaking and hearing in antiquity was a major rhetorical event. People could use oral language in mundane ways such as exchanging information. However, communities often set aside public times when speakers would voice concerns for the whole community. Kenneth Bailey, a Bible teacher who has lived for years in the Middle East, notices that such cultures retain practices for centuries. One such practice, *haflat samar* (an Arabic expression meaning something like "party" or "gathering" for "preservation"), illustrates the role of performance. The *haflat samar* takes place many evenings in the village; people perform material that is important to the community such as proverbs, riddles, poetry, parables, and stories.[14] The *haflat samar* is an informal but somewhat controlled means whereby the community passes along its tradition. The tradition can be modified. Anyone can perform, including women, though men are disproportionately represented.

Activities similar to the *haflat samar* also take place in religious gatherings and in extended family events.[15] Such occasions can last several hours. Thus it is easy to imagine a congregation listening to the Gospel of Mark for the hour and a half it takes to perform. Many people could then reproduce the broad outlines of the story.[16]

In such a culture, the preparation of a manuscript was not the end of one medium of communication (speaking and hearing) and the beginning of another (literature). The manuscript was a prompt for later performances and

13. Alfred North Whitehead, *Modes of Thought* (New York: Free Press, 1938), 32.

14. Kenneth E. Bailey, "Informal Controlled Oral Tradition and the Synoptic Gospels," *Asia Journal of Theology* 4 (1991): 41–44.

15. Kenneth E. Bailey, "Middle Eastern Oral Tradition and the Synoptic Gospels," *The Expository Times* 106 (1995): 364–65.

16. Ibid., 47.

a stand-in for the physical presence of the author.[17] Indeed, most manuscripts of the Second Testament were written with no spaces between the words, without punctuation, and with no paragraph markings. Paul Achtemeier, a former president of the Society of Biblical Literature, points out that the writers of the Second Testament wrote oral clues into the written material (such as indicating a change of subject by a shift in style of expression) to signal the performer how the pieces of the document are related to one another. "What is of greatest importance to keep in mind here . . . is that to be useful, such indications had to make themselves apparent to the ear rather than to the eye."[18] Furthermore, documents frequently were carried from an author to a community by someone who was familiar with the contents and would know how to voice them.[19]

From this point of view, a written text in the Second Testament is an "arrested performance." A text "arrests" or "freezes" an oral-aural moment in time.[20] Today's interpreter needs to release the performative quality of the text for today.

Performance in Exegesis of the Second Testament

The purpose of exegesis is to help the preacher understand and honor the Otherness of a text. The preacher seeks plausible understandings of what a text invites its hearers to believe and do in view of the first-century-CE contexts. Performance can work with the traditional exegetical disciplines to help the preacher apprehend passages in the Second Testament in oral-aural ways that allow contemporary people to experience the text in ways similar to those of people in the first century.[21]

A performance approach uses the common methods of criticism—form, redaction, the various approaches to literary criticism, rhetorical, social science, structuralism, deconstruction, tradition, canonical, ideology, studies in orality, the turns associated with particular groups such as the racial and ethnic, feminist, or the gay, lesbian, bisexual, transgendered, and asexual

17. Dewey, "Textuality in an Oral Culture," 51–52.

18. Achtemeier, *Omne verbum sonat,* 17–18.

19. Ibid., 18.

20. Beverly Whitaker Long and Mary Frances Hopkins, *Performing Literature* (Englewood Cliffs, NJ: Prentice-Hall, 1982) cited in Bartow, *God's Human Speech*, 64, and in Jana Childers, *Performing the Word: Preaching as Theatre* (Nashville: Abingdon, 1998), 49.

21. For further discussion see Shields, *From the Housetops*, esp. 121–28, where he distinguishes between "sermon preparation" and "preparing to preach." For an example of cooperation between performance perspective and more conventional exegesis, see Richard F. Ward, *Speaking from the Heart: Preaching with Passion*, (Nashville: Abingdon, 1992), 47–61.

communities.[22] These disciplines provide information regarding how ancient communities would have taken for granted words, places, characters, mores, relationships, practices, conventions, events, and genres of speech that may be lost or misinterpreted in twenty-first-century North America.

However, traditional exegetical disciplines typically leave the preacher working silently with the biblical passage as a *printed* text.[23] The minister often prepares the sermon in one medium (print) and speaks it in another (oral-aural). In the pulpit, some preachers speak the sermon more in the mode of reading a manuscript than of engaging the congregation in a vibrant oral-aural event. By integrating performance into all aspects of sermon preparation, the preacher can move toward overcoming the hiatus between print-based preparation and oral-aural embodiment in the pulpit.

As Charles Bartow points out, "Performance is not just an act of technical virtuosity following upon scholarly analyses of the work and thereby totally dependent upon them. Instead, it is a type of public criticism that brings fresh understanding to the work."[24] Similarly Jana Childers, a seminary dean, cites Leland Roloff, "Expression deepens impression," and adds that this phenomenon is "particularly true of Scripture texts, so many of which began life in oral form, that the preacher or interpreter/performer cannot be said to know the text until he or she has given it his or her voice and body." In short, "To be known, a text must be performed."[25] The other disciplines help the preacher encounter the text in its Otherness as expressed in oral-aural medium.

22. For discussions of methods of biblical interpretation, see Michael Gorman, *Elements of Biblical Exegesis: A Basic Guide for Students and Ministers* (Peabody, MA: Hendrickson, 2001); Steven McKenzie and Stephen Haynes, eds., *To Each Its Own Meaning: An Introduction to Biblical Criticisms and Their Application*, rev. and exp. ed. (Louisville: Westminster John Knox, 1999); David Bartlett, *Between the Bible and the Church: New Methods for Biblical Preaching* (Nashville: Abingdon, 1999); Stephen Farris, *Preaching that Matters: The Bible and Our Lives* (Louisville: Westminster John Knox, 1998); Joel Green, ed., *Hearing the New Testament: Strategies for Interpretation* (Grand Rapids: Eerdmans, 1995); and Ronald Allen, *Contemporary Biblical Interpretation for Preaching* (Valley Forge, PA: Judson, 1984).

23. Two of the traditional exegetical methods focus on oral-aural dimensions. Form criticism identifies the form and function of small units of material in the "oral tradition" (before the materials were written down) when Jesus's followers used the materials orally in particular settings in life (e.g., teaching, preaching, and evangelism). Rhetorical criticism studies how the biblical writers shaped materials according to ancient conventions of rhetoric (formal and informal) to move the recipients. However, neither school of critics emphasizes performing the text as a part of the work of the contemporary interpreter. Furthermore, contemporary studies of orality in antiquity are calling into question several assumptions for traditional form criticism.

24. Bartow, "Who Says the Song?" 152.

25. Childers, *Performing the Word*, 49.

Performance preparation leads the preacher to read the text aloud as a part of sermon preparation.[26] Indeed, preachers can commit a text to memory and thereby not only develop empathetic understandings of it but also carry the passage in their hearts as they make their way through the week and can feel resonance between the passage and their worlds today.[27]

Reading the text aloud pushes the pastor to slow down and notice the details of the text; reading aloud may call to the preacher's attention matters to be investigated through the exegetical disciplines. "What *does* that word mean in this context in the Gospel of Mark?" Reading aloud can also (in the spirit of Whitehead) help the preacher feel the passage in its visceral and intuitive dimensions, especially as they may have moved listeners in antiquity. Furthermore, by working with the text orally and aurally in sermon preparation, the preacher is preparing to speak it expressively in the service of worship.[28]

Since the texts of the Second Testament were intended to be heard, a minister could profit from hearing someone else perform the passage. A preacher could listen to the text on tape or from members of a clergy colleague group or from a feed-forward group of laity who work with the pastor in sermon preparation.[29]

Charles Bartow speaks of "vocal exegesis." One of my former students refers to "tone of voice exegesis."[30] The tone of voice in which a preacher recites a text contributes to the perception of what the text asks the congregation to believe and do. The same line can be vocalized as a matter of fact, as annoyance, in irony, as a question, in anger, or in one of dozens of other intimations. The traditional critical disciplines help the preacher dis-

26. For detailed consideration of the importance of performing the text as a part of worship and sermon preparation, see Bartow, "Who Says the Song?" 53–94, as well as his *Effective Speech Communication in Leading Worship* (Nashville: Abingdon, 1988), 85–107. Richard F. Ward, *Speaking of the Holy: The Art of Communication in Preaching* (St. Louis: Chalice, 2001), expands on "the three Rs" of performance: reading, recitation, and retelling.

27. Thomas E. Boomershine, *Story Journey: An Invitation to the Gospel as Storytelling* (Nashville: Abingdon, 1988), suggests steps for memorizing a biblical text; cf. *How to Tell and Learn a Bible Story: Step by Step Instructions*, DVD, Network of Biblical Storytellers (Dayton: NOBS, 1997).

28. For systematic help in this regard, see Clayton J. Schmit, *Public Reading of Scripture: A Handbook* (Nashville: Abingdon, 2002); Richard F. Ward, *Your Ministry of Reading Scripture Aloud* (Nashville: Discipleship Resources, 1989); Bartow, *Effective Speech Communication*; Charles L. Bartow, *The Preaching Moment: A Guide to Sermon Delivery* (Nashville: Abingdon, 1980).

29. Shields, *From the Housetops*, 126.

30. Bartow, *God's Human Speech*, 71; Bartow adopted this phrase from his former colleague, W. J. Beeners. The expression "tone of voice exegesis" is from Charles R. Blaisdell, cited in Clark M. Williamson and Ronald J. Allen, *A Credible and Timely Word: Process Theology and Preaching* (St. Louis: Chalice, 1991), 89n34.

tinguish possibilities that were plausible in the first century from those that were not. By performing the passage in different inflections and moods and from different points of view, a preacher may become aware of possibilities for interpreting the text that do not occur in the media of silent reading and silent writing.

Theological Reflection on Performance of the Text

The preacher needs to reflect on a theologically appropriate relationship between how a text asked people in antiquity to respond and how it asks the congregation to respond today. What should the *sermon* encourage the congregation to believe and do? Such critical reflection will likely be guided by the preacher's presuppositions regarding the nature of the Second Testament and the role of that testament in interpreting the divine leading.

We may speak loosely of two poles defining the spectrum of the place of the Bible in theological thinking.[31] I state these poles starkly, recognizing that most preachers fall somewhere in between. At one end are those who believe that the Bible is (to one degree or another) inspired by God, reveals truth that is valid in every time and place, and is internally consistent. For these ministers, the major theological issue is how to *apply* this text today. The sermon should perform a similar application. The preacher needs mainly to update the performance of the text.

Other clergy think of the Bible as written by human beings interpreting God's leading, expressing viewpoints conditioned by ancient cultural contexts, and voicing different theological interpretations. The theological method of such preachers usually involves conversation with the Bible, tradition, and experience with an ear to what makes sense. This preacher does not create a sermon that simply applies or re-performs a text, but must conversationally explore the degree to which what the text asks the congregation to believe and do is true to the preacher's deepest convictions.

Such reflection may lead the preacher to perceive continuity between the convictions of the text and those of the congregation today. In that case the sermon can become an interpretive re-performance. However, the preacher may find points of tension between the convictions of a text and contemporary theological or ethical thinking. In the latter case, the sermon performance should help the congregation understand and experience the contemporary theological perception in dialogue with the text. When the preacher fundamentally

---

31. For a fuller description, see Joseph R. Jeter Jr. and Ronald J. Allen, *One Gospel, Many Ears: Preaching for Different Listeners in the Congregation* (St. Louis: Chalice, 2002), 149–74.

disagrees with a passage, the sermon may become a counter-performance to the performance of the text.

In the latter instance, the preacher does something biblical in character. Richard Ward, a leading performance theorist, notices that in Corinth some super-apostles performed a limited gospel. Paul sent 2 Corinthians 10–13 as an epistolary counter-performance to move the congregation away from embracing the limited and self-serving gospel of the super-apostles toward the Pauline gospel of the cross, resurrection, and self-giving.[32] Similarly, today's preacher may sometimes be called to offer a counter-performance to previous performances attested in the Bible or Christian tradition.

Performance and Interpreting the Letters

Following the custom of antiquity mentioned above, Paul dictated letters to a scribe (e.g., Rom. 16:22; 1 Cor. 16:21; Gal. 6:11; Philem. 19).[33] Ancient letter writers often adopted patterns of rhetoric intended to appeal through the ear to the recipients.[34] The letters of Paul and others thus have an oral-aural quality. Moreover, the letters of Paul, the Pauline school, and other letters were intended to be performed in the gathered congregation, perhaps functioning something like a sermon (e.g., 1 Thess. 5:27; Col. 4:16). We infer from Paul's description of worship in 1 Corinthians 12–14 that services of worship could last all evening, thereby allowing time to perform the whole of a letter. Given the fact that today's congregation typically gathers for worship and preaching in a large building, it may be helpful for the preacher to remember that the early congregations typically gathered in houses. The house church was a more immediate and intimate rhetorical setting than a coliseum or even the typical church building of today.

Moreover, in the oral-aural world of antiquity, letters represented the speaker (writer). Robert W. Funk has even found that letters are a medium "through which Paul made his apostolic authority effective in the churches."[35] The congregation was to perceive the letter and its performance as the presence of

32. Ward, *Speaking from the Heart*, 43–61; cf. Richard F. Ward, "Pauline Voice and Presence as Strategic Communication," *Semeia* 65 (1994): 95–107.

33. Each letter deserves a separate discussion. Because of limitations of space I can speak only generally about them. For further guidance, see Dewey, "Textuality in an Oral Culture," 47–65, and Ward, "Pauline Voice and Presence," 102–7.

34. See Shields, *From the Housetops*, 67–86.

35. Robert W. Funk, *Parables and Presence: Forms of the New Testament Tradition* (Philadelphia: Fortress, 1982), 82. Indeed, Funk finds a formal feature in the letters that he calls "apostolic *parousia*" or "apostolic presence" (e.g., Rom. 15:14–33; 1 Cor. 4:14–21; 2 Cor. 8:16–23; 9:1–5; Phil. 2:19–24; 1 Thess. 2:17–3:3; Philem. 21–22).

the apostle. Funk makes the remarkable observation that "Paul must have thought of his presence as bearing charismatic, one might even say eschato-logical, power."[36] Given this presupposition, Paul expected the performance of the letter to reshape the congregation in the direction of embodying the eschatological community in the present.

To perform a passage from a letter in sermon preparation, and as a part of a service of worship, a preacher needs to take two things into account: the historical context to which the letter was addressed and the rhetorical form of the passage. First, the preacher needs to reconstruct (as much as possible) the congregational issues to which the passage spoke. Each letter was directed to a particular congregation or network of congregations with its own matrix of questions, issues, feelings, tensions, and needs. In some cases we can reconstruct quite a bit about those situations (e.g., at Corinth), whereas other situations are less clear (e.g., at Ephesus). Usually the congregation believed or behaved in ways that did not measure up to the fullness of the gospel. To help the local community become more faithful, the author spoke the letter.

The second thing a pastor needs to take into account is the form or genre of the passage and the function of that form in the rhetoric of antiquity. Many letters in the Second Testament follow a general format: opening (sender/receiver/greeting), thanksgiving or blessing, body of the letter in which the author discusses the major issues that prompted the letter and exhorts the recipients to live according to the gospel, and closing (benediction/greeting). Within these general categories (especially the main body), ancient authors employed more specific rhetorical forms that are often quite helpful to the performer. Such subforms reveal both what the author hoped would happen in the congregation as well as how the passage was designed to bring about that effect. Examples of these rhetorical forms are apocalyptic prophecy, blessing, catalogue of vice and virtue, creed, deliberative argument, doxology, epideic-tic speech, diatribe, household code, hymn, judicial argument, midrash, and topoi.[37] Good commentaries name the form of each passage. Of course, when working with a particular text, the preacher needs to pay attention to how the author of the letter uses the form.

A letter is one side of a conversation between the congregation and the letter writer. To have a sense of the tones with which to vocalize a passage, a preacher needs to be aware of the feelings that were at work in the community as well as the mood invoked by the content and form of the passage. Are the

36. Ibid., 99.

37. An introduction to such forms is James L. Bailey and Lyle Vander Broek, *Literary Forms in the New Testament* (Louisville: Westminster John Knox, 1992), 89–188. Many Bible dictionaries also discuss particular forms.

recipients suffering and in need of comfort? Are they obstreperous and in need of rebuke? Are they confused and in need of a better way of thinking? Does the passage address a touchy situation with humor or irony? Is the author angry? From passage to passage, the tone may vary depending on the dynamics in the receiving community and the purpose of the writer.

As an example of the value of such analysis, consider Romans 3:1–9, a diatribe, that is, a passage that makes its point by means of questions and responses. Stanley Stowers, a scholar of antiquity, joins some other recent scholars in thinking that Romans was written to gentiles in the Roman congregation who disdained the Jewish members in the community and even Judaism itself. They argue that Paul sought to encourage gentile believers to respect their Jewish compatriots and to recognize that Jewish people would be saved as Jews (i.e., without joining the Jesus movement). Some Jewish people did not acknowledge the validity of the gentile mission. Romans 3:1–9 is a dialogue in a form recognized by people in antiquity. This form employs a dialogue between an imaginary Jewish teacher and Paul in which the apostle seeks to convince *gentiles* who hear the dialogue that God will keep the divine promises to the Jewish people though some of the latter have not recognized the validity of the gentile mission.[38] While preparing the sermon, the preacher could vocalize the passage as a dialogue between two voices as follows. In the service of worship, the preacher could do the same, or two performers could bring the passage to expression as an actual dialogue. I have added some explanatory remarks [in brackets].

> Imaginary teacher: Then what advantage has the Jew? Or what is the value of circumcision? (Rom. 3:1).
>
> Paul: Much, in every way. For in the first place the Jews were entrusted with the oracles of God [that is, the promises of God to bless all people, Jewish and gentile]. What if some were unfaithful [that is, did not recognize the validity of the gentile mission]? Will their faithlessness nullify the faithfulness of God [and result in God not saving them]? (Rom. 3:2–3).
>
> Teacher: By no means! Although everyone is a liar, let God be proved true, as it is written, "So that you may be justified in your words, and prevail in your judging" (Rom. 3:4, quoting Ps. 51:4b).
>
> Paul: But if our injustice [the Jewish reluctance to acknowledge the gentile mission] serves to confirm the justice of God, what should we say? That

---

38. Stanley K. Stowers, *A Rereading of Romans: Justice, Jews, and Gentiles* (New Haven: Yale University Press, 1994), 165–75.

God is unjust to inflict wrath on us? (I speak in a human way.) (Rom. 3:5).

Teacher: By no means! For then how could God judge the world? (Rom. 3:6).

Paul: But if through my falsehood God's truthfulness abounds to [God's] glory, why am I still being condemned as a sinner?[39] And why not say (as some people slander us by saying that we say), "Let us do evil so that good may come?" [i.e., "Why should we not just sin all the more and thereby support God's plans?"][40] Their condemnation is deserved! (Rom. 3:7–8).

Teacher: What then? Are we any better off? (Rom. 3:9a).

Paul: No, not at all; for we have already charged that all, both [Jewish people] and Greeks, are under the power of sin [and both Jewish people and Greeks receive the mercy of God]. (Rom. 3:9b).

This passage likely coheres theologically with the deepest convictions of many preachers about God. The sermon then could re-perform the text calibrated to contemporary issues.

Performance and Interpreting the Gospels and Acts

The Gospels and Acts are to be read (e.g., Mark 13:14; Matt. 24:15; Luke 1:1–4; John 20:30–31; Acts 1:1–2), which in the rhetorical culture of the first century means that they functioned as oral-aural communication.[41] Writing the text, as noted earlier, did more to create a means to preserve the performance than to transpose the material into print culture.

The Gospels and Acts manifest characteristics typical of oral-aural style in which speakers tend to add motifs to one another more than to subordinate some motifs to others. The oral-aural medium tends to be aggregative more than analytic; that is, the speaker tends to get a notion across by telling different versions of it more than by analyzing it. Plots develop less linearly and more episodically, associatively, and in parallel and concentric narrative structures. Oral-aural style is repetitive. While oral-aural communicators tend to pass on tradition more than create it, they do modify tradition. The audience often identifies with more than one character in the story. The language and imagery

39. In Romans 9–11, Paul explains how Jewish reluctance to embrace the gentile mission has actually worked to advance that mission.
40. Stowers, *Rereading of Romans*, 173.
41. See Shields, *From the Housetops*, 35–66.

of oral-aural world communication leans toward acoustical expressions more than visual.[42] These materials do not so much make an argument in logical fashion as they create an impression.

Performance studies in league with redaction and literary criticisms imply a caution regarding a common practice in sermonizing today: the preacher usually works with a single text. While this custom has much to commend it,[43] the performance of the whole of Mark, Matthew, Luke-Acts, and John has cumulative effect. Preachers often focus so intently on the individual text that they lose important resonances between the particular passage and the larger performance setting of the whole Gospel.

When preparing to preach on one passage, a preacher can do some simple things to help keep the larger oral-aural world of the Gospel in mind. The preacher can read the *whole Gospel* aloud and can listen to it on tape or in a live setting. (Such an exercise takes only about an hour and a half for Mark and about two and a half hours for Luke-Acts). A sensitive listener can hear connections between the passage and the whole. Furthermore, a concordance frequently helps preachers notice key words that link various parts of the text.[44] Commentaries and other helps lead the preacher to recognize how parts of the Gospel narrative are mutually interpretive. Along the way, the preacher may realize that the sermon must take account of other passages, words, images, and themes in order to capture the fullness of what the text asks the listening community to believe and do.[45]

Many of the letters are patently addressed to particular congregations about specific (and often easily identifiable) concerns so that a preacher can easily name performer, audience, and purpose. By contrast, the situation to which a Gospel was directed is often harder to reconstruct. The Gospel writers allude indirectly to the circumstances they were addressing. Furthermore, Joanna Dewey makes an observation that is especially suggestive to a minister preaching from a performance point of view:

42. Joanna Dewey, "Mark as Aural Narrative: Structure as Clues to Understanding," *Sewanee Theological Review* 36 (1992): 48–51; cf. A. B. Lord, "Characteristics of Orality," *Oral Tradition* 2 (1987): 54–62.

43. E.g., Ronald J. Allen, "Why Preach from Passages in the Bible?" in *Preaching as a Theological Task: World, Gospel, Scripture*, ed. Thomas G. Long and Edward Farley (Louisville: Westminster John Knox, 1996), 176–88.

44. Unfortunately, English translators sometimes render the same Greek word with different English words in different texts, or translators sometimes render different Greek words with the same English word. Consequently, this task is best carried out with a Greek concordance of the Second Testament or with an analytical concordance that alerts the English reader to the Greek that lies behind the English translations.

45. On this subject, see Ronald J. Allen, *Wholly Scripture: Preaching Biblical Themes* (St. Louis: Chalice, 2004).

Today we are trained to read for information. We tend to understand the gospels as giving us information about Jesus and/or [the world of Jesus's early followers]. Our emphasis generally is on the *referents* of the story, not on the story as story. Yet the act of hearing a narrative performance or attending a play or other live performance is much more a participatory experience of entering the world of the story and possibly being transformed by it.[46]

In the optimum performance situation, the listener enters the world of the narrative created in the telling of the gospel, experiences that world via the imagination, and emerges from the narrative able to think afresh about the listener's own immediate world. Participating imaginatively in stories prompts listeners to imagine consciously and/or intuitively how more faithfully they could perform their lives in their own worlds as informed by the performance of the gospel narrative.

To be sure, the Gospels and Acts contain straightforward statements and imperatives. While the preacher may be attracted to the immediate accessibility of such propositions, they are always embedded in narrative settings. To honor the performative aspects of these texts, the interpreter should hear them in their narrative settings.

These insights are suggestive for preaching. When the individual passage or the longer gospel story is appropriate to the preacher's convictions about God, the preacher might want not so much to explain the text as to perform a sermon that is itself an imaginative world that the congregation can enter. When a passage runs against the grain of the preacher's beliefs, the sermon needs to perform a critique of the viewpoint of the text as well as offer a positive alternative. Of course, we should not rhapsodize uncritically about this possibility. Sometimes the gospel witness is best served by a sermon that discusses the narrative in propositional analytical terms.

The Gospels and Acts are made up of smaller forms such as allegory, apocalypse, beatitude, call narrative, commissioning story, conflict story, epiphany, exorcism, genealogy, provision miracle, rescue story, revelatory discourse, sentence of holy law, and speech.[47] Not only does each of these forms have a different rhetorical purpose, but each Gospel writer places, shapes, and uses the forms for the aims of that Gospel. Such information often offers the preacher important clues regarding how to perform the text. As a part of performative exegesis, a preacher needs to investigate the content of a text and how the text speaks to the community to which the Gospel is written.

---

46. Dewey, "Mark as Aural Narrative," 56.
47. Such forms are discussed in Bailey and Vander Broek, *Literary Forms of the New Testament*, 89–188.

A preacher then needs to understand the various elements of a text with an ear toward how people would have responded to them in the community to which the Gospel was spoken.

For all passages in a Gospel, the preacher needs to pay attention to the following. The preacher can usually get information about these matters from Bible commentaries, dictionaries, and other interpretive helps.

- The form of the passage (e.g., beatitude, call story)
- The function of that form in the oral-aural culture of antiquity and in the Gospel from which the pastor is preaching
- Characteristic elements of the form
- The setting described in the passage (e.g., wilderness, house, roadside, synagogue, temple) and the significance of that setting in the book from which the sermon comes
- The characters in the text, how they appear elsewhere in the Gospel, and how the Gospel writer intended for hearers to think about them
- The plot, that is, the movement of action or thought from the beginning of the text to its end, with particular attention to complications, actions and reactions, climax, and resolution
- Key words and images and how they resonate with other passages in the Gospel
- What happens emotionally and intellectually to the listening community when hearing the story
- The feeling-tone of the text (e.g., joyous, sorrowful, angry, determined)
- How the passage addressed the circumstances and dynamics of the community to which the Gospel was written

The preacher explores these disparate elements to ascertain likely possibilities for performing the text as part of exegesis. The preacher wants to know how the Gospel writer hoped to move the hearers. The preacher can then reflect critically on the degree to which such a goal is appropriate to what the preacher most fully believes to be true of God's purposes for the world today.

One phenomenon common to all four Gospels and Acts deserves special comment: these materials frequently caricature Jewish people (especially Jewish leaders) in a negative light.[48] When performing the text as a part of prepara-

---

48. A work that systematically looks at these elements is Ronald J. Allen and Clark M. Williamson, *Preaching the Gospels without Blaming the Jews* (Louisville: Westminster John Knox, 2004).

tory exegesis, the preacher can honor disdainful, hostile, and sometimes even sinister portraits of Jewish people. However, to perform this picture uncritically as the reading from Scripture in the service of worship or as a part of the sermon is to reinforce anti-Judaism and even anti-Semitism. I have come to think that neither lector nor preacher should simply perform such passages. Rather, in a teaching moment in connection with the performance of the text as the Scripture reading or in the sermon itself, or both, the lector or preacher needs to critique these polemics as historically unreliable, unjust, theologically inappropriate, and hurtful to Jewish people.

The story of the widow who puts "two small copper coins, which are worth a penny" into the temple treasury in Mark 12:41–44 is an example of the importance of a performance approach to exegesis. The Markan Jesus warns the disciples, "Beware of the scribes" (12:38). The widow, according to Jesus, "put in everything she had, all she had to live on" (12:44). Preachers typically intone this passage in such a way as to revere the widow and to imply that today's congregation should follow her example.

Some interpreters, however, hear the story another way.[49] By way of form, the text is a pronouncement story, that is, a brief narrative involving Jesus and others that culminates in a short, pithy saying of Jesus intended to provide the hearers with direction for life. The setting is the temple, the leaders of which are nearly always viewed negatively in the second Gospel (e.g., Mark 11:15–17). The characters are the disciples (who hear the story), the scribes, and the widow. Listeners identify with the disciples and hear the teaching directed to the disciples as teaching directed to them (listeners). The widow is evidently poor and, therefore, should be a person who *receives* support from the community. The Gospel of Mark nearly always interprets the scribes in a negative light (e.g., Mark 1:22; 2:6, 16; 3:22; 7:1–5; 8:31; 9:11–14; 10:33; 11:18, 27; for exceptions, 12:28–34; 14:1, 43, 53; 15:1, 31). In Mark 12:38–40, Jesus warns against the self-important scribes who "devour widows' houses." By devouring widows' houses, the scribes violate one of Judaism's most important axioms—to care for widows. By putting "in everything she had, all she had to live on," the woman bankrupts herself and would have to sell her house to be able to live. The scribes thus "devour" her. Mark uses this story to warn the community against the scribes. Since Mark wrote after the destruction of the temple (Mark 13:1–3), the story does not imply that the community would be unfaithful without the temple; indeed, the story

---

49. For details see Allen and Williamson, *Preaching the Gospels without Blaming the Jews*, 162–64, building on Addison G. Wright, "The Widow's Mite: Praise or Lament—A Matter of Context," *Catholic Biblical Quarterly* 44 (1982): 256–65.

implies that the unfaithfulness of the scribes and the temple leaders led to its destruction.

To perform the text exegetically, the minister would intone it as a warning against the scribes and the widow-devouring system of the temple. The preacher might deliver the last line in a tone of accusatory incredulity, as if to say, "Can you believe she out of her *poverty* has put in everything she had, *all she had to live on?*"

Performance and Interpreting Other Materials in the Second Testament

Two other documents deserve brief mention. Most scholars think Hebrews was a sermon directed to a Hellenistically oriented community. Using traditional patterns of Hellenistic rhetoric, the preacher who spoke "To the Hebrews" shapes each part of the sermon for a particular rhetorical purpose.[50] When developing a message for today, then, the minister needs to note the particular rhetorical function of each text within the larger work.

Although the book of Revelation has some characteristics of letters (e.g., Rev. 1:4–5a), it is more an apocalypse with a permeating oral-aural-visual message for congregations that perceived themselves suffering under the Roman Empire. The author refers to the public reading and hearing of the book (Rev. 1:3; 22:17–18). John received the vision in the midst of worship (Rev. 1:9–20). The apocalypse was put together as an "oral enactment" whose sound-word-images make use of numerous oral-aural elements (e.g., techniques that facilitate speaking and remembering).[51]

Such qualities inspire David Barr to observe that through the performance of the text, the congregation experienced imaginatively a symbolic universe. The latter "enlightens the audience, giving them a new understanding of their world." Even as they endure persecution and look for the coming of the apocalypse, "They live [already via the performance] in a new reality in which lambs conquer and suffering rules. The victims have become the victors." According to Barr, the performance of the text empowers the congregation no longer to see themselves suffering "helplessly at the hand of Rome," but now to see themselves "in charge of their own destiny and by their voluntary suffer-

---

50. For an up-to-date treatment, see Judith Hoch Wray, "An Exhortation to Faithfulness: Hebrews," in *Chalice Introduction to the New Testament*, ed. Dennis Smith (St. Louis: Chalice, 2004), 281–305.

51. David Barr, "The Apocalypse of John as Oral Enactment," *Interpretation* 43 (1986): 249–56.

ing they participate in the overthrow of evil and coming of God's [realm]."[52] The last book of the Bible is the epitome of performance. The preacher and congregation who do not actively perform it simply cannot receive it in the depths of human perception intended by John.

Allowing for the hyperbole that sometimes accompanies new discoveries, Werner Kelber calls attention to the importance of this discussion: "While there is no such thing as face-to-face encounter with a text, the mouth-to-heart engagement in oral communication fosters personal and intimate relations. The spoken word, emanating from interiority and entering another interiority, creates a deep-set bonding of speaker with auditor. 'Sound unites groups of living beings as nothing else does.'"[53] Week by week, ministers seek to preach sermons with such depth-penetration and community-building power. By integrating performance theory into the center of interpreting the Second Testament in conjunction with credible exegetical and theological methods, the preacher increases that possibility.

52. David Barr, "The Apocalypse as a Symbolic Transformation of the World: A Literary Analysis," *Interpretation* 38 (1984): 49–50.

53. Werner Kelber, *The Oral and the Written Gospel: The Hermeneutics of Speaking and Writing in the Synoptic Tradition, Mark, Paul and Q*, new ed. (Bloomington: Indiana University Press, 1997), 146; Kelber is quoting Walter Ong. For further development of implications for preaching see Shields, *From the Housetops*, 149–60.

7

The Use of the Body in the Performance of Proclamation

TODD FARLEY

Through performance, scriptural texts evoke worlds "real enough for people to enter, to believe in and to be changed by."[1] Charles Bartow shows us that inside every text we read there is an "arrested performance,"[2] where what once was alive is frozen in words on a page: "blood turned into ink."[3] An age ago, the lives and times of prophets and kings were recorded on parchment. The actions and antics of saints and scoundrels were translated onto the written page. The passions and spirit of the people of God were inscribed—turned into ink. Hundreds of years have passed, and we hold the book that tells of the passion and spirit, action and antics of a people long dead—yet their words still speak to us today through the power of the Holy Spirit. We seek not only to read the words they wrote, but to enliven them, so that the ink "may be turned back to blood."[4] This chapter will focus on the body that speaks, the body that re-embodies ink. We will examine how—through the body—we communicate to those who hear *and behold* our proclamation.

1. Charles L. Bartow, *God's Human Speech: A Practical Theology of Proclamation* (Grand Rapids: Eerdmans, 1997), 97. Bartow is quoting Don Geiger.
2. Ibid., 98.
3. Ibid., 121.
4. Ibid.

There is no culture in which the body is not communicative. Every human being has the natural tendency to laugh, to cry, and even to dance. The human being was created to communicate the invisible idea—to make the invisible visible. How else would we know when people are happy or sad unless they show it or vocalize it (vocalization being in itself a physical process)? How can we offer our "spiritual worship" if not through the body? For it is through and in the body that we live this spiritual life, as Romans 12:1 states:

> Therefore, I urge you, brothers [and sisters], in view of God's mercy, to offer your bodies as living sacrifices, holy and pleasing to God—this is your spiritual act of worship. (NIV)

It is part of our essential being to use our bodies as part of our reasonable and spiritual worship of God. As Luther said,

> Worship is not a function of the mouth but of the whole body. It is to bow the head, bend the body, fall on the knees, prostrate oneself, and so forth, and to do such things as a sign and acknowledgement of an authority and power; just as people bow in silence before secular princes and lords. . . . From this understanding of outward worship you will also understand what Christ meant by true spiritual worship. It is the adoration of bowing of the heart . . . [and] where worship is offered from the heart, there follow quite properly also that outward bowing, bending, kneeling, and adoration with the body.[5]

Gesture and movement are likewise essential to the preacher, for each preacher speaks both audibly and visually to the hearing and watching congregation. John Wesley indicates the importance of integrated and honest gesture for the preacher:

> That this silent language of your face and hands may move the affections of those that see and hear you, it must be well adjusted to the subject, as well as to the passion which you desire either to express or excite. It must likewise be free from all affectation, and such as appears to be the mere, natural result, both of the things you speak, and of the affection that moves you to speak them. And the whole is so to be managed, that there may be nothing in all the dispositions and motions of your body to offend the eyes of the spectators.[6]

5. Martin Luther, *Vom Anbeten des Sakraments des heiligen Leichnams Christi* (1523), Weimarer Ausgabe 11: 445ff., as quoted in Peter Brunner, *Worship in the Name of Jesus*, trans. M. H. Bertram (St. Louis: Concordia, 1968), 333.
6. John Wesley, "Of Gesture," Letters & Writings. Directions Concerning Pronunciation and Gesture, Section 4, *Collected Works of John Wesley* (1872).

What Wesley points out is that the gestures made while preaching should be so married with the words as to be true and sincere, and so as not to appear contrived or "affected." This has long been the law of good orators. In 1654 a book called *Chironomia: Or, the Art of Manual Rhetoric* was written by John Bulwer. In it Bulwer tells of an ancient Roman's virtuosity in the art of gesture and public speech:

> [The] most actively eloquent was Q. Hortensius the orator; one could not tell whether they should most desire to run to *hear* or *see* him speak, his presence and aspect did so adorn and become his words, and assist his periods to accomplish all their numbers; and again, his verbal expressions were so conformable to this gesture and so elegantly administered unto his hand, that for certain, Aesop and Roscius, two famous actors of those times, were often observed to crowd into the assembly when he was speaking, [so] that they might by imitation transfer some of his expressive gestures from the forum to the theatre.[7]

The fact is that gestures made by any public speaker not only augment the words spoken but visually speak nuances not found in uttered words. Communication through body and use of gesture naturally takes place, regardless of whether the preacher intends it. The purpose of this chapter is to help the preacher develop an intentional use and understanding of gesture through techniques that come from the world of physical theater.

The Preacher's Zero

The first impression a person makes on an audience establishes how that crowd will identify the person thereafter. In public speaking, the audience will examine and evaluate the speaker before she ever speaks. That evaluation becomes the starting point for the audience's reception of what will be said. In order for the speaker to make a good first impression, one that will open the listener to hear all that the speaker wishes to communicate, the first stance should represent the speaker's natural and neutral state. In mime, we refer to the neutral stance of the performer as a *double zero*. Double zero refers to "zero emotion on the face" and "zero emotion on the body." It is conceptualized as an empty canvas upon which the movement artist paints his or her gestures and postures. These gestures in turn communicate thought and emotion to the observing audience. Double zero is akin to being "at attention" in the army,

7. John Bulwer, *Chirologia: Or, the Natural Language of the Hand*, and *Chironomia: Or, the Art of Manual Rhetoric*, Landmarks in Rhetoric and Public Address (Carbondale: Southern Illinois University Press, 1974), 167–68.

ready for action. A variation of the performer's double zero is the more basic *zero* position. A person's zero position is a person's natural and neutral stance. In preaching, a zero position is the stance a preacher takes behind the pulpit, hands to the sides or resting on the pulpit itself—or, if there is no pulpit, the establishing position taken on the platform from which the address is to be made. Like any performer, the preacher begins with an empty canvas which will be colored by her words and imprinted by her actions—the canvas will be viewed and read by the congregation.

The speaker's zero position becomes the reference for all other movement and positions. In other words, the preacher's establishing posture and position on stage becomes the point of reference, the starting place, and the normative standard for all other postures and positions. All movement and gesture take place from and return to this zero. The speaker's zero is established in three areas:

1. Posture: the establishing stance of the speaker
2. Rhythm: the overall speed at which movements are begun, executed, and ended
3. Gesture: those willed movements of the hand, face, and body that communicate a thought to the observer

Every speaker has a common posture, rhythm, and gesture vocabulary that he regularly employs. The most common of these will establish the speaker's zero. Movement away from this zero can take a positive or negative value, for example:

1. The preacher who moves his hands constantly (let's call him John) establishes *movement* as the zero. When such a preacher stops moving the hands in order to make a point, the absence of movement creates what can be called *negative value movement*. The absence of movement for this speaker makes a strong statement.
2. The preacher who rarely moves her hands (let's call her Jane) establishes *non-movement* as the zero. When such a preacher gestures with the hands, her use of movement creates *positive value movement*, which also makes a strong statement. Every preacher establishes her own zero, and a corresponding movement rheostat. The diagram below demonstrates how this would look.

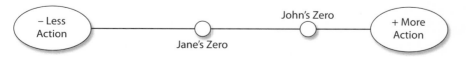

Here, we see that John is generally more active when he speaks than Jane. Though it means that John is generally more animated, it also means he has less positive potential for dynamic expression in comparison with Jane's dynamic potential. And more movement does not necessarily mean better communication; sometimes less is better. Generally, it is better for the zero to be more centered—like Jane's. John's one advantage is that when he chooses to be completely still, that stillness will be very strong, stronger than Jane's.

In preaching, communication works best when movement and gesture are wisely chosen. An unskilled or undisciplined speaker will create a haphazard effect. The movements and gestures made during a sermon should be full of meaning and purpose, directly related to the sermon itself, not to the comfort of the speaker.[8] A speaker who gestures excessively can be like a person who speaks too much—in the overabundance of words the meaning can be lost.

Body Symbolism

> Human consciousness makes human gestural activity a design and not a simple instinctual response to external or internal stimuli. There is style or strategy in the rhythm of human body movement. This measured motion is intimately connected with speech (verbal gesture).[9]

In every culture of the world, the parts of the body have symbolic and communicative meaning. Sometimes cultures understand these meanings differently. For example, giving a gift with the left hand in North America is fine, but in the Philippines, it is considered vulgar. In many cultures a bodily gesture means the same thing, such as waving the hand in greeting, lifting the hands in surrender, bowing the head in rejection or lifting it in pride, and kneeling in humility, or standing at "ready." The natural function of a particular part of the body suggests what it will generally symbolize. The following is a list of bodily parts and their common figurative meanings.

8. Comfort gestures include scratching the head or body, rocking back and forth, pacing, playing with objects such as pens, rings, and clothing. Displacement gestures are also common in novice speakers. A displacement gesture is one made when the speaker gets lost, confused, or distracted: the gestures that might be made include comfort gestures and other gestures such as the shuffling of the sermon notes.

9. E. Elochukwu Uzukwu, *Worship as Body Language: Introduction to Christian Worship: An African Orientation* (Collegeville, MN: Liturgical Press, 1997), 3.

The Head

> When Jesus had received the wine, he said, "It is finished." Then he bowed his head and gave up his spirit. (John 19:30)

Because of the function of the brain, the head is generally understood as a gestural signifier for life, leadership, intelligence, and intellectual direction. But the position of the head can also signify the use of the senses. For example, if one cocks the head to avail the ear, the head signifies hearing. If the eyes are turned toward an object, the head signifies seeing. The head can also project toward that which it observes, hears, smells, and tastes. Or it can pull away, indicating being repulsed or involved in contemplation. Sometimes the head can indicate more than one thing at a time, as when it tilts to the side when contemplating or observing with more than one sense. For the public speaker, the head should be held neutrally, straight ahead, or with a slight lift directed toward the middle of the audience. For example, with an audience in a balcony, the head should be held in a position to be seen by both those in the orchestra's front row and those in the balcony's top row. Once an initial head position is chosen, it is established as the zero. Then, all expressions and movements begin from and return to that zero.

The Face

> The whole spectrum of human moods is reflected in the face and its expressions.[10]

The face is the most communicative part of the body, and also the first to lie. The speaker's facial expression should start in an emotional zero with only a touch of expression relative to the topic to be discussed. The facial expression should welcome the audience into the conversation. Expressions should start first and foremost in the eyes, and then naturally radiate to the rest of the face. Once the speaking begins, expressions flow as needed and should be perceived as natural, using theatrical expressions only when they are known to be an "act," or an obvious representation of characters or their emotions. For example, when a speaker is dramatically recounting a biblical story, the face might take on the facial expressions of the characters or portray their emotional state. Character expressions or "masks" are fine when well acted

---

10. Silvia Schroer, Thomas Staubli, and Linda M. Maloney, *Body Symbolism in the Bible* (Collegeville, MN: Liturgical Press, 2001), 85.

or intentionally emphasized for effect: the audience enjoys the "act" if it is known to be intentional. Overuse of facial expressions will cause the audience to become calloused to one's more meaningful and subtle expressions. They may also be suspicious of contrived expressions. The worst thing a speaker can do with the face is to overexaggerate his or her own expressions—this is called mugging. Such an act will be perceived as insincere and destroy the credibility of the preacher.

The Neck

> The neck could be stiff, powerful, and iron-like, but it could also be put in a noose.[11]

The neck carries the weight of the head and emphasizes any head position. The neck can communicate pride, self-confidence, and stubbornness when stiffened; but when exposed, it is associated with vulnerability. The importance of the neck is seen when people do not support the head correctly, projecting it forward like a goon, or slumping like a floppy bore.

For the public speaker's zero, the neck should hold the head straight and not thrust the head forward or backward.

The Chest

> But the tax collector, standing far off, would not even look up to heaven, but was beating his breast and saying, "God, be merciful to me, a sinner!" (Luke 18:13)

The chest represents the visual breath—life. And because of the Western symbolism of the heart, it also represents love and emotions. When an emotion is extroverted, the chest fills and projects forward or is lifted upward. When the emotion is introverted, the chest is drawn inward or downward. On a man, the chest has been a traditional symbol of strength, and for a woman, motherhood. The chest is touched to identify "self." For the public speaker's zero, the chest should be well supported by the waist and neither overfilled nor collapsed. This will give the speaker the ability to communicate with the chest when needed.

11. Ibid.

The Waist

> Righteousness shall be the belt around his waist, and faithfulness the belt around his loins. (Isa. 11:5)

The waist is the center of the body, the symbolic seat of the soul, appetites, and desires. It is from the waist that the deeper breath (soul) is expressed. For many movement artists, it is the place where movement starts and balance is found. Gestures that involve the waist are those that include breath and communicate general health: a sharp intake of the breath (such as seen in shock) usually starts in the waist; hunger and pain are symbolized by touching the stomach with the hand. For the public speaker's zero, the stomach should be held in—with the effect of "pulling up" or supporting the chest.

The Pelvis

> So Hanun seized David's servants, shaved them, cut off their garments in the middle at their hips, and sent them away; and they departed. When David was told about the men, he sent messengers to them, for they felt greatly humiliated. (1 Chron. 19:4–5)

The pelvis is the foundation on which the upper body sits. It is also a symbol for gender and humanity; in medieval art, the devil could not have a human bottom and sported a tail instead. The gestures that involve the pelvis are those that are vulgar and sensual, and that express engagement/disengagement. The pelvis also indicates intent to move: the direction the pelvis faces usually indicates the direction the person wishes to take. If the pelvis is turned away from a person or object it can communicate removal, distancing, or being "closed" to others. If the pelvis is facing toward another person or object it can communicate one of the following: engagement, confrontation, "openness," and possibly sensuality. If the pelvis is thrust forward, it could communicate aggression, sensuality, or strong posturing (as seen in the Spanish matador). For the public speaker's zero, the pelvis should be facing the public, not turned away—which could indicate a removal or disengagement. The hips are considered part of the pelvis, but have less to do with overt sensuality (unless swayed in walking). When the hands rest on the hips it can communicate a resigned rest or—when the hands are fisted—firm resolve.

The Arms

The arms facilitate the movement of the hands and exaggerate the hands' communication. By themselves, the arms represent the ability to work and achieve tasks. As a consequence of their natural symbolism toward work, the relaxing of the arms communicates rest from work, inability to work, or disengagement from work. The arms uplifted are known nearly universally as a sign of surrender—for they can achieve little while upheld. Extending the arms outward communicates giving or engaging. Drawing the arms inward communicates receiving or withdrawing. Arms that are dropped to the side, loosely swinging, appear listless and devoid of power and strength. For the speaker's zero, the arms should be controlled or purposely placed—usually to the sides or resting on the podium/pulpit.

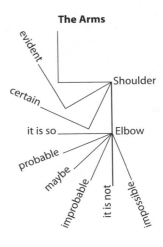

The Arms

The Hands

> The souls of the righteous are in God's hand: in whose hand are both we and our words. (St. Augustine on Psalm 119)

The hands are the second most communicative part of the body. Many times they are also the least controlled—to the hazard of the speaker. The hands communicate concepts of power, means, direction, detail of thought or concept, manipulation, ability, and control. The open palm generally signifies concepts of something being *released-toward-another* or being *open-to-receive-from-another*. The closed fist usually signifies the concept of retaining or gathering force. The positions of the fingers themselves usually relate to advanced character identification, identification of labor, and the giving of detail.

There are two considerations for the appearance of any hand gesture: *hand position* and *hand design*. A *hand position* is the isolated shape taken on by the hand itself. A *hand design* includes the hand position and adds the shape of the arms and rhythms used to execute a gesture. The same hand position can be used in many hand designs, which communicate completely different thoughts. For example, a flat hand position (called *palette hand*) can be used in many designs: the arms lifted up to the sides of the body with the palms

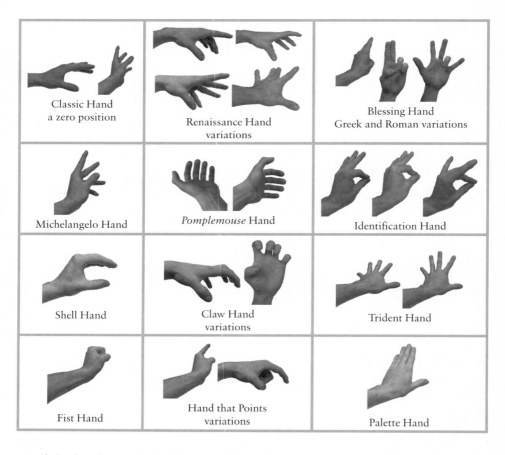

Classic Hand a zero position	Renaissance Hand variations	Blessing Hand Greek and Roman variations
Michelangelo Hand	*Pomplemouse* Hand	Identification Hand
Shell Hand	Claw Hand variations	Trident Hand
Fist Hand	Hand that Points variations	Palette Hand

of the hands remaining horizontal communicates "What?" The arms lifted diagonally forward with the palms on the diagonal facing the people is an "invitation," while the arms thrust violently forward with palms toward the public communicates "Stop!" Hand gestures have three common elements: *hand position, hand/body design,* and *rhythm.*

Master mime Marcel Marceau states that there are more than ninety-nine positions of the hands; most speakers use fewer than half a dozen. The use of the hands in speaking has been analyzed and discussed throughout the ages, yet remains a common problem for the speaker. The greatest question seems to be how to use the hands so it appears natural rather than contrived. The answer is to become acquainted with the possibilities and practice until the positions become second nature. The speaker's best zero hand position is naturally relaxed to the sides or placed on the podium. Above are illustrations of some of the most-used hand positions.

The Legs

A lie has no legs, and cannot stand; but it has wings, and can fly far and wide. (Bishop Warburton)

The legs are primarily used to communicate concepts of direction, transportation, possession, and dominion. The thigh is associated with strength and might. The inner thigh is considered intimate and even sensual. The slapping of the upper leg or knee can communicate laughter or self-mockery. When the legs are bent (*en plie*), they communicate the idea of being stable or grounded or even "under the ground"; e.g., demons are many times played with bent legs and are imagined as being from "under ground." When the legs are straight (*en tondue*) and feet are flat on the floor, they communicate being "on the ground"; e.g., human beings (straight legged) are earthbound, thus the legs are played straight. When the legs are placed together and lifted above up onto the toes—being *en eleve*—they communicate the concept of being "in the air"; e.g., angels are many times played *en eleve* (on their toes) because they are imagined above the ground, or in the air. Much of the symbolism of the legs is associated also with the feet, which are discussed next. The speaker's zero has straight legs, standing with flat feet slightly apart and the body's weight evenly balanced between them.

The Feet

The foot, much like the hand, had a symbolic power of its own in Israel: it was associated with subjugation, domination, and the seizure of others' property. To "tread someone or something under the foot" was regarded even then as an act of the greatest humiliation.[12]

The feet are the foundation of the body and communicate the domain of a person. The feet have long been a symbol of ownership and possession, for only one person can stand in the occupied space. When the feet are placed together they occupy a smaller space and are considered nonassertive, in contrast to feet that are apart and communicate a dominant and assertive stance. The speaker's zero has already been mentioned under the heading of the legs. The speaker should not shift weight from foot to foot, which appears as nervousness; instead, he or she should balance the weight between both feet, or intentionally use *les equilibre* as later described.

12. Schroer, Staubli, and Maloney, *Body Symbolism in the Bible*, 85.

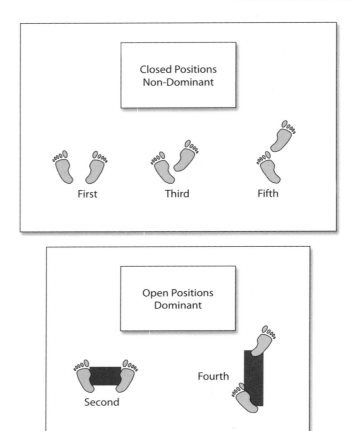

The Back

> Then there gathered unto him all the men of war, whom Demetrius had put away, and
> they fought against Demetrius, who turned his back and fled. (1 Macc. 11:55)

The back communicates vulnerability, rejection, refusal, and burden when turned away, or conversely, resolve, strength, and decisiveness when straightened. Rarely does a speaker turn his back toward the audience; however, there are times when it is effective. Turning the back gives the audience time to think and measure the speaker's response to a presented idea, and to process their thoughts. For example, if a speaker states something that will be considered a harsh fact and then turns her back to the audience—it is as if she has left them with the fact and is vulnerable to their responses. If after she turns her back, she walks away and looks over her shoulder, it is as if to say "are you following me, do you get what I have said?" Or if she suddenly turns to face the audience, it is as if to catch them unaware and to confront them with what has been said. Or if she slowly turns, it is as if she is about to unfold the harsh truth and reveal its profound depths. The back is also shown to the audience when the grief is too hard to face and the tears are hidden, or conversely, when one is trying to hide an emotion such as laughter (revealing it in the movement of the back, rather than the facial expression). For the speaker's zero, the back should be held upright, and the speaker should rarely turn his or her back to the audience.

The Shoulders

> They tie up heavy burdens, hard to bear, and lay them on the shoulders of others; but they themselves are unwilling to lift a finger to move them. (Matt. 23:4)

The shoulders are the symbol for the bearing of burdens and stress. Speakers, actors, and movement artists alike can lift the shoulders to indicate stress and tension. Otherwise they should be relaxed in a normal posture. The preacher should start with a zero position that has the shoulders pulled back and down in a relaxed position. Shoulders are lifted to show the unknown burden of a question, such as a statement of "I don't know." The hands are brought to the shoulders to show the burden born by the person. The hands brush off the shoulders to free themselves of the burden or its residue. A speaker can massage his or her own shoulder to show tension and its need for release or the need of relaxation from wearisome work.

Equilibrium, Time, and Space

In mime we have a position called *les equilibre*, also referred to as the *statiques*, or "balances." With the body straight, you can balance over the ankles to allow the body to move forward, backward, and sideways. Each of these positions communicates a different concept to the observer. Forward balances give an impression of aggression and engagement. Backward balances give an impression of being withdrawn, disengaged, or relaxed. Side balances give an impression of reflection or disorientation. Concepts of time are also signaled by the *equilibres*. Timelines are a common way time has been imaged; in body positioning, references to time are created by leaning. A backward balance, or reference behind the person, is seen as a reference to the past. A center balance is seen as a reference to the present. And a forward balance is seen as a reference toward the future. Hand gestures augment and identify detail on how far back, how emphatically present, and how far forward in time the concept is found. For the speaker's zero, the equilibrium should be balanced only slightly forward. The following diagram is from a bird's-eye view, and it illustrates the basic communication of *les equilibre* and the significance of space as it relates to timelines and thought.

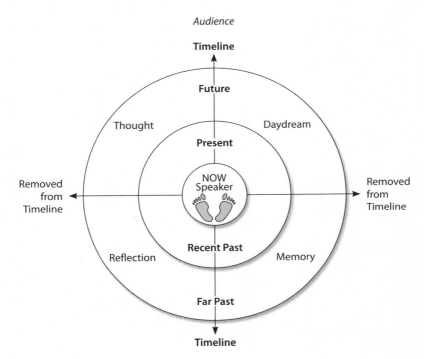

Conclusions on Body Symbolism

Gestures and body positioning are elements of a complex vocabulary of physical speech. Their use is not widely understood by speakers. But observers are typically aware of their meanings when they are effectively used. There is not space here to examine all the possible gestures and various meanings found in the body. The intent has been simply to identify the major concepts associated with basic body movements and relate them to the work of the preacher. Now we turn to the use of rhythm and the speaker's use of symbolic space.

Rhythm: Emotion, Thought, and Reaction

We naturally associate emotions and thoughts with rhythm. Is surprise fast or slow? Fast. Is daydreaming fast or slow? Slow. Is indecision fast or slow?

Both fast and slow. Likewise we associate *thought* and *reaction* with degrees of rhythm. Reflection is identified with slower rhythms while reaction is identified with faster rhythms. In everyday life, people's movements demonstrate small degrees of variation between fast and slow—showing great contrasts only in extreme situations or sports. In physical theater, the degree that rhythms vary is exaggerated in order to create greater contrast—contrast helps the audience read rhythm differentiations. Without clear contrasts in rhythm, the physical movement becomes mundane and humdrum.

There are two basic rhythms that work in combination with, or without, muscular resistance:

1. Fast: communicates the *reactionary*
   a. with muscular resistance: forceful, violent, ecstatic, emotional
   b. without muscular resistance: carefree, release, childlike play
2. Slow: communicates the *thoughtful*
   a. with muscular resistance: contained, controlled, mounting or suppressed emotion; heavy, physical effort
   b. without muscular resistance: graceful, calm, relaxed, light, floating, dreamy

Every person has a "rhythm" at which he or she moves through life. We naturally recognize this in others, identifying some people as "nervous," others as "calm." We associate characters with rhythms: we would expect the Pied Piper to play fast and "bright" rhythms and would describe him as "light on his feet"; we would describe a thieving sneak to have sharp and fast movements; we would expect Shakespeare's Juliet to have smooth and graceful rhythms full of breath and life.

Such assessments are based on a person's overall rhythm pattern, the rhythm zero. Like movement, each speaker will have a tendency toward rhythm patterns and signatures. Speakers often find it difficult to control and understand their own rhythms; many find it hard to perceive and self-evaluate their rhythm patterns. By comparison, gestures are easier to analyze. Gestures can be seen by the one creating them, whereas one's own speed is hard to measure. To overcome this difficulty, the speaker should view himself or herself on video. This provides the needed distance of being "outside of oneself" and enables one to analyze the viewed rhythm. A person's natural rhythms are not necessarily the right ones for public speaking. Most of the time a speaker should start with a "calm" rhythm and build from that zero. There are many exceptions, however. For example, a person may "burst onto stage" for action themes such as resurrection and healing. Contrarily, a person might proceed slowly to the podium before delivering a lament.

Each movement a speaker makes has a rhythm, but that rhythm must come to an end, must have a *movement punctuation*. Movement punctuation helps the observer take time to think, while stressing the point made by the presenter. Here are a few *basic movement punctuations* and a few applications:

1. The *stop*: a full and smooth arresting of movement. The rhythm ends and the body stops moving. A stop shows the end of a finite thought and makes a statement.
    a. The *perfect stop*: the whole body ceases to move. This effect is statuary and is a good technique for creating complete calm.
2. The *non-stop*: the movement slows down to the point that the audience does not perceive an end. A non-stop is used to show infinite ideas such as "glory" or "beauty."
3. The *toc*: a *toc* is a sharp, quick movement, a single jerk or spasm of muscle. It shows a definite and emphatic stop. If a *stop* says "no," a *toc* says "NO!"
    a. The *toc motor*: a jerk or muscular impulse that begins a movement, most common when we lift a leg or "push off" from leaning on something. It is a strong way of starting a movement off with force or emphasis, a "GO!"
    b. The *toc finale*: a jerk or muscular spasm that ends a movement, most common when making contact with a solid object. The *toc finale* is a definite and emphatic way of ending a movement. It is like shouting "THE END."
4. The *breath* could be called a *non-stop motor*. The breath gently starts the movement. This is effective for more lyric and reflective starts. It is considered a "deeper" and more thoughtful start than *toc motor*—the *toc motor* appears more external. The breath would be used to show that you are relaxed, welcomed home, filled with life, etc.

There are some advanced rhythms that the speaker uses, such as *crystallize*, where the "idea" solidifies or the "lightbulb turns on." To *crystallize*, start relaxed and then tighten all the muscles in the process of executing the full movement, ending with a taut frozen position (*crystallized*). The *tremble* is an advanced rhythm used to show extreme emotion, such as when Jairus is told by the messenger that his daughter has died: he falls to his knees "trembling." To tremble, use extreme and tight muscle contractions accompanied by jagged breathing (if not speaking).

Coloration is another useful rhythm technique. The simplest way of thinking of *coloration* is "big, bigger, biggest." Coloration is needed when the presenter is repeating the same idea over and over again. When the audience sees or hears what they have seen or heard before, the result can be that they lose interest—"been there, done that." To stop this loss of interest or engagement, we *colorate* one aspect of the idea while keeping the integrity of the concept. Examples of *coloration* and *decoloration* (the reverse process):

1. A single voice sings, then a duet, then the choir: coloration.
2. The longest text is read; a medium text is read; a short text is read: decoloration.
3. I read a phrase standing still; I read a phrase with arm/hand gestures; I read a phrase and move from the podium to center stage; I read a phrase and walk into the congregation; I return to the podium (back to audience), slowly turn and read the next phrase standing still. This is an example of coloration with a quick decoloration—sometimes less is more, and the best climax.

Rhythms that are new to your body are difficult to learn, but very possible. Use a video to help see what your rhythms look like. Observe the rhythms of people around you and note how the rhythms people use reveal emotions, thoughts, reactions, and age.

The Creation of Symbolic Space

Like the mime, the preacher enters onto the platform with only the body to perform the text. The stage is empty—with the exception of the sacerdotal furnishings. As the preacher reads or speaks, the platform and congregation are filled with ideas, concepts, and imagined persons and places. As the congregation listens, they begin to create *significant space*, even *symbolic space*. *Significant space* is created by assigning a *place* by the gesture of the hand or focus of the eyes. For example, if the speaker gestures that Jesus is on the right and Satan on the left, later in the sermon, when the speaker gestures to the right, that space will be identified as Jesus's or "the good side," while the left will be identified as Satan's or the "bad side." When purposefully used, this strengthens emotional and conceptual values in the mind of the observant listener.

To conclude this chapter and demonstrate its techniques, we will take a look at a physical interpretation of Matthew 25:31–46. There are four characters, which are all played by the speaker; each character has a specific "space" on the platform.

Characters	Physical Appearance/Statue (Zero)	Space
Jesus	Body's zero: stands upright, "pulled up"	Podium/Center Stage
	Hands' zero: classic, renaissance; Will use: blessing, fist, demi-fist (claw), Michelangelo, hand that points	
	Rhythm zero: controlled, calm, but ready to respond	
	Punctuation zero: breath	
	Feet's zero: 1st or 3rd	
Narrator	The speaker's zeros and gesture set	Podium, but also roams
Sheep	Body's zero: more natural or slightly weighted in shoulder as if burdened	Stage Right of podium
	Hands' zero: shell or classic	
	Rhythm zero: more intermediate and natural	
	Punctuation zero: the stop	
	Feet's zero: 1st and 2nd	
Goat	Body's zero: curved or overly upright (pious)	Stage Left of podium
	Hands' zero: identification or prayer	
	Rhythm zero: fast, *tocs,* sharp mechanical movements	
	Feet's zero: 5th or 4th	

Other Identified Characters and Spaces

- Audience/congregation represents the gathered peoples who are separated
- Choir or other ministers on stage represent the hosts of heaven
- Center of platform represents the "seat of judgment"
- Down Stage Right represents the Sheep and the Good (heaven-bound)
- Down Stage Left represents the Goats and the Bad (hell-bound)

Matthew 25 Text	Actions (Rubrics)
[31]"When the Son of Man comes in his glory,	Start by looking at the text; as it is read, look straight up toward heaven.

Matthew 25 Text	Actions (Rubrics)
and all the angels with him,	Still looking up, look to the left and right.
then he will sit on the throne of his glory.	Place hands on the top sides of the podium.
³²All the nations will be gathered before him,	Look at the congregation.
and he will separate people one from another as a shepherd separates the sheep from the goats, ³³and he will put the sheep at his right hand and the goats at the left.	Bring the hands into a prayer position (palms together), then extend the arms forward, turning over the palms so that they are away from each other, facing outward, and separate the right and then the left to the diagonal sides. (Bird's-eye view)
³⁴Then the king will say to those at his right hand, 'Come, you that are blessed by my Father,	Bring the right hand forward into "Blessing Hand," and turn the head toward the right followed by the hand.
inherit the kingdom prepared for you from the foundation of the world;	Lift left hand in "Classical Hand" onto the forward diagonal. Roll right hand over toward the right.
³⁵for I was hungry and you gave me food,	Left palette hand touches stomach.
I was thirsty and you gave me something to drink,	The middle finger of the left hand touches the mouth (Classical Hand).
I was a stranger and you welcomed me,	With both hands on chest and head down, open arms to sides and look to the right where the "Sheep" are imagined.
³⁶I was naked and you gave me clothing,	With both hands, touch shoulders and thighs.
I was sick and you took care of me, I was in prison and you visited me.'	Touch the forehead with the right hand as if taking your temperature, then caress the right side of your face.
³⁷Then the righteous will answer him,	Look toward the audience, as you step sideways two feet, arch the arm to the right side. 
'Lord,	Both hands in Classical Hand stretch toward the "narrator's spot" (the podium), as the body turns to the left (toward the podium) and head looks up above the podium.

Matthew 25 Text	Actions (Rubrics)
when was it that we saw you	With hands open to the low diagonal, lift into the high diagonal.
hungry and gave you food,	Touch the stomach with the palm of the hand, close into a fist and open the hand as you extend it toward the "Jesus spot" (the podium).
or thirsty and gave you something to drink?	Touch the lips with the middle finger, and as the hand moves from the lips, form the hand in a C as if holding a cup and extend the hand toward the Jesus spot.
[38]And when was it that we saw you a stranger and welcomed you,	Move the hand horizontally with a sweeping gesture toward the audience from left to right. Indicate one place in the audience stage right, and then indicate a place to your right side as if giving an invitation. Finally, look back at the Jesus spot in puzzlement.
or naked and gave you clothing?	Cross over the arms with one hand on a shoulder and the other on your waist. Close hands in a fist, then extend arms in front of you as if holding clothes, first extending toward the audience then toward the Jesus spot.
[39]And when was it that we saw you sick or in prison and visited you?'	Place the right palm on the top of the head and the left palm on the abdomen. Take two heavy steps toward the audience. And as you step forward, straighten up, extending the arms in welcome toward the audience, and then turn back to face the Jesus spot.
[40]And the king will answer them,	With the back to the audience, step back in to the podium (back still toward audience) and turn the head over the left shoulder, looking to the left with the body turning to follow the head position (the whole body is now facing stage right).
'Truly I tell you, just as you did it to one of the least of these who are members of my family, you did it to me.'	Smile and gesture toward the right to the "Sheep spot" and then continue to sweep the audience with a horizontal gesture from right to left. Then touch your own chest. Keep the body facing toward the right (toward the Sheep).
[41]Then he will say to those at his left hand,	Change the expression of the face from smile, to sorrow, to deep sorrow as you turn the head (but not the body) to look over your left shoulder toward stage left—the "Goat spot."
'You that are accursed, depart from me	Put the head down as you sharply point with your left hand toward stage left (with a fast rhythm ending in a *toc finale*).
into the eternal fire prepared for	Lift your left hand and shake it as if to mimic a flame,

Matthew 25 Text	Actions (Rubrics)
the devil and his angels;	then draw the hand downward into a fist. 
[42]for I was hungry and you gave me no food,	Turn and face stage left, the Goat spot. Touch the right palm to the stomach, turn over hand and push away from body, palm toward Goat spot.
I was thirsty and you gave me nothing to drink,	Touch the left middle finger (in classical hand) to lip and then turn the hand over so palm faces away from body and push hand toward the Goat spot.
[43]I was a stranger and you did not welcome me, naked and you did not give me clothing,	Step toward the Goat spot and open the hands (palms up) to the sides of the body (the whole body is facing stage left and the Goat spot). Lift hands horizontal toward the Goat spot and push away as you step back toward the podium as if rejected. Cross the body with the hands: right hand on shoulder, left on waist.
sick and in prison and you did not visit me.'	Place the hands on the sides of the podium and lean in as if resting your weight on the podium: head hangs down while shaking "no."
[44]Then they also will answer,	Straighten completely and walk over to the Goat spot, stage left. Sweep the left arm vertically up then down toward the Goat spot as you step into it. Change body position to the Goat's zero (either hunched or arrogantly "pulled up" in a pious position).
'Lord,	The "Goats," with a puzzled expression and a bit frightened, look up to the Jesus spot. Alternate between wringing hands and a prayer position.
when was it that we saw you hungry or thirsty or a stranger or naked or sick or in prison,	Open the hands from the prayer position about a foot and bend "open" at the wrist (palms will be tilted upward). Cock the head to the side. With the arms well away from the body, have the fingers touch the stomach, then lips, then shoulder/waist, then cover the mouth and open the eyes wide on "prison."
and did not take care of you?'	Continue to look "wide-eyed and innocent" at the Jesus spot as you turn your body away (turning left toward stage left). You will end up looking over your right shoulder at the Jesus spot. As you turn, open your hands to the sides with the palms horizontal and lift the shoulders up: this will give the impression of an exaggerated question with hypocrisy.
[45]Then he will answer them,	Completely straighten up and walk back to the podium, looking at the audience as you walk. Then morph into the Jesus character.

Matthew 25 Text	Actions (Rubrics)
'Truly I tell you,	Turn and face the Goat spot. Reach out sideways with the hands in what will look like a half-formed crucifix position, and walk toward the Goat spot.
just as you did not do it to one of the least of these,	With your right hand and a horizontal sweep, gesture toward the audience (palm up) from left to right.
you did not do it to me.'	Now turn toward the audience and walk downstage or onto the front floor.
[46]And these will go away into eternal punishment,	Gesture back to the Goat spot while facing forward, draw the left hand from the high diagonal down to the low diagonal and shake the hand briefly as if on fire (as before). A sad expression is on the face.
but the righteous into eternal life."	Turn and gesture back to the Sheep spot with the right hand on the low diagonal, palm down, turn and face the audience and lift, keeping the low diagonal of the hand (palm down), turn the palm over to face upward when it is positioned toward the audience and lift it "heavenward" as if lifting the audience to heaven. Smile.

The story of the Sheep and the Goats provides a clear example of how a text can be presented using the skills of the actor and mime. I would also argue for the preacher to use gesture in sermons, gesturing to stress a point or word, identifying a significant idea in space (assigning it a "spot"), and using the rhythms of the body in accompaniment with the rhythms of speech. Indeed, volumes have been written on the speaker's gestures, and this chapter only introduces ideas for consideration and practice.

In summary, the body is a communicative tool for preaching. Wherever an audience is present, the speaker must be as aware of what the body communicates as what his or her words communicate. Many preachers have trained their voices in preparation for preaching and learned to choose their words skillfully yet fail to realize that their bodies often belie what they verbalize. Every performer of the Word must realize that turning "ink into blood" involves the body in movement.

8

Finding Voice in the Theological School

RICHARD F. WARD

It is not "good" voices or "bad" voices that I am listening for, but voices that come from somewhere near the heart and that do not seem afraid to be heard.

Barbara Brown Taylor, *Birthing the Sermon*

The introductory class in preaching has assembled. It is a small class by design to allow plenty of time for practice, interaction, lecture, and discussion of the art of preaching. This is the first time the class has met, and the professor's opening question now hangs in the air: "What is the primary goal you have for your study of preaching during this term?" One student, a woman in her late forties, breaks the ice and answers: "I want to find my own voice." Other heads nod around the circle.

What is this student asking for? To "find" something implies that it has been "lost." She assumes that some "original" voice has been "lost" in the course of her development as an adult, and now she needs to retrieve it in order to fulfill the expectations of her professional role. Her search has some urgency. She and the congregations she will serve have expectations for vocal performance that are shaped by the values and aesthetics of an increasingly complex communications culture. "Ordinary" voices do not seem "good enough" for the demands of the marketplace. Digital technologies transmit voices that are crisp and clear of distortion. Celebrity speakers and broadcasters dominate the airwaves, setting standards (for good or ill) for speaking in public. The energized barrage of digitalized voices making sales pitch after pitch leaves listeners skeptical of truth claims and hungry for authenticity. They long for voices that belong to people with whom they can be in a trusting relationship. Listeners want the energy, clarity, and variation their technology gives them but they also want *embodied* voices to address them in an atmosphere of confidence and trust. Our student wonders: Can I *be myself* as a preacher and proclaimer of the Word? What definitive *sounds* will come from my heart and will that are congruent with the performance of my role?

Where shall our student look for this "voice" she feels she has lost? And where will those of us who teach her look for viable patterns of instruction? Will we look into manuals full of drills and exercises for voice improvement? Perhaps, but it is clear from her tone and attitude that she is asking for a good deal more than "I want to learn some techniques for speaking properly." She is expressing a desire for what classical rhetoric remembers as *pronuntiatio*, the art of bringing a speaker's thought to expression through voice and gesture.

In giving instructions to our students about bringing their thoughts to expression in the preaching classroom, we have relied too heavily on the metaphor of voice as instrument without ongoing theological reflection on the task of teaching about the use of voice. As a consequence, the training of the voice for preaching remains marginalized in the curriculum of the theological school. The gospel we are committed to and proclaim calls for a particular kind of expression. Among the concrete particularities of that expression is the sound of someone speaking to the assembly, a modulation of thought through volume, pitch, rhythm, and cadence. Preaching is gesticulation in God's direction, an enactment that involves the totality of thought, body, and imagination.

Talking to students about finding their voices means drawing on a rich interplay of metaphors and associations. The metaphor of voice as instrument has expanded into a cluster of associations. "Voice" has become emblematic of an embodied Self and synonymous with identity, authenticity, and presence. Stephen H. Webb puts it this way: "The voice can be said to embody the body, because all parts of the person, from feelings to thoughts and impulses, are expressed through the voice."[1]

New associations about "voice" help to dispel confusion about the theological underpinnings of our practice, a confusion that often led homiletics

1. Stephen H. Webb, *The Divine Voice: Christian Proclamation and the Theology of Sound* (Grand Rapids: Brazos, 2004), 58. Webb is here describing the work of Kristen Linklater, *Freeing the Natural Voice* (New York: Drama Publishers, 1976).

and speech into turf battles and power plays over whose prerogative it was to do vocal instruction. For many charged with the responsibility, vocal education and training were onerous and tedious. Sometimes they were understood as remedial education. The tedious nature of instruction was a consequence of borrowing vocal techniques and pedagogies from the disciplines of theater and performance studies without considering the theological implications for doing so. Theology had displaced rhetoric as the queen of subjects long ago in the theological school; it was associated with the *content* of what was said, not *how* it was said.

The bifurcation of theology from agency still haunts the hallways of the theological school, but it will not do in addressing the needs of the students in our classes. This woman like so many others who travel through our classrooms is expressing a desire not only to speak *well*, that is with adequate volume, pitch, and articulation, but also to speak *faithfully*, that is, she wants to speak in ways that are faithful to her interpretation of the gospel and authentic to her own personality and experience. She wishes to prepare herself *in the totality of her self* for the theological task of embodying and enacting a transforming Word and presence in the congregations she will serve.

Where will her search for authentic voice and presence take her? And where does that search take us, if we are charged with giving her guidance and instruction? *Consideration of voice pushes us to make an expedition into the theological undercroft of the homiletical household.* Our methods of teaching homiletics as well as our rhetorical and performance practices have theological consequences. It is best that we have a grasp of what those theological assumptions are. *We need to impress on our students that questions about "voice" are theological ones, not only for them but also for those of us who teach them.* When we explore questions of *how* we speak sermons and texts, we are on the threshold of some larger ones: Why do we speak? Why are *we* the ones who are speaking? What shall we say? And under what circumstances will we be speaking?

In this chapter I mean to go on that expedition through the undercroft to look for fresh ways of shoring up the theologies of communication that nourish our work with "voice." What I will not do is try to duplicate Jana Childers's excellent suggestions for how vocal training can become part of classroom instruction in the preaching arts.[2] Nor will I review or recast Mary Lin Hudson and Mary Donovan Turner's seminal work in *Saved from Silence*.[3] I will

2. Jana Childers, *Performing the Word: Preaching as Theatre* (Nashville: Abingdon, 1998).
3. Mary Lin Hudson and Mary Donovan Turner, *Saved from Silence* (St. Louis: Chalice, 1999).

only point and make reference to Stephen H. Webb's and Charles L. Bartow's expansive practical theologies, which take up the question of voice.[4] Rather I plan to situate my chapter in the interstices between these fine works. The light I will carry with me into the undercroft will be small but focused. I plan to aim its beam on three images that I have found instructive for us and for our students who are looking to "find their voices" for preaching.

The first image is from our recent past. The year is 1992 and the place is Princeton Theological Seminary. Charles L. Bartow has been named to the first Carl and Helen Egner Professorship at Princeton. He is giving his inaugural lecture and is tracing the history of speech instruction at Princeton. Above the discipline, he says, were a variety of banners as it marched through the seminary in the last century: elocution, expression, oral interpretation, or simply speech communication. These banners identified their practitioners who crafted pedagogies that responded to the challenges posed by the theological and communication environments surrounding the proclamation of the Word.

Bartow's look back into the rich history of speech instruction at Princeton is instructive to all of us who aim to help students find their voices for preaching. Evoking the legacies of James Rush, Leland Powers, W. J. Beeners, and now Charles Bartow helps to break open the easy assumption that teaching voice to theological students is marginal to theological education. It is a continuation of a rhetorical and performance tradition that feeds the art and practice of preaching, but also a tradition that is too often neglected or forgotten. What Bartow shows us is how these figures in the history of instruction were operating out of a set of religious assumptions about the human predicament.

A common theme punctuates these varied traditions of instruction and reflection: that proclamation and service of the Word as embodied in the created order and expressed in communities of faith is in response to the divine initiative of God's unmerited grace. "Responsiveness" is a key term in the oral arts. Ears are tuned for the promptings of God's Spirit in texts, traditions, culture. Bodies are trained to become so alert to the affective stirrings of human expression in order to give form to thought and desire through gesture and movement. A voice is a sounding of the individual and collective soul when it awakens to divine presence. In the pedagogies that flow from these precepts, one thing seems clear: speaking the Word is an effort of collaboration between human and divine. Toward that effort, God risks disclosure by letting go of the privileges of Otherness. Human beings let go of sin, that is, whatever it is

---

4. Webb, *Divine Voice*; and Charles L. Bartow, *God's Human Speech: A Practical Theology of Proclamation* (Grand Rapids: Eerdmans, 1997).

that prevents us from witnessing and giving expression to God's disclosure. Faithfulness on God's part and on ours depends on our degree of availability to the covenantal bond we share with God.

Introducing those men and women who represent the tradition of speech instruction in the theological school can become a prompt for discussing latent theological assumptions the students are making about their voices and bodies. We usually give scant attention in the preaching class to the history of preaching, much less to speech education. Consequently when a student asks whether we might help her find her "voice," we are at a loss for what to do. It is as if no one has ever thought about it before. Seeds for developing a profound practical theology of voice for preaching that meets current needs lie in part in the fertile ground of remembered practices and theories of performance studies. I can think of two ways I would draw on that history to address that student's concern with "voice."

I would first use the remembered assumptions of speech instruction to discuss goals and virtues for preaching; second, I would build on conventional practices to develop appropriate exercises for exploring what is "natural" about the voice. Suppose, for example, that I am developing the syllabus for the class I have imagined at the beginning of this chapter. I anticipate that in the first or second session of the class some values-laden terms are going to surface. Students will use words such as "authenticity," "accessibility," and "availability" to talk about the virtues they associate with good preaching. I will use the legacies of our forebears in speech instruction to show how the contemporary insistence on authenticity reflects earlier concerns with what is "natural" over against what is "affected." From that vantage point, we will look critically at the viability of some of the practices offered by the "expressionists"[5] to arrive at a way of speaking that is "natural" and therefore "authentic." We will see how those practices were designed to meet the needs of a culture that was shaped by the aesthetic sensibilities of a Eurocentric, print-based generation. To what degree do these practices help us develop speaking voices appropriate for a digitalized and pluralistic age, shaped by the aesthetic sensibilities of postmodernism?

One exercise I have used to develop the virtue of authenticity in speaking is called the "talking in church" exercise. In it I ask those students who are willing to participate in the exercise to draw a piece of paper out of an offering plate. The topic is in the form of a note passed in church from one person to

---

5. In Charles L. Bartow's "In Service to the Servants of the Word: Teaching Speech at Princeton Theological Seminary," *Princeton Seminary Bulletin* 13, no. 3 (November 1992), he provides a summary statement of what the school of expression assumed: "It [expressionism] assumes that nearly all people have voices and bodies capable of expressing fully whatever is on their minds," 279.

another. What they would read is something like this: "Tell me about the biggest mistake you ever made in your life" or "Who was your favorite uncle?"

The exercise has the effect of playfully catching students off guard. They do not have the time or inclination to step into a preacher role but are tricked into being themselves in front of others. Boundaries between private and public selves are transgressed, and the exercise very often releases both laughter and intimate disclosures. At some point early in the discussion, we point out to the students what came naturally to them as they brought thought to expression, particularly through vocal mannerisms. We are also able to identify patterns of vocal and physical behaviors that obstructed the performance of the thoughts and flow of images. We now have a context and point of reference for assessing the student's progress in the more complex tasks of public reading of Scripture and sermon performance as the class develops. This exercise reflects our indebtedness to the legacy of expressionism. It is a legacy that begs to be uncovered in our explorations of preaching and oral performance of literature.

The exercise also becomes the occasion for some theological reflection. What are the theological implications for privileging the concrete particularities of human experience as it relates to preaching? Is it possible that when we become audiences for another's bearing witness to their experience, we are doing so through the eyes of God? What about the struggle to be heard? Are we not participating in a divine struggle to be heard and understood through the language, symbol, and imagery of lived experience? Is the human voice an emblem of a divine spark within the human soul? How does that lived experience affirm or conflict with the values of God's gospel?

Stephen Webb presses another theological trajectory in considering an exercise such as this one. In assessing the work of Kristen Linklater, Webb maintains that the "human voice is never natural," that is, since (as Christianity teaches) it is never free from sin, no voice is untouched by human falsity and pretension.[6] Webb reminds us that the complex cultures of human communication and performance we are negotiating are indeed a web knit together by the grace of a righteous and merciful God. We will never find the perfect resonance of a perfected soul. What is natural about the human voice in the presence of God is the cry from the heart for mercy.

Charles Bartow asked near the end of his inaugural lecture, "Where do we go from here?" now that the discipline of oral interpretation "has gone the way of performance studies."[7] In the years since the publication of this

6. Webb, *Divine Voice*, 59.
7. Bartow, "In Service to the Servants of the Word," 284.

lecture, Bartow has helped to thoroughly ground performance studies not only in speech pedagogy, but also in Reformed theology.[8] Those of us who have been professionally mentored by Charles Bartow throughout his career have taken his question of direction to heart. Where *have* we gone from the point of that lecture? And where have we taken the discipline of performance studies in our work in the theological school?

Here I want to offer my second image for the chapter. This time it is a biblical one. I use this to demonstrate how a performance-centered view of biblical interpretation has informed not only my practice of oral interpretation of Scripture but also how that practice can be used for the vocal empowerment of our students.

Take a look at Mark's brief account of Jesus healing a man who is without hearing and has a speech impediment (7:31–37). It will show one way that biblical exegesis and vocal pedagogy can converge and suggest a method of instruction. First, take note of where Jesus is in the story. Not only did the Spirit drive him into the wilderness early in the Gospel (1:12) but now it is also driving him beyond his comfort zone in Galilee and into "Tyre and Sidon," the territory of the hated gentiles. Eventually this same Spirit will drive him to Jerusalem, where he will take up his cross.

At this point in the story Jesus is in the region of the Decapolis, the same area where he cleansed a man of a legion of demons (Mark 5:1–20). Misunderstanding Jesus's directive to "go and tell everyone what God had done for him," the man, rescued from madness, attributes the healing to Jesus (v. 20). In Mark's Gospel, Jesus controls the wind, the seas, and even the unclean spirits, but even he cannot control the message. Now Jesus confronts the reality that perceptions about who he is and what his ministry is about are out before him in some ways that are troubling to him. Apparently these misconceptions are mirrored in the Markan community, which is choosing to recall this story for interpretation. Jesus's task according to this Gospel is to look for every opportunity to clarify through his words and actions the radical claims his ministry will make on those who follow in his footsteps.

Jesus remains in unclean territory (one of Mark's symbols for that which is assumed to be outside the favor of God). He has just returned from an encounter with a gentile woman whose faith is so impressive and so persistent that not only is her daughter released from bondage to an "unclean spirit," but Jesus himself is also released from the restrictions he has placed on his ministry to confine it to his fellow Jews.

8. See especially Bartow's seminal book *God's Human Speech*.

In this account, Jesus confronts bondage of a different sort. A man is brought to him who is in bondage to silence. If I am a part of a theological culture that conceives of God primarily as sound and Word—as Mark's listeners certainly were—I would see this man's situation as dire indeed. Not only does he live in the midst of people with unclean lips (Isa. 6),[9] but in not being able to hear or speak, this man certainly appears to lie outside the reach of a vocal and highly expressive God. Jesus breaks the grip of his followers' assumption that this man is unclean because (1) he lives in gentile territory, and (2) he does not have the ability to hear or speak clearly. Jesus uses what is available—a bit of spittle and the recognized pattern of a healing touch—to accomplish what others think is impossible. When Jesus touches the man who is without hearing and speech, the bondage to silence is broken, and presumably the man is able to function in the oral-aural realm that Jesus has ushered in. What the disciples, witnesses, and auditors of this divine action see is Jesus's performance of freedom. To be given one's voice (as Jesus does for this man) is to be set free.

This simple account has helped me see the situation of many of my students in a different light. It also has helped me clarify what the nature of my work with them is to be as they look for their voices.

By the time my students come into the preaching class, they have had training in other parts of the curriculum. They have had some courses in biblical exegesis, for example. They are able to write fairly well and usually have good minds and imaginations. They have plenty of raw material. Yet I am struck by how many of them feel "unclean" when it comes to the task of preaching. The preaching ministry calls them to be accessible and accountable in ways that cause fear, anxiety, and self-doubt. Many feel that even though they have some skill in exegesis, they have difficulty with hearing the sounds of God in Scripture, tradition, or personal experience. This is in part because of the overemphasis on Scripture as a printed medium and lack of attention to its orality. The fact that Scripture comes into their experience as a text that they pore over in silent or written reflection flattens its expressive power to fully engage them. How can a textualized tradition carry the sound of God *unless it is somehow vocalized*? Unless engaged vocalization occurs, the primary metaphor for our experience of God shifts from the ear (presence) to the eye (Word).

Some feel mute; that is, they lack the capacity to give oral expression to sounds emanating from their own souls. Others simply feel that some perceived

9. The prophet Isaiah seems to be a source for Mark, as he quotes him in his first chapter in combination with other biblical texts.

defect in character keeps them out of God's favor. We can make use of this healing story to help students restore their hearing and speaking by setting goals for themselves and beginning to practice them.

First, let's have the students learn the story well enough to recite it and offer a performed interpretation of the text. Redirecting students' focus away from themselves and their perceived inadequacies by means of a text will encourage them to grapple with the demands the text will place on them—not the demands they are placing on themselves to come up with and speak a sermon so early in the course. The experience also gives them *sound* and *voice* to work with in interpretation. Stepping into the shoes of the biblical narrator places students in a position to read differently than the way they are probably accustomed to. Just as it is in the story, hearing and speaking are conjoined. Stephen Webb puts it this way: "Hearing is a dynamic relationship in sound that calls forth speech."[10]

How the narrator *sounds* is not something the text gives us on the surface. Neither is it found through use of a method of interpretation that does not take the oral character of the Scripture into account. A meaningful *sounding* of the text has to be discovered, then expressed using the materials a student has available, namely, the voice and the body. The text presents the teller with a set of attitudes and perspectives that are quite different from the teller's own. They emerge from a different conceptual world, yet one to which a student seeks entry. As the student teller's work proceeds through the imagery and narrative structure of the text, the student begins to make some discoveries about the performance of freedom:

1. The student discovers that it is possible to be set free from both pulpit and page and therefore use the voice and body more expressively in oral interpretation.
2. The student discovers that the sounds released from the page by means of the voice and body are tied to questions of meaning; inflection, pace, and pitch can change a listener's experience of what a text means. As a student begins to shape a sermon, he or she will begin to understand that *how* the sermon is spoken is crucial to a listener's experience of what it will mean.
3. The student will discover that the voice (as part of the body) is not simply an instrument for delivering a message; the voice is a probe for exploring its meaning.

10. Webb, *Divine Voice*, 60.

4. The legacy of oral interpretation as it resonates here teaches this: the practice will help us become better exegetes, not simply more competent in our roles as lectors.

Not only is this biblical text suggestive for our students but it also suggests something to those of us who teach them. How many of us are mute before our students' questions of voice because we do not feel qualified to take them up? I have previously suggested that we have been deaf to our own traditions of instruction and training in voice. Rather, we have listened to those in the culture of the theological school who believe that voice is a subject that belongs at the margins of the curriculum—left to specialists and therapists, not to permanent faculty.

A speech therapist would certainly be an asset to any program in preaching. As I write this, however, I realize that the culture of the theological school is changing dramatically. The resources of faculty time and available funds seem to be shrinking, and a specialized program of voice instruction is a luxury that few schools can afford.

Moreover, both students and faculty are expected to accomplish more tasks in order to meet new institutional realities. Faculty workloads are heavier, and students' attempts to juggle employment, family, and study make the concentration and focus required of a disciplined program of voice instruction even more difficult. Classes in "vocal performance for preaching" to be offered by the homiletics faculty are the ideal solution, of course. Yet what faculty members have had such instruction in the course of their own training? And if they did, did they have the interest to embrace it? Where does this leave us? Shall we go on ignoring the needs of our students who want to speak clearly, as does the man in the biblical story?

What the story suggests to me is that Jesus used what was available to him to accomplish the performance of freedom. One thing we do in fact have is a facility with textual exegesis and interpretation. We are now beginning to realize the implications of the interface between those textual traditions and the traditions and conventions of oral performance that helped to shape them. We can work with those insights to develop interpretive practices that will help train our students' voices to be more responsive to a text's effect. Specialized programs of drills and exercises, while valuable, are not the only resources we have when it comes to helping students find their voices. The demand of doing performed interpretations of biblical texts for preaching makes use of exegetical skills to introduce students to different soundings of the Word, soundings and utterances that can expand their capacity for vocal gestures that open rich fields for interpretation. The enterprise of voice instruction stands to benefit from the performance turn that biblical hermeneutics has taken.

Left unchecked, the approach I am developing will become strictly a speaker-centered or even a text-centered one. The performance turn that Bartow named in his lecture has wider implications. Performance studies, following other postmodern tendencies, tries to locate many centers and fields of meaning in human communication.[11] In a performance-centered, theologically grounded perspective on voice, we need to account for audiences. The student of ministry who is charged with finding his or her own voice for preaching is also charged with helping the congregation find theirs.

The third image I want to shine a light on is that of people gathering for worship. From this image we derive a ritual view of communication that will inform our development of a practical theology of voice. The sacred ceremony is the place where our students, the sacred texts, and the audience "find" their respective voices. In this arena we learn that the "voice does not come from deep within us but rather emerges in the give-and-take of listening and speaking to others."[12] Finding voice is a corporate enterprise.

James Carey has distinguished the ritual view of communication from the more dominant transmission view in American culture. Though both views have religious roots and attitudes, the latter has served Protestants in the development of theologies of communication where the sermon was prominent. Imagined as a conveyor belt, communication was seen as a linear process whereby a speaker developed a message that was transmitted through space to reach a listener. Along the way toward reception, the speaker has to overcome certain noises, that is, all those things that limit the capacity of a listener to hear and understand the message.

Carey points out how well this model of communication serves the values and aesthetics of industrial cultures that are concerned about transporting or delivering goods across great distances to profitable markets. "It is a view of communication," says Carey, "that derives from one of the most ancient of human dreams: the desire to increase the speed and effect of messages as they travel in space."[13] The payoff? Control, not only of space but of people.

11. Here I am following the definition of communication advanced by Ronald J. Pelias in *Performance Studies: The Interpretation of Aesthetic Texts* (New York: St. Martin's Press, 1992), 11–12. "All human communication possesses a performative and dramatic nature; that we typically view performance as a communicative event distinct from ordinary talk, an artistic act that exists in a variety of forms and settings; and that performance is a social and cultural event that has the power to solidify and modify cultural values."

12. Webb, *Divine Voice*, 59.

13. James Carey, *Communication as Culture: Essays on Media and Society* (New York: Routledge, 1992), 17.

For Christian evangelicals, this gave an underpinning for their desire to follow Christ's commission to preach the gospel to every living creature (Matt. 28:19) by speaking the gospel across the chasms and noise of human sin, namely, those resistances and distractions that impede true discipleship.

It is easy to see how voice can become commodified by this model of communication in ways that serve the values of a consumer culture. It can also lead us to develop very poor theological understandings of human communication. Speech instructors in every age and particularly in ours have resisted the commodification of the human voice by insisting through our practice that the voice could not simply be assessed, analyzed, and trained apart from the bodily self. Practitioners who served the disciplines of communications and homiletics while they were dominated by a linear-transmission model made tentative moves to push past the model (or more to the point by going underneath it) by going as deep as they went wide. The space through which messages traveled included not only the space *between* speakers, listeners, and God but also the *space of the speaker's soul*. Speakers of the gospel were not always as imperialistic as the linear-transmission model would seem to encourage us to believe. In the 1940s, H. E. Luccock encouraged his own students of speech and preaching to seek "the soul of delivery." Under the banner of "expressionism," for example, speech teachers encouraged students of preaching to let go of those habits that prevented them from fully speaking what was on their hearts. Apparently, some of the noise that obstructed the clear declaration of the gospel across space and time arose from the speaker's own soul.

We have also held to the tenets of a theology of sound that suggests God's voice emanates from a "person" (as in one of the "persons" of the Trinity) or, if you prefer, a "presence." God's voice cannot be abstracted from God's character, which is as mysterious as it is knowable. God's voice is disclosed in human experience through narrative and sacramental performance.

Carey's ritual view of communication lends coherence and insight to these tendencies in speech instruction to go more deeply into the processes by which messages are developed, understood, and interpreted. The focus is not solely on the speaker but also on the ceremony that "draws persons together in fellowship and commonality."[14] Transmission of information and interpretation still takes place, of course, but it does so within a web of communicative activity which the Christian can imagine as being highly charged with the Holy Spirit and the Word walking among the people.

Within this theological framework we can reimagine the roles of preachers, presiders, oral readers of texts, and audiences. The ritual view of communication

14. Carey, *Communication as Culture*, 18.

helps us see even the congregation as performers rather than passive recipients of the gospel of God.[15]

We can imagine sacred texts as being marked by the communion of saints whose presences are given voice and enactment by the readers who serve them. The preacher's struggle to find something to say becomes iconic, that is, emblematic of the congregation's struggle to be heard and seen as witnesses to the gospel they profess.

When I am introducing these insights to the students in the classroom, I will first show them various images of medieval priests or deacons giving direction to the players in the mystery plays of that era. The drawings or engravings often feature a robed or vested figure holding a book or script in hand and a baton. He looks like an orchestra conductor who holds a score and gives instruction on how music is to be played. According to the conventions of the time, the robed figure in the drawing would, in the course of a rehearsal or even a performance of a mystery play, give instructions to the players on how the lines should be spoken and what actions or behaviors the players should use in performance of their roles. I ask students to use this image as they lead congregations through the performance of liturgical prayers and texts. What attitudes, tones, and inflections shall we use in our performance of worship? How do we represent through our voices and bodies the range of human experience as we perform the church's language of prayer? I have found that when students take on the role of director of the church's performance of its liturgy and show in their own performances what appropriate tones, sounds, and attitudes they wish for the performance of liturgical texts, their voices and bodies become more responsive to the texts themselves.

Voice instruction in the theological school is animated by this principle: *voice is the modulation of incarnational truth.* As central as that axiom seems to be in theological education, voice instruction faces significant challenges. Homileticians who practice their vocations in seminaries affiliated with the old-line Protestant denominations are faced with shrinking budgets, rising tuition costs, and expansion of faculty responsibilities. They feel inadequately prepared to teach voice in the preaching course since few of them have had formal training, and administrators are reluctant to provide the funds needed to hire specialists. The shift from print-based to electronic media and the acquisition of new technologies for digital amplification tend to make vocal pedagogies designed for a former communications era irrelevant. Students

---

15. I am indebted to Nicholas Lash's notion of the "church as performers of the Gospel" as it enacts the gospel's promises, claims, and calls to action not only in worship but in everyday life. Nicholas Lash, *Theology on the Way to Emmaus* (London: SCM, 1986).

pressed for time and resources do not develop the concentration and disciplines necessary for improving vocal production. Consequently, with rare exceptions, the use and training of the human voice has virtually dropped off the list of priorities in the theological school. Even now, the senior administrator stops me in the hall following the student chapel and says: "We have to do more to help our students *project their voices*!"

This line of thinking and reasoning is too focused on methodology and not enough on theology. It does not adequately take into account insights from our collective interdisciplinary experiences of teaching in theological schools. Embedded deep within the institutional psyche of the theological school is the notion that teaching voice is non-theological, a system of instruction outside the primary concerns of the school and one that can therefore be dismissed as unnecessary. It might even be seen as a luxury that a beleaguered administrator can ill afford.

The task for those of us charged with students who want to find their voices is to first *do our theological homework*. What is theological about our current practice? What is theological about our legacy of instruction? Are these theologies adequate for the task? The second responsibility is to *make better use of what knowledge we have*. To do that we need to "be opened" (Mark 7:34) not only to the latent theologies of sound that undergird our practice but to the resources of our own traditions of instruction. These traditions and practices can be reframed and further developed into pedagogies that meet the challenges we face in the digitalized communications culture that surrounds us. And finally, let us listen to the voice of one who mentored many of us: "We are here as servants of those we teach, putting at the disposal of our students whatever technical knowledge we may have, so that [they] may understand more fully and more competently undertake the ministry of Word and sacrament for the church that calls them."[16]

---

16. Bartow, "In Service to the Servants of the Word," 274.

9

The Preacher's Creative Process

Reaching the Well

JANA CHILDERS

It is a fortunate preacher who has never encountered a dry well. Most preachers are very familiar with what it feels like. Preacher-talk abounds in metaphors for the phenomenon: we "come up empty," "hit the wall," "go dry," and "short-circuit." We "dig deep," "hunker down," and "pull ourselves up by our boot straps." Our problem is with the "blank screen," the "blank page," and the "blank mind." If only we could "get in the groove," "get things flowing," or "unstop the dam." It was Aimee Semple McPherson who said it eighty years ago, but it could have been said by many another preacher in many another age:

> Dusty, musty, wrapped in the mummy-like grave clothes of formalism and modern theology, without an "amen" in the soul or a "hallelujah" upon the lips, without the soft flowing pearls of erstwhile tender tears of conviction upon her cheeks, sits the professing church of Jesus Christ today, like a garden drooping; like a fountain that has ceased its flow; and offers but the poor apology of a bucket of muddy water from a hardly reached well.[1]

1. Aimee Semple McPherson, *Foursquare Correspondence Courses* (Los Angeles: Bridal Call, 1928), 2:9–10.

Though she is speaking ostensibly about the state of the church, one cannot help but hear the preacher's angst. If the church is in desperate trouble, a preacher might well blame modern theology first, though not for long. If the church is languishing without "an 'amen' in the soul or a 'hallelujah' upon the lips," it is not just the fault of formalism. Preachers and preaching are to blame. At the very least, preachers and preaching are responsible for the cure. It is the preacher's job to reach the well.

"Reaching the well" is just one way to talk about the need to access the spiritual resources for preaching that lie beneath the surface. Beneath the surface of the text, the preacher and the community are the riches that make the life-and-death difference in preaching. To tap them means coming up with living water. To fail to reach them means dying of thirst. This is, of course, the province of the Holy Spirit—where miracles and cries of *aha* and splendiferous insights happen. It's the realm of *mysterium tremendum* and unspeakable holiness. It is the realm of mystery. Closing your eyes and averting your face is a natural response. But it is a realm that preachers are obliged to know something about. Interestingly, though it may never be possible and perhaps not desirable to plumb the depths of the subject, there are a number of ways to approach the phenomenon of the preacher's creative task.

Deep Translation

Missiologist Andrew Walls describes the mission of the church as

> living on someone else's terms, as the gospel itself is about God living on someone else's terms, the Word becoming flesh, divinity being expressed in terms of humanity. And the transmission of the gospel requires a process analogous, however distantly, to that great act on which Christian faith depends. Cross-cultural Christianity . . . has to go beyond language, the outer skin of culture, into the processes of thinking and choosing and all the networks of relationship that lie beneath language, turning them all to Christ. . . . This is *deep* translation.[2]

What is true of mission is true by extension of its essential tool—preaching. The "deep translation" Walls describes is, in fact, part and parcel of all authentic Christian preaching. The realm that is beneath the outer skin of language, the realm of "the processes of thinking and choosing and all the networks of

2. Andrew Walls, "Christian Scholarship and the Demographic Transformation of the Church," in *Theological Literacy for the Twenty-First Century*, ed. Rodney L. Petersen and Nancy M. Rourke (Grand Rapids: Eerdmans, 2002), 170–71.

relationship that lie beneath language" is another way of talking about the realm that creative preachers strive to tap every time they preach. This is true because all preaching is cross-cultural preaching. All preaching operates in a way that is analogous to the incarnation. All preaching depends for its success on "deep translation": on the ability of the preacher to draw on the realm beneath language and reach the listener in that same realm. If homiletician O. C. Edwards is right that the purpose of preaching is to permit Christ to become the dominant symbol of the unconscious, then the preacher getting beneath his or her own skin is an obvious first step.

Actio Divina

In his seminal volume, *God's Human Speech: A Practical Theology of Proc-lamation*, Charles L. Bartow lays the theoretical and theological foundations for preaching that traffics in the realm beneath the skin. The Word of God "is not *verbum* but *sermo*, not *ratio* but *oratio*. It is lively, face-to-face, oral-aural discourse and suasory action. . . . It is *actio divina*, God's self-performance."[3] For Bartow, preaching is incarnational activity that occurs at the intersection of *actio divina* and *homo performans*. Where Walls sees "deep translation," Bartow sees action. Preachers are "actors, too, in the ethical, not simply the-atrical, sense of that term, taking action to facilitate other people's enacted obedience. For God's word heard means that you do not just stand there; you *do* something."[4]

For Bartow, as for Walls and others who hold an incarnational view of preaching, preachers are actors whose own bodies and experience, speech and action participate in the gospel process—i.e., the process by which the Word of God moves forward across the face of the earth and from age to age. For Bartow, the stuff of the preacher's life—that which she or he brings to preaching—is altered at the crossroads of *actio divina* and *homo perfor-mans*. When the preacher's "projections of self come face to face with the self-disclosure of the divine . . . what we would be is transformed into what God would have us be."[5] However, both use of self and refinement of self are implied in Bartow's model; we are not talking about *loss* of self here. So, Bar-tow says, the God "who is merciful in judgment yet just in divine compassion, burns away the illimitable self as with flames that cannot be quenched. But

3. Charles L. Bartow, *God's Human Speech: A Practical Theology of Proclamation* (Grand Rapids: Eerdmans, 1997), 26.
4. Ibid., 122.
5. Ibid.

at the same time, [God] restores and refines the finite self till it burns with a radiance beyond its ken."[6]

What remains for those of us who accept an incarnational view of preaching and appreciate Bartow's distinctive accent on action is the question of how the self is used in preaching. To be sure, the most dramatic and observable aspect of the phenomenon is the one Bartow so eloquently describes—a fiery transformation. But the aspects of the process that occur before, during, and after that moment are of interest too. They are the moments that may tell us something about how to reach the well, about how to move in the realm of the Holy Spirit, about how to use what is beneath one person's skin to reach another.

This chapter makes the claim that preaching that reaches the listener at the realm that lies beneath language depends on the preacher's tapping of the resources of that realm during the preparation of the sermon. It explores models of creativity to find methods useful in this task. It also puts forward the notion that performance is not only a way of testing and embodying the discoveries of the creative process, but a tool in the creative process itself.

A Brief Review of Creativity Theory

Researching models of human creativity can be a rewarding task. For one thing, one finds in the testimony of artists, scientists, and other creators examples of all one's own neuroses—an oddly reassuring experience. For another, the sheer multiplicity of models is encouraging—suggesting to the desperate psyche that the cure for writer's block is out there somewhere. And, finally, people who write about the creative process are themselves, by and large, a colorful lot. Some, in fact, are quite pithy. A. A. Milne, for example, describes his own process somewhat wryly when he says, "One of the advantages of being disorderly is that one is constantly making exciting discoveries."[7]

The study of the creative process, like the creative process itself, is both inspiring and daunting. The troubling side is suggested by Nietzsche: "One must still have chaos in oneself to give birth to a dancing star."[8] That remark points to the white, soft underbelly of the field. It's also the only reason some of us read pleasant little tomes proposing models of human creativity. We want to know how to manage the chaos. We read watching for clues to the

6. Ibid., 123.
7. A. A. Milne, quoted by Franklin C. Baer at http://www.bemorecreative.com/fq-intro .htm.
8. Friedrich Nietzsche, *Thus Spoke Zarathustra*, in *The Portable Nietzsche*, ed. and trans. Walter Kaufmann (New York: Viking Penguin, 1954), 129.

questions posed by self-doubt, dry wells, and failures of imagination. Those of us who treat our own neuroses by reading about others' may study creativity on two fronts: the literature and the lore. There is succor on both sides. The following section of this chapter rehearses the development of creativity theory and explores highlights of each approach.

The history of formal academic interest in human creativity is a relatively short one. It was not until the late nineteenth century that scholars began systematic investigation of the subject. After Freud and Jung introduced the notion of the unconscious, certain questions naturally arose. Questions that hadn't really made sense to voice before suddenly began to suggest a promising line of inquiry. Where does inspiration come from? How does imagination work? Why do some people seem to be more creative than others? Is there anything people can do to improve their capacity for creativity?

One of the earliest models of the creative process was proposed in 1926 by Graham Wallas. It is worth mentioning because it bears a striking resemblance to more than half the models proposed since. Wallas describes four stages of human creativity:

1. Preparation: the stage in which the problem or issue is defined
2. Incubation: the stage in which the problem or issue is laid aside
3. Illumination: the moment in which the new idea emerges
4. Verification: the stage in which the solution is tested[9]

Of particular note is the blend of critical and associative activities Wallas describes. His view of creativity involves more or less equal parts of rational activity (primarily seen in stages 1 and 4) and imaginative activity (primarily seen in stages 2 and 3). This casual mixing of these two elements flew in the face of popular thinking. Since Socrates, rationality had been understood as a hindrance to creativity—something likely to come between the artist and the heavenly muse. Wallas's model demonstrated that creative and analytical thought could be seen as complementary. This constituted a significant and enduring contribution to the field. The question of the precise nature of the admixture of rational thought and imaginative association would occupy those writing in the field over the next three decades.

In the years following the publication of Wallas's model, theorists' interest was drawn increasingly to the role played by unconscious processes and uncontrollable events. The creative process was seen along Darwinian lines as a function of random variations and natural selection. So, it was pointed out,

9. Graham Wallas, *The Art of Thought* (New York: Harcourt Brace, 1926), 80.

although Alexander Fleming "discovered" penicillin, there was an important element of chance in the way it showed up in the petri dish. Yes, theorists acknowledged, George de Mestral invented Velcro, but it was a walk in the woods and the cockleburs that adhered to his cuffs that "gave" him the idea. By 1953 when Alex Osborn introduced the notion of "brainstorming" (in Berkeley, California), the unconscious and the random were held in high esteem, and the creative process was viewed by many as something quite outside the control of human beings.

World War II brought the first round of significant funding for and serious interest in creativity research. The United States Department of Defense anted up, hoping for better technology and more effective leaders. However the fifties and sixties saw little advancement in creativity theory, and by the midseventies, academic interest had become focused on empirical methods and measurable phenomena. Social scientists distanced themselves from the seemingly subjective field of creativity, reinforcing the popular belief that the study of creativity was both fuzzy and futile.

During the fifties, however, Frank Barron, a young research psychologist at University of California, Berkeley, carried out an ambitious research project that would help to reestablish the field and mark him as its leading expert. Barron's work focused on interviews with well-known artists, scientists, and other creative geniuses. A rigorous research method called "holistic assessment" was used to draw creative people into three days of intense interviews, experiments, test-taking, and group discussion. Barron describes it as "a hardwork, overtime party. . . . [The subjects] were often outrageous, eccentric, uninhibited, rule-challenging, norm-rejecting cases of self-possession and self-assertion. Picture if you will an intuitive introvert with a lot of dash, a big bank account, a skipping wit, a disrespectful attitude toward true-false questionnaires, and an assured place in cultural history. Do that, and you can imagine what we poor psychologists were up against."[10]

Barron's model, published decades later at the end of his active research career (1988), represents a key moment in the development of creativity theory. Employing the birth metaphor, it is described in four stages:

1. Conception: the stage in which a prepared mind receives the problem
2. Gestation: the stage in which the process develops on an intricate timetable

10. Frank Barron, introduction to *Creators on Creating: Awakening and Cultivating the Imaginative Mind*, ed. Frank Barron, Alfonso Montuori, and Anthea Barron (New York: Putnam, 1997), 3.

3. <u>Parturition</u>: the stage in which the new idea or solution is born
4. <u>Bringing Up Baby</u>: a period of further development[11]

Not only is the balance between critical and associative thought restored in Barron's model but the question is seemingly laid to rest. The viability of creativity theory as an academic discipline is established and its use as an instrument for personal and social gain demonstrated. In addition, Barron's life project succeeded in focusing the question of the academy on the relationship between creativity and the quest for meaning. Barron, of course, knows the answer. Creativity, he affirms, "is an attempt to penetrate the mystery of self, and perhaps the even greater mystery of Being."[12]

Also working on creativity theory during its years of unpopularity—the 1970s—and also interested in the mystery of self was Mihalyi Csikszentmihalyi, a Hungarian-born theorist at the University of Chicago. Csikszentmihalyi's work was fueled by the question of drive. During a research project on the subject of motivation (what motivates creative people to create?), he hit on the idea of asking the study's subjects to carry beepers. As the beepers were activated randomly through the day, subjects were asked to write down what they were doing and how they felt about it. When Csikszentmihalyi fed the data into a computer for analysis, he discovered that creative people who are performing at their peak seem to enter another world. "Time is distorted, a sense of happiness and well-being overcomes them." They enter what Csikszentmihalyi calls a state of "flow"—"when things seem to go just right, when you feel alive and fully attentive to what you're doing."[13]

A follow-up study on high school mathematicians explored the question of unrealized creative potential. The students Csikszentmihalyi examined were all equally talented in math. However, one subgroup had abandoned interest in the subject while the other went on to take advanced courses, compete in tournaments, and excel in the field. The difference between them, Csikszentmihalyi discovered, was an ability to tolerate solitude: "Most people cannot put up with solitude for very long. After a few minutes and certainly after a few hours, they start to feel a kind of psychic entropy. They are unable to coordinate their thoughts and feelings and actions in orderly ways. . . . To

11. Frank Barron, "Putting Creativity to Work," in *The Nature of Creativity*, ed. Robert Sternberg (Cambridge: Cambridge University Press, 1988), 80.

12. Barron, introduction to *Creators on Creating*, 2.

13. Quoted in Anne C. Roark, "The Secrets of Creativity," *Los Angeles Times*, November 12, 1989, 12.

keep from feeling unhappy or bored, they pick up a telephone or turn on the television."[14]

Csikszentmihalyi's work helped solidify a focus on the artist's experience (what Barron had called "the mystery of self") and made key contributions to the understanding of how artists access their inner experience.

The end of the twentieth century saw two significant developments in creativity research which stemmed from significant external influences on the field. First, corporate America became interested in the study of creativity as the US military had been decades before. In the name of quality improvement—and in the quest for more innovative leaders and better problem solvers—corporate money flowed. MBA programs and Silicon Valley joined Ma Bell, Chevron, and IBM as sites of intense interest in the field. The Scan-Focus-Act Model of creativity is typical of the dozens of models catalogued during this period. It proposes a simple process that describes creativity in three stages:

1. Scan: look for options and gather information
2. Focus: make a choice
3. Act: try out the model

The approach, its authors hasten to say, is characterized by a variable time frame. However, as is obvious from the simplicity and brevity of the model, variability—or flexibility of any kind—is not its most notable feature. Scan-Focus-Act's process, like many of the business-driven models proposed in the nineties, focuses instead on parsing and measuring creative activity. Such models share a common understanding of human creativity as recursive, fractal, cyclical, and nonlinear. The "measurability" of creativity demonstrated by these models served at the end of nearly a century of study to emphasize creativity's accessibility, if not its predictability.

The second significant development in creativity theory during this time was the establishment of a link between mental illness and creativity. In a 1987 landmark study, Dr. Nancy C. Andreason, professor of psychiatry at the University of Iowa College of Medicine, documented the connection. Her research involved thirty faculty members at the University of Iowa's Writers' Workshop, the country's oldest writing program. She had expected to be able to make a correlation between schizophrenia and creativity in writing. However, her research showed a striking correlation with depression instead. Eighty percent of the writers studied were clinically depressed, compared with only 30 percent of the control group of nonwriters. More striking still was

interesting

14. Ibid., 13.

the discovery that nearly half the writers were diagnosed with a severe form of depression—referred to then as "manic depression"—compared with 10 percent of the control group. Two years later, a study by Kay Redfield Jamison at Johns Hopkins University of forty-seven English poets, novelists, and playwrights produced similar results.

If business-driven models of creativity showed it to be a viable field of investigation, the study of its physiology suggested that investigation could reveal—at least someday—its very roots. Creativity, once seen as ephemeral and fuzzy—a subject unfit for serious academic research—had developed into a legitimate field of inquiry. In one century, the understanding of what creativity is and how it may be studied shifted several times and on several fronts. By the end of the first century of formal academic interest, three major developments were notable. First of all, creativity's accessibility had been demonstrated. No longer the province of mystery, creativity turned out to have plottable, measurable, and investigatable aspects. The pattern of creativity itself was found to be describable—eight to ten major models and scores of minor ones were proposed for the task. Secondly, the understanding of the nature of creativity changed. It moved from being understood as an experience other than and antithetical to rational thought to being understood as the product of analytical and imaginative thought held in tension. Finally, the origins of creativity were reexamined. No longer something from above, creativity began to be understood as something from within.

Key Findings in the Study of Creativity

Both the academic literature in creativity and the informal writings of those who are themselves creative have much to tell dusty, thirsty preachers about reaching the resources below the surface. Perhaps the most reassuring of all is the experts' belief that there is a well to be tapped. It is present and cultivable in most everyone, they claim, and there are disciplines that will improve the creative ability of anyone who will adopt them. This section of the chapter explores three key observations from the literature and lore on creativity and applies them to the challenges faced by preachers.

Tapping the Well: The "Cultivability" of Creativity

The well is there for the tapping, the theorists claim. Frank Barron's lifelong study of creative people yielded numerous insights, this among them. His publications describe conditions, personal qualities, and skills that support creative work. First of all, he notes, there are a number of ways to be creative. Originality, fluency, adaptive flexibility, spontaneous flexibility, sensitivity to problems, and expressional fluency are all aspects of what is commonly called "creativity." Most people excel at some and not others, but skills for improving each may be developed.

Perhaps more importantly for parched preachers, Barron is able to identify the common characteristics of creative people. It is an encouraging list, suggesting again that though some people may start life with advantages in one or more areas, much of creative work relies on muscles that can be built up. Creative people, Barron found, are more likely to have the ability to work independently, high energy, flexibility, an introverted/intuitive nature, and the desire to create. As has been mentioned, some correlation with manic depression was also found. Of all Barron's discoveries about the characteristics of creative people, though, his work on the question of the role of intelligence is most striking. He was able to show repeatedly that in creative work, a modest IQ is plenty, and there is no benefit for creativity to having an IQ higher than 120.

Finally, Barron's conversations with geniuses yielded one further insight into what makes creative people tick. He asked them to talk about the conditions that supported or were required for their creative work. They mentioned balance, space, and the ability to operate outside the reach of society and its strictures. But the overriding theme in these conversations was the importance of freedom, which was cited more than any other single factor as essential to creative work.

When Barron's findings about the characteristics of creative people are compared with Csikszentmihalyi's results in the same areas of study, it is immediately obvious that the two researchers are describing the same phenomena. Where Barron talks about flexibility, Csikszentmihalyi talks about openness to new experiences and the willingness to take risks. Where Csikszentmihalyi notes the importance of being able to tolerate solitude, Barron mentions the ability to work independently. Where Barron lists a tendency toward introversion and intuition, Csikszentmihalyi notes the tendency to think in images. The overlap of the two lists suggests that openness and a capacity for introversion are essential characteristics of creative geniuses. For the purposes of this chapter, it is important to note that both are cultivable. Preachers' wells are renewable and extendable, research suggests. No one has an excuse for settling for rote, perfunctory, or trivial preaching. The well is there. Preachers who are not happy with their God-given ability in the area of expressional fluency may be well advised to look for creativity in other aspects of their personality. A sensitivity to problems, for example, may be cultivable by those who are willing to spend some time in their studies with an out-loud performance of the text. Rehearsing a text by matching one's own voice and body to the needs of the text to be expressed is an excellent way to strengthen one's sensitivity to textual nuances, questions of connotation, and other pastoral issues—in other words, to its "problems" and opportunities.

Deepening the Well: The Importance of Creating Space

The idea that holding rational and imaginative thought in tension produces creativity is an idea about "space." Space is what is produced by juxtaposition, that is, by holding opposing elements in tension. It is as essential to creative work as freedom. Indeed, in a sense, it is freedom. When artists and other creative people talk about the need for space, they are talking about the importance of creating the essential condition for creative insight—psychic, psychological, spiritual, and often physical space. They are talking about deepening the well.

Wallas's model refers to this phase of the creative process as "incubation," and Barron's labels it "gestation." Both locate this phase just prior to the "aha" stage, the moment of insight. The necessary precondition for insight is a period of "space," they claim. Mystic and philosopher J. G. Bennett explains:

> If I have some question which I cannot answer by the ordinary processes, by calling upon what I know about a subject, and I have satisfied myself that I do not already have the answer, then it is no use in going on looking for it. I have become habituated, by doing this for many years, to quite quickly stop looking for an answer and to go to this other, opposite, condition of putting the whole thing away except for *the question*. I stop all thinking "about" the subject, even to the extent of chasing away any thoughts that seem interesting or suggestive. Even the question ceases to be present in the form of words. . . . All that remains is *the need to find an answer*. . . . I suppose that it really is this abhorrence of a vacuum (i.e., created by preventing the mind from wandering off to other subjects) that draws the mind to some new thought or new insight, and makes for this spontaneous or creative step that I am looking for.[15]

For the artist then, space operates the way a vacuum operates. Juxtaposition and tensiveness help to create space. Space is more than openness and blankness, however. When artists and creativity theorists talk about space in this sense, what they are talking about is more like a charged force field than a vacant lot. Space creates the necessary precondition for generativity, insight, and newness.

15. J. G. Bennett, "Living in the Medium," in *Creators on Creating*, 77–78.

The concepts are not the province of artists alone. Theologians as disparate as Harvey Cox, Jürgen Moltmann, and Gordon Lathrop make use of the notion of juxtaposition (although the word may be most famously associated with philosopher William Coleridge's work on creativity). It is valued for its ability to create a venue—for a spark, for human play, or for worship. As preachers, we might say that it is valued for its ability to create an arena for the Holy Spirit. The elements of worship, Lathrop claims, have meaning as they are juxtaposed to each other. He continues, "I have thought that a certain space is created when one thing is held in tension with another . . . that this space can enable our enacted symbols to hold us—and from that place of holding to propose to us both re-readings of the world and consequent actions for justice."[16]

It is not surprising that theologians and others interested in spiritual experience have cottoned on to the concept of space. From the beginning, people of faith have understood the need for a time and place apart. Countless numbers of the Christian faithful have followed Jesus's example, seeking out the desert or the mountains as an arena for communion with God. Judaism has an even longer tradition, of course, of valuing the space of wilderness and journey. The sixteenth-century metaphysical thinker Rabbi Isaac Luria was known for his teaching about God's "withdrawal" from the world. His doctrine of *tsim-tsum* (the Hebrew word for withdrawal) claimed that God made space in the world for human beings to learn and grow—to develop into the creatures they were meant to be—by a unique blend of divine withdrawal or space-making and divine presence.

For contemporary preachers attending to their own creative processes, there are few tasks more challenging than making space. Psychic, psychological, spiritual, and physical space may all be required at one time or another for preaching—and are sometimes required all at once—yet most preachers' lifestyles permit little time and afford little opportunity for solitude. Space in terms of time is not easy for a preacher to create. However, where time is not available, tensiveness may be. Where mountains are too far away to access, juxtaposition may be rather close at hand. The creative preacher can make space anywhere and often with the fairly small blocks of time available by performing pieces of the biblical text and juxtaposing character, voice, context, and rhetorical situation one against the other.

A preacher can ask: What happens to this line of the text if I say it in this tone of voice? Or this? What happens to this character if I picture him face-

16. Gordon W. Lathrop, "*Ordo* and Coyote: Further Reflections on Order, Disorder and Meaning in Christian Worship," address given at the Academy of Liturgical Studies, San Diego, California, January 2006.

to-face with Jesus or with his back turned? What happens to this truth claim in the text if I plop it into my rhetorical situation? What happens to this line of Jesus if I hear him saying it to my Mrs. Young or Elder Park? There are many ways to create space. The theorists remind us that the creator first makes space, then waits to see what will pop into it.

The Shape of the Process: Stepping into the Water

To say that the creative process is fractal, recursive, and nonlinear is to say that it does not appear to be orderly. It does not cooperate nicely with the artist or with those studying the process itself in achieving predictability, harmony, or sense. It does not lend itself to neat steps and cause-and-effect sequencing. Though the creative process can be described (or else what did Frank Barron give his life to?), the first thing one has to say about it is that it appears to be irregular. The second thing, though, that Barron and his colleagues would want to say about it is that it is not as irregular as it appears.

"Recursive" refers to a pattern or experience that "runs" over and over. "Fractal" processes are those that seem to repeat irregularly but actually are measurable. "A fractal is a rough, fragmented geometric shape that can be subdivided in parts, each of which is (at least approximately) a smaller copy of the whole. Fractals are generally self-similar (bits look like the whole) and independent of scale (they look similar, no matter how close you zoom in)."[17] In other words, in a recursive, fractal process there are fluctuations, shapes, and patterns that at first glance seem to be unpredictable, but, given the right instruments, are measurable and do reoccur. There is a wholeness to the entity or process that is not immediately obvious. Coastlines, mountain ranges, stock market fluctuation, and software are examples. If the creative process is fractal and recursive, it means that even though it is not easily controlled, manipulated, or orchestrated, it has integrity, is ultimately accessible, and perhaps, on a good day, is even manageable.

None of this should surprise preachers. Any preacher who has ever "preached above his or her head" or taken a dog of a sermon into the pulpit only to have it fly knows how irregular the preaching process can be. Any preacher who knows anything about the ways of the Holy Spirit knows this. When she comes, she comes on her own timetable and in her own way. She is neither predictable nor tidy. She has never been known to drop a good sermon into a preacher's consciousness in Roman numeral outline form. She, in fact, needs an editor.

17. "Fractal." Dictionary.com. Denis Howe, *The Free On-line Dictionary of Computing.* http://dictionary.reference.com/browse/fractal.

The Holy Spirit does not break her insights into bite-sized thoughts or put them in order. Ann and Barry Ulanov explain:

> Where our speech proceeds in sequences, the spirit moves in simultaneities. Where we demand some reasonable association of ideas, or even of emotions, looking almost always for antecedents to explain consequences, the spirit gathers everything up at once and deposits it in one massive offering to our understanding. We are, all of us, creatures of parts, used to beginnings, middles and ends because our lives are divided that way, and our language and our way of taking in language follows the same logic of process. But the spirit is one and undivided.[18]

In other words, the way of the Holy Spirit with preachers may be described as nonlinear, recursive, and fractal.

If that is a fair description, it may be because the well on which creative geniuses draw, and the well over which the Holy Spirit hovers with its—ah—bright wings, are the same. Karl Rahner, among others, has observed that the Holy Spirit seems to favor the realm of the human unconscious. Though her work on us and with us can be witnessed in every conceivable realm, her movement in the unconscious is most striking. Whether the Holy Spirit has any such preference is something, I imagine, that will never be known for sure this side of heaven. But one reason to believe it may be so is that the disciplines that artists use to access the unconscious mind bear a striking resemblance to certain spiritual disciplines. We call those disciplines prayer. Whatever you call them, their track record in feeding creativity is impressive.

To access the unconscious mind, artists say, it is necessary to still the conscious mind. This helps create the condition for the activity of the unconscious to "come forward." The effect is like a curtain in the psyche parting, some say. What is usually front and center and loud and preoccupying—the activity of the conscious mind—moves aside, allowing the creative riches of the unconscious to cavort and juxtapose, free associate and pinwheel: in short, to play upon the stage. Psychologists disagree over the details of just how the conscious and unconscious work together in the creative process. Abraham Maslow, for example, sees the unconscious as a first step and the conscious as a second; he calls them "primary" and "secondary" creativity. Jung sees the two in balance and warns that imbalance leads to spiritual disintegration. James Hillman is interested in the intersection of the two as a "third realm, a sort of conscious unconscious." However, there is no disagreement about the strategic importance of the unconscious to creativity.

---

18. Ann and Barry Ulanov, *Primary Speech: A Psychology of Prayer* (Atlanta: John Knox, 1982), 108.

Three artists' observations about tried-and-true methods for accessing the unconscious are worth noting here: First, it is important to eliminate strain. Trying too hard is guaranteed to keep one stuck in the mud of the conscious mind. For this reason, creative writing guru Julia Cameron requires "morning pages" of those who follow her method. First thing every morning, one sits at the desk, pen or pencil in hand, and writes until one has covered three full pages. There are no rules about what one writes. It is perfectly fine to write, "I hate this. This is a stupid exercise. I have nothing to say," over and over again if one likes. The only rule is to keep the hand moving across the page. No cross-outs, no pauses, no lifting the hand from the paper is permitted. The exercise reduces the strain of facing the blank page. Similarly, some actors practice a "clean ball" discipline. The handing off of lines or the interplay of action between actors on stage is imaged as a "ball," and actors are coached to avoid sweating or squeezing or otherwise straining over the ball as it is passed from one to another. The goal is to hand it off "clean."

For preachers, eliminating strain can be achieved through the physical activity involved in the out-loud performance of the text and the oralizing of the sermon composition process. The classic model of the preacher composing the sermon in the study as he or she paces the floor is one that has much to commend it. Preachers might well add to this the kind of focus on breath that other performance artists use to calm the body from the inside out. Muscle relaxation exercises, breathing exercises, and physical movement can do much to relieve the strain many preachers bring to the creative process.

Secondly, it is important to eliminate distraction. Distraction is the very thing that rouses the conscious mind, preventing the unconscious from coming forward. Dramaturge Arthur Hopkins claims that it is often the small things—the nonessentials—that distract an audience, breaking the psychic spell the director and actors hope to cast:

> I eliminate all gesture that is not absolutely needed, all unnecessary inflections and intoning, the tossing of heads, the flicking of fans and kerchiefs, the tapping of feet, the drumming of fingers, the swinging of legs, pressing of brows, holding of hearts, curling of moustaches, stroking of beards and all the million and one tricks that have crept into the actor's bag, all of them betraying one of two things—an annoying lack of repose or an attempt to attract attention to himself and away from the play.[19]

Hopkins's comments are concerned with the audience's experience, but the same rule applies to the artist or the preacher in the throes of creating. Elimi-

19. Arthur Hopkins, *How's Your Second Act?* (New York: Samuel French, 1948), 14–15.

nation of distraction is essential to the creative process. This is one reason so many sermon insights come in the shower or the car. But there is another.

The third thing that all those who attend to the creative process know is that there are a couple proactive ways to induce access to the unconscious, both of them known to the preacher as aspects of the oral composition and rehearsal—in other words, as aspects of the "performance"—of sermons. The first completes the explanation about all those sermons born on freeways and in shower stalls: it is possible to lull the conscious mind with repetitive muscle movement. Large-group muscle movement works especially well— running, jogging, walking, vacuuming, sweeping, etc.—but even the kind of smooth repetitive movement that is involved in steering a car or washing one's neck is effective. This, of course, is the swinging watch principle. Repetitive movement lulls. But when one's own muscles get involved, the lulling effect is seemingly deepened.

Another example of the proactive strategies artists employ for accessing the unconscious is the writer's practice of entering into the process at the same time every day. Anne Lamott is among those who believe that the unconscious can be trained to kick in at a set time. This, again, is familiar territory for preachers. Near the end of his life, a mentor of mine told me that he "had a 10 a.m. Tuesday appointment with the Holy Spirit for sixty years and had never been stood up once."

For the thirsty preacher who is willing to be attentive to his or her own creative process, to develop disciplines to support it, and to experiment freely with the use of voice and body in the quest to reach the well, the news is good. God has, it seems, built into the preacher equipment that will support the process. Used in the service of the Word, blessed by the gracious action of the Holy Spirit, it is hard to imagine a richer source of resources for preaching.

10

What Comes Next?

Performing Music and Proclaiming the Word

C L A Y T O N J . S C H M I T

When I was three, my mother was concerned for my memory. She had good reason. One night, after having been put to bed to say my prayers, I spoke out loud: "Now I lay me down to sleep." Then I called out to my mother in her bedroom: "Mama, what comes next?" After a half dozen attempts, and getting no further on my own, my four-year-old brother, infinitely wiser than I and eager to get to sleep, said: "Clay, just say 'amen' and go to sleep!"

What comes next? is a question all preachers need to contend with. It has to do with learning the steps in working with a text, crafting a sermon, reworking its language, internalizing its moves and structure, and performing the prepared pulpit materials with logic and clarity upon delivery. At each stage, we need to develop habits for knowing what comes next and for determining what does not come next. All preachers learn sooner or later that one of the keys to effective proclamation is determining what to leave out.

Learning what comes next is an issue that all artists face. How could an actor proceed successfully if she did not know which line follows which in a dialogue? How could a sculptor finish a work if he did not know which tool to use after the heavy chisel work was done? Musicians are keenly in need of an understanding of what comes next; music cannot proceed or succeed if after each note the performer needs to ponder, "What comes next?" Music teachers are rightly frustrated by the common habit of students who pause at every mistake: "Wait," they say, and start the passage again. Students eventually learn to press on through a mistake so that the music continues. Learning this is learning the difference between preparation and performance.

Musicians, as a matter of training and habit, acquire sometimes prodigious skill at knowing what comes next. Think, for example, of a concert pianist sitting between an orchestra and an audience, poised to play a piano concerto. The virtuoso pianist will have the piece memorized and will know, in body and mind, precisely which notes follow which, how and where those notes and passages fit into the orchestral score, precisely when to begin, to reenter, to pause, to slow, to look to the conductor for partnership in interpretation, and so on. The layers of knowledge of what comes next are uncountable. Vladimir Horowitz, it is said, even knew when to throw in a mistake, given his conviction that "perfection itself is imperfection."[1]

How do musicians achieve such habits of mind and body? And is there anything that can be learned from the performance of music that will help preachers understand the theology and practice of their art? Can reflection on the "what comes next" of music provide insight for the "what comes next" in the shaping and delivery of a sermon? I contend here that there *is* something to be learned and will try to demonstrate some of what preachers might gain through a close look at the nature of music and the habits of musical performance.

Our line of inquiry here follows a line recently developed by a new school of theological investigation. It seeks to use the arts as a lens through which we can see theological issues more clearly. Headmaster of this school is Jeremy S. Begbie, director of the Theology Through the Arts research project at Cambridge University.[2] As a musician, Begbie gives special attention to the relationship between music and theology. In *Theology, Music and Time*,

---

1. The Vladimir Horowitz Web site, http://web.telia.com/~u85420275/trivia.htm.
2. The cover notes from Jeremy S. Begbie, *Theology, Music and Time* (Cambridge: Cambridge University Press, 2000), present him thus: "Jeremy S. Begbie is Vice Principal of Ridley Hall, Cambridge. He teaches systematic theology at Ridley Hall and in Cambridge University. He is Director of 'Theology Through the Arts,' Center for Advanced Religious and Theological Studies, Faculty of Divinity, University of Cambridge. Jeremy Begbie is a professionally-trained musician, and has performed extensively as a pianist, oboist and conductor." His other books include *Voicing Creation's Praise: Towards a Theology of the Arts* (London: T&T Clark, 1991); and *Resounding Truth: Christian Wisdom in the World of Music* (Grand Rapids: Baker Academic, 2007). He has also edited several volumes on theology and the arts, including *Beholding*

he shows that music can demonstrate theological ideas and instruct us in reconsideration of theological assumptions. Music can, as he says, "serve as a means of discovering afresh and articulating" theological truths.[3] While many have undertaken to explore the ways that music demonstrates—via analog and metaphor[4]—theological ideas, doctrines, or principles, there is much yet to be learned from the way music functions and what that announces about theology and theological activities. The purpose of this chapter is to follow the trajectory of this reasoning, seeing music not merely as an analog for preaching but to inquire about music's essential qualities and discern from them theological principles that can inform the theology and the task of preaching. Specifically, I will examine two issues relating to musical performance: (1) the insight that music exists only as an activity that is externalized, and (2) the qualities of anticipation and inevitability in musical performance. Through these, I hope to demonstrate ways in which music can refresh our perspectives on the theology and performance of preaching.

Preaching and Proclamation

Before proceeding to the main issues, I pause here in order to reassert the word *proclamation* as a synonym for preaching in this chapter.[5] This term, popularized by C. H. Dodd in his published lectures on preaching, *The Apostolic Preaching and Its Developments*, has been criticized as "a fancy synonym for preaching," which overlooks preaching that is didactic, exhortational, prophetic, and so forth.[6] While not my main purpose here, I am eager to dispel two false assumptions about bringing the Word of God to life in worship. The first is that the category of performance is inappropriate to discussions of preaching and worship. Preaching, so the thinking goes, should never be reduced to theatrics, mere techniques employed by inauthentic performers so as to entertain or manipulate an audience. *Proclamation* reminds us that preaching has something to announce, namely, the kerygmatic word of hope found in Jesus Christ and through the promises of the Christian and

---

the Glory: Incarnation through the Arts (Grand Rapids: Baker Academic, 2001); and *Musical Theology* (Grand Rapids: Eerdmans, 2007).

3. Begbie, *Theology, Music and Time*, 93.

4. See, for example, Mike Graves, *The Sermon as Symphony* (Valley Forge, PA: Judson, 1997); and Kirk Byron Jones, *The Jazz of Preaching* (Nashville: Abingdon, 2004).

5. David Buttrick, "Proclamation," in *Concise Encyclopedia of Preaching*, ed. William H. Willimon and Richard Lischer (Louisville: Westminster John Knox, 1995), 385.

6. Ibid.

Hebrew Scriptures. Proclamation is in the indicative mood;[7] it announces some important ideas. As David Buttrick says, proclamation underscores "the character of the gospel as news, good news of a new state of affairs in our world."[8] If preaching is announcement of God's love for humankind, it cannot afford to be done poorly. The oft-cited crisis in preaching today[9] suggests all too strongly that many preachers do perform their work ineptly on a regular basis. To be a "preacher" today has come to imply a certain laziness, an attitude that nothing crucial is at stake in sermonic discourse; preachers appear to be living illustrations of the irrelevance of the spoken word.[10] More than ever, then, preachers need—as each author in this book will argue—every good technique at their disposal to bring the good news of Jesus Christ to bear on the lives of people. In proclamation, as in newscasting, theatrics may be employed in urgent service to breaking news. (Of course, *techniques* is a friendlier word than *theatrics*.) The breaking news for preaching is the powerful in-breaking of God's love on the world. Proclamation embraces the urgency of preaching and opens us to the use of techniques that best enable us in our *good news* casting. As Charles Bartow reminds us, "it is imperative that we attend to [God's] self-disclosure with all the means appropriate to it."[11]

The second false assumption that proclamation helps address is that preaching is a negative and dismissible enterprise. "Do not preach to me," a person will say, or we may complain that someone is speaking in a "preachy tone." Such comments imply that preaching is inseparable from judgmentalism.[12] The term *proclamation* does not bear this legalistic connotation. Because it

---

7. Paul Scherer, *The Word God Sent* (New York: Harper & Row, 1965), xi. See also Charles L. Bartow, *God's Human Speech* (Grand Rapids: Eerdmans, 1997), 129.

8. Buttrick, "Proclamation," 385.

9. See, for example, *What's the Matter with Preaching Today?* ed. Mike Graves (Louisville: Westminster John Knox, 2004); and Ron Boyd-MacMillan, *Explosive Preaching: Letters on Detonating the Gospel in the 21st Century* (Waynesboro, GA: Paternoster, 2006).

10. "Our age has more regard for the artist than for the orator," reports Eddie Gibbs, *Church Next: Quantum Changes in How We Do Ministry* (Downers Grove, IL: InterVarsity, 2000), 26.

11. Bartow, *God's Human Speech*, 3. Even Karl Barth, well known for his challenge regarding preaching techniques, knew that a certain artistry is required to bring the Word of God to life. This can be seen by anyone who reads his sermons. He confesses this, as well, in his *Church Dogmatics*: "The sermon demands an orderly language which is appropriate from the standpoint of content as well as expression. Form and content, then, are not to be separated in preaching. The right form is part of the right content." Karl Barth, *Church Dogmatics* (Edinburgh: T&T Clark, 1936), I/1:120.

12. "Judgment without grace," observes Richard Lischer, "has contributed to these entries in *Webster's New International Dictionary*: Preach = 'to exhort in an officious or tiresome manner' and Sermon = 'an annoying harangue.'" *A Theology of Preaching: The Dynamics of the Gospel* (Eugene, OR: Wipf and Stock, 1992), 44.

does not presuppose judgment, proclamation suggests proper distance and balance between pronouncement of the law and the announcement of good news. It indicates, as we shall later discuss, the contour of grace and the inevitable shape of preaching.

There are two additional benefits to be derived from our use of the word *proclamation* in this chapter. *Proclamation* suggests, in a way that *preaching* cannot, that there may be modes of announcing the good news that are not strictly oral discourse. We might acknowledge that a certain song, hymn, or anthem *proclaims* the gospel, whereas it would feel awkward to suggest that these forms *preach* the good news. There are many modes of proclamation, oral discourse being the chief one. Our inquiry here has to do with what might be learned about preaching from another art form, one that can also provide means for proclamation. Proclamation not only implies other modes for announcing the good news, it suggests that they might inform one another and occasionally work together to proclaim the gospel. Finally, proclamation allows us to move beyond another misuse of the word *preaching*. The commonly heard exclamation, "That will preach!" is typically ascribed to the wrong things. It is used in reference to humorous lines and poignant sermon illustrations as opposed to the story of God's love. Only one thing will preach: the promises of God revealed in the Scriptures. All other things are techniques and tools we use in our attempts to proclaim the gospel.[13] Proclamation reminds us that there is something urgent to be proclaimed and only *that* will preach. For these reasons, the words *preaching* and *proclamation* will be used throughout this piece more or less interchangeably.

Preparing, Performing, and Archiving: Activities of Preaching and Music

In preaching, what comes first? Preparation. The classic understanding here is of preaching turning the ink of Scripture into the blood of a human orator[14] before the live gathering of a body of listeners, or, when believers, the living body of Christ. Any homiletical work that precedes delivery of the sermon

13. Karl Barth is well known for his claim that the best preachers can do is *attempt* to proclaim the Word. It becomes proclamation only when the Holy Spirit enters into the work. See Karl Barth, *Homiletics* (Louisville: Westminster John Knox, 1991), 44.

14. Bartow, *God's Human Speech*, 63: "With startling clarity T. S. Eliot indicated what is going on . . . when he remarked that it is the purpose of literature to turn blood into ink. William Brower was no less vivid and on target when he said that the purpose of speaking literature is to turn the ink back into blood. So let it be with the Bible in the pulpit in our Lord's Day worship."

(including the making of a manuscript or pulpit notes and the rehearsal of written material)[15] is preparation for the moment of proclamation.[16]

What comes next? Performance. Preaching, as is well known, is an oral-aural activity essential to the church.[17] No amount of postmodern concern for the slipping place of the spoken word and the rising preeminence of art and moving images in today's culture can supplant the basic mode of proclamation we call preaching. Paul Scherer's conviction from nearly a half century ago still holds: "there is not today, there never has been, and *there never will be* any adequate substitute for preaching."[18]

For preaching to be an oral-aural event, it must be performed.[19] It does not exist merely as thoughts in the mind of a preacher, or words written on a page. Preaching exists only when the preacher's thoughts or written words are brought to life in sound. A preacher's work in his or her study and the work of exegeting a congregation[20] through the pastor's active engagement in ministry are preliminary activities that point toward, but cannot be called preaching. Paul Scott Wilson describes these activities as being on the back side of the "now" of the sermon's delivery. A preliminary but significant aspect of the proclamation of the Word does occur prior to performance as the preacher personally hears the Word proclaimed through his or her study and preparation of the sermon. But the chief moment of proclamation occurs when the preliminary matters give way to the principal matter of delivering the message to God's people. Sermon preparation involves internal, often private work. But preaching is principally a public exercise, an externalization of internal thoughts and activities. Though speaking more generally of all human speech, the way Walter Ong has described this process holds well for preaching. He said that speech is "an inwardness that is simultaneously an utterance or

15. For preachers committed to what is variably called textual, scriptural, biblical, or expository preaching, these preliminary matters consist of prayer, first reading of texts, reflection and meditation on the texts, technical reading of texts, exegesis of context (congregational, local, national, and global), construction of sermonic theme and logic, writing of the sermon, rewriting of the material, and vocal and physical rehearsal of the message. Needless to say, these activities are not a single night's work.

16. Charles L. Bartow considers the moment of proclamation an event: "Preaching is not just the proclamation of an event—even of The Event; it *is* an event—a happening, an experience. . . . Preaching has to do with what yet may be." *The Preaching Moment* (Nashville: Abingdon, 1980), 18.

17. See Clyde Fant, *Preaching for Today* (New York: Harper & Row, 1975), 112–26; Bartow, *The Preaching Moment*, 103; and Bartow, *God's Human Speech*, 3.

18. Scherer, *The Word God Sent*, xi, italics added.

19. Richard Ward, *Speaking from the Heart: Preaching with Passion* (Nashville: Abingdon, 1992), 76–77.

20. See Leonora Tubbs Tisdale, *Preaching as Local Theology and Folk Art* (Minneapolis: Fortress, 1997), 56–90.

'outerance' or 'outering.'"[21] Until the inward thoughts and preparation of the preacher are uttered (outered), the sermon does not exist.

And what comes next? Archiving. Any transcribing of a sermon (including saving a manuscript or notes from the performance) constitutes a librarian activity: collection, storage, retrieval, and distribution for later use. As Eugene Lowry and others have noted, a sermon manuscript is the corpse of a sermon that once lived.[22] There may be many good reasons for archiving sermons. But they are not preaching's purpose. Again, archiving reaches inward. It retrieves that which was uttered (outered) and pulls it back for private use. It is an activity that follows preaching's main, external activity.

If preaching is the performance of the Word of God, then what of Scripture itself? Is the written record of the biblical text also to be considered mere archiving? Stephen Webb, a keen expositor of Karl Barth's theology, shows that, like Luther, Barth would consider the written word of Scripture secondary to oral proclamation of it. Quoting Barth, Webb says: "Barth anticipates performance theories of interpretation when he argues that, for Scripture, 'the writing is obviously not primary, but secondary. It is itself the deposit of what was once proclamation by human lips.'" Webb concludes, "It is the sound of Scripture that saves us, not its appearance on the printed page."[23]

The point in seeing preaching as two internal sets of activities surrounding one external activity is that performance of the Word is the central and culminating element of proclamation. The sermon does not consist of preparation, but surely emerges from it. The manuscript or pulpit notes are not the sermon, but indicators of its language and logic. They are clues to a performance but cannot contain the moods, rhythms, inflections, and physicalities of the sermon event. The later use of a sermon's written or audio/video record—for evaluation, publication, meditation, as a repository for illustrations, or as the recycling of previous work—is devotional at best and academic at most.

The truth of this, however apparent, is brought into sharper relief when we see how the aural presentation of music demonstrates a theological and homiletical idea: some things fully exist only when brought to life in the world of sound. We find this idea captured in the very first part of the kerygmatic

21. Walter Ong, *The Presence of the Word* (Minneapolis: University of Minnesota Press, 1981), 309.

22. See Marguerite Shuster's chapter in this book, "The Truth and Truthfulness: Theological Reflections on Preaching and Performance."

23. Stephen H. Webb, *The Divine Voice: Christian Proclamation and the Theology of Sound* (Grand Rapids: Brazos, 2004), 177. Walter Ong would agree: "The greater reality of words and sound is seen . . . in the paradox that sound conveys meaning more powerfully and accurately than sight. If words are written, they are on the whole far more likely to be misunderstood than spoken words are." Ong, *Presence of the Word*, 115.

message, where it is recorded that God created all things through sound: God said, "let there be light" (Gen. 1:1). When we consider the creation of music, we find that within the process of composition resides a present echo of original creation.

Creation as Outward Expression

Before there was any created order, there was God (Gen. 1:1) who, in some divine way, thought of a universe. It came to be only when God spoke. The compositional idea of cosmos came into existence as the Creator performed those thoughts through spoken word. While this is clearly metaphor—human attempts at description of impossibly removed concepts and events—the Scriptures enforce this anthropomorphism of holy Word and exalt it to the level of doctrine. Jesus was the Word, Scripture tells us, who was with God in the beginning (John 1:1–3). An equation is drawn in Scripture between God's first spoken Word in Genesis and the Word of John's Gospel.[24] Stephen Webb captures this equation by saying that "Jesus is God's natural voice."[25] He says further that "the idea that God speaks means not only that Jesus Christ was the voice of God in the incarnation but that the very same Jesus Christ has always been God's voice."[26] This doctrine of God's utterance is pushed even further in the writings of Paul where he proclaims that it is through ongoing proclamation of the Word that creatures are brought to faith ("So faith comes from what is heard, and what is heard comes through the word of Christ," [Rom. 10:17] and made to be new creations in Christ [2 Cor. 5:17]).[27] Whatever the godly thoughts or compositional ideas (to extend the anthropomorphic figure) that existed prior to creation, they were merely preparation for the utterance that became creation. When God spoke, it was a performative Word, accomplishing precisely that which it articulated.[28] Creation occurred when God's thoughts were given utterance, or outward expression in sound.

24. This equation is noted as a tenet of faith: "Christians believe," says Stephen Webb, "that the voice that created the world is the same voice that sustains and saves it, so that the history of sound, as it is orchestrated by God, has a vocal richness that harmonizes every dissonant note." Webb, *Divine Voice*, 15.

25. Ibid., 69–72.

26. Ibid., 196.

27. Stephen Webb summarizes the doctrine this way: "God can do anything God wants, but according to the Bible, God ordinarily chooses to accomplish the work of salvation through the spoken word." Ibid., 167.

28. *Performative* is used here in the sense developed by J. L. Austin in *How to Do Things with Words* (Cambridge, MA: Harvard University Press, 1975). For an explanation of how this term applies to preaching, see both John Rottman's essay in this book, "Performative Language

Moreover, creation was not complete until, in its final scene (Gen. 1:26–31), God created humankind. The creative process was not fulfilled until God had made someone to receive it. With its reception came its care, what we call stewardship. Humans, though creative, were not able to add anything material to creation (procreation merely redistributes existing molecules), but they did become the archivists, those who saw to the careful use and perpetuation of the God-breathed document we call the cosmos.

The Genesis account of creation has left its trace in the process of creating music. Again, humans create nothing material in composing music. Sounds merely play with the movement and placement of existing molecules. But musical composition contains an echo of the pattern of divine creation. It begins with the private, internal reflection of a composer and proceeds through stages of composition. But music comes fully into being only when it is played, externalized, and received by some audience.[29]

Music as Externalized Activity

Music making, or "musicking," as Christopher Small coins it,[30] consists of many activities, and some of them are quite internal. Thinking musical thoughts, exploring musical ideas that might lead to composing, musical composition and arranging, even musical practice involve internally oriented activities. They occur in the mind of individuals, in the private creative activities of selection and evaluation of musical symbols, or in the nonpublic rehearsal of musical works. While these activities are important for the creation of music, they do not exist for themselves. They are merely preparation. They occur as prelude to music's primary function: performance. This is music's key external quality. The internal activities exist for the sake of the external. "Performance," Small observes, "does not exist in order to present musical works, but rather, musical works exist in order to give performers something to perform."[31]

We can even go so far as to say that music, as an entity, is merely an abstract concept *until* it is externalized. Music does not concretely exist as musical

and the Limits of Performance in Preaching," and Clayton J. Schmit, *Too Deep for Words: A Theology of Liturgical Expression* (Louisville: Westminster John Knox, 2002).

29. Roger Scruton explains the purpose behind the composition of music: "The composer's intention is not to produce a pattern of sounds, but to create a living musical movement. Even when writing for himself, the composer is writing for an audience: for music is the intentional object of human experience, and exists only as heard." *The Aesthetics of Music* (Oxford: Oxford University Press, 1997), 451.

30. Christopher Small, *Musicking: The Meanings of Performing and Listening* (Hanover, NH: Wesleyan University Press, 1998), 11.

31. Ibid., 8.

thoughts in the mind of a composer or performer. It does not exist as musical notation in a score. It does not exist as a musician manually executing fingerings on an instrument or blowing noiselessly into a horn or miming the bow movements on a violin. It exists only when it is performed (rehearsal performance is to be included in this distinction, for the act of playing for practice still brings the music to aural life). Moreover, performance implies musical execution (playing or singing) *and* hearing. Music cannot be said to occur unless it is heard, for that is its purpose and its fulfillment.[32] As Gordon Graham says, "music has to be heard; no other grasp of its content is possible."[33] Listening to music is part of music's externalization. The flow of activity is from inward to outward: typically, music is conceived in the mind of a composer, conveyed by means of notation and score to a performer, practiced and learned through rehearsal, performed at some point for one or more persons (even if the musicians play only for themselves), and heard by that audience. Its being received is the ultimate condition of music's externalization.

We often refer to a musical score as the music itself. "This is wrong," says Peter Hill. "Scores set down musical information, some of it exact, some of it approximate, together with indications of how this information may be interpreted."[34] But scores and sheet music are merely archives of musical ideas. Roger Scruton, in his magnificent study *The Aesthetics of Music*, puts it simply: "Performance is the art of translating *instructions* to produce certain sounds into an organization of tones."[35]

There appear to be clear parallels between God's creation of the cosmos and the human creation of music. But the parallels are more than mere analogy. They are traces of the very nature of creativity captured in a human way through the composition of music, and reflective of what is called for in the

32. Francis Sparshott is helpful here, especially in response to those who argue that music does not require an audience: "The simplest and most obvious way of specifying the end and means of music is to say that it exists to provide something to listen to, and does so by specifying ways of providing sounds for listening. This cannot be got round by the fashionable device of saying that music exists to be performed and not heard . . . because the only straightforward way of specifying what is performed, or what differentiates a musical performance from other forms of physical exercise, is that it is the production of a sequence of sounds and silences, and sounds exist only for the ear, which in this case is presumably an attentive and therefore listening ear, whether or not what one attends to is what one is doing oneself." Francis Sparshott, "Aesthetics of Music: Limits and Grounds," in *What Is Music? An Introduction to the Philosophy of Music*, ed. Philip Alperson (University Park: Pennsylvania State University Press, 1994), 51.

33. Gordon Graham, "Music and Mission," an unpublished paper presented for the Music and Theology Colloquium, January 29–February 1, 2004, Ely, England.

34. Peter Hill, "From Score to Sound," in *Musical Performance: A Guide to Understanding*, ed. John Rink (Cambridge: Cambridge University Press, 2002), 129.

35. Scruton, *Aesthetics of Music*, 441, italics added.

process of proclamation. Some things exist only when brought to life in the world of sound. Creation is one of them. Music and preaching are others.

By noting these echoes of divine creativity in music, we are drawn to see more clearly some homiletical ideas. First, understanding the creative process in relation to music releases us from the false assumption that preaching, as a thing made for an aural world, can be made without adequate preparation. In music, bringing notes or words to life in a composition process calls for the composer first to see a text or idea worth setting, and then to select according to the "logical rightness and necessity of expression"[36] those aural symbols that most adequately express the idea. Bringing them to life in rehearsal involves the performer(s) applying critical revisions (reworking of interpretation, phrasing, breathing, and so forth) that make for the most adequate performance of the piece. These preparatory activities of perception, selection, revision,[37] and rehearsal are not the musical event, or at least not the main event. Yet they are critical to the successful performance of the piece.

This is instructive for preachers and an especially good reminder for those whose habits become lax. Effective proclamation, as an outward, performative event, relies on preachers who prepare in appropriate ways for the preaching moment. All of the elements that we have identified as preparation above are necessary to the occasion of delivery. They are not incidental nor beside the point of preaching. They are the necessary base on which a meaningful sermon event is constructed. Certainly God can make use of careless work and can turn inept attempts to good purpose. That is God's prerogative. As Webb reminds us above, "God can do anything God wants" (see n. 27). It is hard to conceive, however, that it is God's desire to call preachers to the urgent task of proclamation, only to be satisfied with the work of those who shirk preparation and rely solely on the imagination in the preaching moment.[38] God clearly intends to inspire the work preachers do in the study as well as that which takes place in the pulpit. There are some gifted preachers who can proclaim the Word effectively as an instance of spontaneous spiritual gift. We have heard of a few: Peter was one; Paul another. There may be others. Peter Storey tells that as a young preacher, he had the gift to extemporize sermons brilliantly with little or no preparation. As he relied overly on this gift, Storey reports, God revoked

---

36. Susanne K. Langer, *Feeling and Form* (New York: Charles Scribner's Sons, 1953), 39.

37. The aspects of creativity are explored with regard to the writing of sermons in Schmit, *Too Deep for Words*, 96–114.

38. When asked why she always preaches from a manuscript, Barbara Brown Taylor remarked, "I may diverge [from the manuscript] but I have a wild imagination and when I let that go in the pulpit, I am usually sorry." Gateway Films, *Great Preachers: Barbara Brown Taylor*, Odyssey Productions, 1977.

it. He is a highly successful preacher today, but it is always a matter of arduous preparation.[39] Like Storey, some may have spiritual gifts for communication, but preachers should not assume too great a connection between apostolic gifts and the yeoman gifts required for faithful proclamation.

The second thing we learn from understanding the process of creativity as it relates to aural things is this: that which is brought fully to life in the world of sound must be received by some audience in order to reach its completion and fulfillment. God spoke the universe into being for the delight and care of humankind. Music is created to be played and to be perceived. Sermons are written to be preached and heard. The urgency of proclamation is not satisfied in the creation of written materials. However useful devotional artifacts may be, faith comes—as Paul, Luther, Barth, and others have argued—through hearing. Preparation and archiving without reception through performance make for empty activities; they create a vehicle that fails to deliver its contents.

We discover a third homiletical insight in examining the process of musical production. What preparation and archiving describe is not something static, but a spontaneous event that changes with each performance. The presence of an audience, its level of responsiveness, the type and size of performance space, the idiosyncrasies of the instrument (less for a violinist who brings her own instrument to a performance than for a pianist who does not), the technique and preparation of fellow musicians, the impulsive nature of musical interpretation, and consideration of many more issues make each performance unique and appropriate to the moment. A musician's preparation and use of a score provide a template for a given performance.[40] Habits of execution are developed that bring notation to life. But humans are not automatons, and no habitual behavior is a precise duplication of a previous action. Habits allow us to select actions appropriate to the moment, to improvise (as we will consider below) in such a way that a successful performance proceeds, regardless of shifting circumstances.

Preachers also need to acquire good habits that lead to successful performance. Here too, preparation and manuscript or sermon notes provide the general contour of proclamation. The well-rehearsed preacher will be able to bring the sermon to life in appropriate ways each time the sermon is delivered. The dialogical nature of preaching demands that the speaker be attentive to

39. Peter Storey is a former bishop of the Methodist Church in South Africa and was a principal voice in the struggle against apartheid. See his book for examples of sermons he preached during that period: *With God in the Crucible* (Nashville: Abingdon, 2002).

40. See Stefan Reid, "Preparing for Performance," in *Musical Performance*, ed. John Rink, 102.

the audience and its shifting response so that the message can be adjusted, improvised, and received successfully by the listeners.

The habits of successful preachers are learned through the training of one's mind, body, and voice. They are informed, as well, by careful attention to the use of the preaching environment, including pulpit, microphone, pulpit materials, chancel space, and so forth. These habits are honed through periods of training and practice, as well as through the practice of each sermon. Sometimes, good preaching habits can be acquired by observing the work of others and borrowing techniques that might inform our own performances. Preachers may borrow good techniques from other preachers, but also from performers in other art forms. To use the techniques of theater or musical performance in the pulpit is not to be false or imitative. It is to acknowledge that other performers know things that preachers should know.[41] Though we may borrow techniques, even theatrics, from others, they become ours through practice, in the same way that a guitar player learns flat-picking techniques from a teacher and practices them until they are a part of the guitarist's own style and range of skill.

The issue of habit brings us to our second area of investigation. The question What comes next? has to do not only with the broad movements of preparation, performance, and archiving. It has to do with a performer's habits that release music's qualities of inevitability and anticipation.

Inevitability and Anticipation in Musical Performance

How does a musician know, when bringing a piece of music to life, what comes next? Through knowledge of music's conventions, a performer acquires a sense of musical inevitability and a corresponding sense of anticipation regarding where the music needs to go. One of the most basic conventions, for example, is that a dominant seventh chord wants to resolve to a tonic chord (the strong five-one impulse).[42] At the end of a hymn, the harmonization of a

41. Jana Childers indicates the value of preachers learning from other performers in a chapter titled "What Actors Know," in *Performing the Word: Preaching as Theatre* (Nashville: Abingdon, 1998), 99–117.

42. For those unfamiliar with the canons of music theory, a brief explanation: Western music theory is based on harmonies built on the eight tones (an octave) of the musical scale. The notes in a C major scale, for example, are C, D, E, F, G, A, B, with a return to C as the eighth tone (the white keys on a piano). The first (and last) tone is called the *tonic*, or home tone. The fifth tone is called the *dominant*, since it is the most dominant sounding tone after the tonic. Chords are typically constructed as triads, two notes added in harmony to a first. For example, in the key of C major, the tonic chord consists of the first, third, and fifth notes in the scale, namely C, E, and G. The dominant chord is built on G, with B and D added. There

concluding "Amen" is constrained by another convention: the plagal cadence, where the subdominant chord resolves to the tonic (four-one).[43] The most basic convention in Western music is this: as the end of a piece approaches, both performer and audience know that it is not finished until the final tonic is sounded. It is anticipated by all; it is inevitable. If this convention is upset, something surprising is heard and the music will sound novel or incomplete. Why are Peter Schickele's fictitious P. D. Q. Bach compositions funny? They play on the expectations of musical convention and surprise us with changes that upset them. All of Western music is the unfolding of conventions: from the sequencing of chords, to the chord substitutions of jazz, to the use of the tone row and its inversion,[44] to J. S. Bach's use of numerology in his melismatic[45] sequences, to the ABA shape of the sonata allegro form.[46] All music is built on conventions that create a sense of inevitability which in turn advances a sense of anticipation in the performance. The performer, by knowing musical convention and how it applies (or is violated within a given piece of music), knows what comes next, what follows that, and how a piece goes on from

---

is a natural musical inclination for the dominant chord to be followed by, or be resolved to, the tonic. This is the *five-one resolution*. This is such a strong impulse that people totally unfamiliar with music theory will hear the need for the tonic to follow the dominant. This is heightened when a fourth note is added to the dominant chord for suspense. By adding a note seven steps above the dominant we create a *dominant seventh chord* (G, B, D, and F in the key of C major). This chord not only leans toward the tonic, but insists on being resolved to the tonic. Any ear familiar with any form of Western music will hear this necessity and note a mistake or oddity in the music if it is violated. There is a charming anecdote which tells that the students of J. S. Bach would succeed in getting him out of bed in the morning by loudly playing a *dominant seventh chord* on the organ and fleeing. Bach would be so disturbed by the lack of resolution that he would spring from his bed, rush to the organ, and play the corresponding *tonic chord* to resolve the lingering tension.

43. In the key of C major, the fourth tone, F, is the subdominant. It is the next most prominent note after the tonic and dominant. Musical custom has determined that hymns conclude with an "Amen" that is accompanied by two chords, the subdominant to tonic resolution, the four-one, or so-called plagal cadence. Again, the convention is so strong that if a hymn were concluded by a five-one "Amen," even the untutored listener would hear it as a mistake.

44. The tone row is a technique used by twentieth-century composers who felt restricted by the typical conventions of music theory. They began to construct compositions around other conventions, including the more or less random assignment of notes to a compositional row of tones. Using the twelve tones (all white and black piano keys) in a given octave, they would establish a row, then have it played in inversion, reversion, and so on. This is one of the conventions of "atonal" music.

45. A musical melisma is a succession of quickly moving tones within a musical phrase, usually set to a single sung syllable in vocal music. For example, "Alleluia" might be set in a musical phrase with several notes assigned to the first syllable and a single note for the others, as in "A-a-a-a-a-a-lle-lu-ia."

46. "Sonata allegro" is the term used to describe the most common symphonic compositional form.

there. The performer thinks ahead, as does a good chess player, and knows intuitively that the body must perform by habit the next note, chord, riff, or expression because what is anticipated is that which has a certain inevitability. For concert music, what is inevitable is the unfolding pattern of forms, notes, and expressions that the composer has orchestrated and indicated in the score.

For jazz, what is inevitable is that which conventionally belongs to a given performance style. Dixieland jazz has different conventions than fusion jazz and progressive jazz. Within each genre, however, there is a set of improvisational expectations that the performer learns and applies as the music unfolds. The jazz improviser knows the harmonic structure of a piece and what can be played upon it. The player feels the tonal shape of the music, anticipates the moves of the harmony, and builds a structure of sound upon it. It will be different each time, yet distinctively similar each time.[47] The jazz musician is committed to the belief that "there are always a million and one ways" to play a melody.[48] Jazz conventions indicate which variations fall within conventional range. To push beyond those expectations—to play the melody inverted, for example, or to slip beyond an established tonality—would be to push the melody beyond recognition. It may still be acceptable as some form of jazz, but it is not anticipated by all jazz conventions.

There is a sense of anticipation and inevitability in listening to music as well. For the listener, the anticipation may be understood in a general way insofar as the listener is familiar with the musical idiom being performed. There may be the expectation that a symphony will unfold in four movements. (Those unfamiliar with the symphonic conventions may find themselves embarrassed when they applaud between movements.) Or the listener will know, by virtue of repeated exposure to the form, that music in the blues idiom conventionally unfolds to a repeating twelve-bar chord progression.[49] Even if the listener is untutored in music theory, he or she will anticipate the shape of the blues, know that certain qualities within it are inevitable, and be surprised (if not annoyed) if the conventions are violated. In cases where the listener has great familiarity with a piece, such as Handel's *Messiah*, the listener knows the inevitable shape of each movement and will receive each part with anticipation.

47. I once had the opportunity to perform with celebrated jazz saxophonist Terry Herrington (known best as the saxophone voice of Lisa on the television show *The Simpsons*). After one particularly beautiful improvisation in rehearsal, I noted that it was a shame we couldn't have captured it by recording or in notation. Herrington humbly remarked, "That's okay. The next one will be just as good." And it was.

48. Jones, *Jazz of Preaching*, 83.

49. The basic 12-bar blues progression in the key of C, for example, would consist of these chords: C, C, C, C7, F7, F7, C, C, G7, F7, C, C.

There is, in most cases, a sense of joy in hearing familiar pieces unfold as expected. If it were not the case, musicians would only play novel music and the recording industry would dissolve.

By what means does the musician acquire the ability to play the inevitable and anticipate its necessity? This comes through long periods of practice and the acquisition of appropriate habits. What Samuel Wells says about the formation of habits in theater performance holds equally well for musicians. Through practice, performers achieve a sense of "relaxed awareness." In such a state, they can create an instinctive and appropriate response to that which leads up to each given moment. In the theater setting, the habits of relaxed awareness function in this way:

> There is trust and respect for oneself and the other actors. There is alertness and attention. There is fitness and engagement. There is an understanding of narrative—of what is an end and what is a beginning of a scene or story. There is an ability to keep the narrative going and to explore a situation. . . . There is an aptitude for . . . sensing the shape of the story.[50]

In musical performance, similar qualities apply. There is knowledge of one's instrument and trust of one's fellow performers. There are alertness, engagement, an understanding of the narrative shape of the music, what constitutes a beginning and an end, and the aptitude for keeping the music going. "A person with skills of this kind has gained them through years of training."[51] These considerations are especially important in the case of improvisation. Though improvisation "is perceived to be about spontaneity," Wells reminds us, "[it] is in fact about years of experiments. It . . . is about long preparation before following instinct. . . . This state of readiness, the alertness that comes from years of disciplined preparation, is the condition to which improvisers aspire."[52]

The relaxed awareness to which musical performers aspire comes about through the creation of habits of the mind and body. These habits allow for music to be learned in three ways. Aaron Williamon describes them: First, they acquire an aural memory, whereby performers "hear compositions in the 'mind's ear,'" enabling them to "anticipate upcoming events in the score and make concurrent evaluations of a performance's progress." Second, there is a visual memory that impresses notational images on the "mind's eye" of the performer. Third, performers acquire a kinesthetic memory, that is, "finger,

---

50. Samuel Wells, *Improvisation: The Drama of Christian Ethics* (Grand Rapids: Brazos, 2004), 80.
51. Ibid., 81.
52. Ibid., 80.

muscular or tactile memory," which "enables performers to execute notes automatically."[53] These kinds of memory provide the musician with the capacity to know where one is in a given musical moment and where the music needs to go. The ear receives the current harmonic structure and instinctually anticipates where it is headed. The eye sees the music, or the mind's eye recalls it, and the mind anticipates which notes and expressions are to follow. The hands and body experience the articulation of a given moment and anticipate how next to move as a matter of habit.[54]

Inevitability and Anticipation in Preaching

We find, in considering the inevitability of music, that there are qualities that musicians and listeners anticipate. This sense of musical expectation also applies to preaching, where anticipation takes on theological significance and informs the way sermons are prepared and performed.

In preaching, there is a certain theological anticipation and inevitability to the shaping of a sermon. Unless a sermon is to be perceived as "preachy," it will present a natural unfolding of the logic of salvation. The sermon will have the same shape as the structure of the scriptural record: fall and redemption. The fact of sin leads, in Scripture, inevitably toward the necessity that God will provide a means by which to reconcile humankind. The structure of salvation, whereby God gives God's self to atone for human sin, creates a gravitational force of grace that pulls those caught in the fall, or free fall of sin, toward itself. This is the great "five-one impulse" of the law and the gospel. As a dominant seventh played as the penultimate chord in a piece of music leans toward and wants to capitulate to the tonic, so the declaration of the law leans toward the inevitability of grace and wants to capitulate to its resolving power.

The proper balancing of the judgment and gospel tones in preaching is a theological convention. The naming of sin must be followed by the pronouncement of grace. This is the divine dialectic[55] that all preaching

53. Williamon here follows Edwin Hughes, who has identified in performers the qualities of aural, visual, and kinesthetic memory. Aaron Williamon, "Memorising Music," in Rink, *Musical Performance*, 118–19.

54. The learning of the patterns of this instinctual hand/body behavior are explored in fascinating detail in David Sudnow's *Ways of the Hand: The Organization of Improvised Conduct* (Cambridge, MA: MIT Press, 1993), a study in which he describes the process of learning to play jazz on the piano. His work has been mined for theological insight by Begbie in *Theology, Music and Time*, 224–33.

55. Lischer, *A Theology of Preaching*, 33–43.

announces. While there are few liturgical principles that are universal these days, there is at least one: if people are to be convicted of their sin, a statement of forgiveness must follow. Confession and absolution cannot be separated. This, as Gerhard Forde insists, is what preaching must announce: "A sermon does indeed include explaining, exegeting, and informing, but ultimately it must get around to and aim at a doing, an actual pronouncing, declaring, giving of the gift. In proclaiming the Word, our goal is *absolution*, the doing of the deed that ends the old and begins the new."[56] After a preacher articulates the human condition, what comes next? Announcement of the gospel.

This does not mean that sermons are prohibited from improvising on these themes. They can be stated in as many ways as there are preachers, multiplied by the number of occasions on which they preach. *Every* sermon needs to be a fresh structuring of this motif. But each sermon will express a version of this dialectic or it will not be *actio divina*, the kerygmatic Word that God self-performs through the speech of a preacher.[57] As Peter Storey once said, "Before you preach your sermon, read through it. If it does not contain good news, tear it up!" When the sermon takes liberty with this convention, it becomes something other than proclamation. It may be a lecture, a pop psychology pep talk, a religious essay, or a list of the old "Helpful Hints for Hurtful Habits."[58] Even when the sermon attempts to expound a biblical text, it can still lose its way and defy the theological convention of balancing the law tone with the gospel. In *A Theology of Preaching*, Richard Lischer identifies seven confusions of the law and gospel that are found in preaching. One of them, "judgment without grace," is described this way:

> The incessant launching of lightning bolts from the pulpit gives God a bad name. It exalts what the Reformers called God's "alien work," that of condemnation, to a position of unwarranted superiority. This kind of preaching tries to accomplish with the law what only the gospel can do. It scares the hell out of people, but fails to scare them into heaven. . . . When it falls upon receptive hearts, the preaching of judgment without grace produces sheer terror.[59]

Our goal in preaching is not to produce terror, but to instill hope; to create a hearing in which the good news can do its transforming work on receptive hearts.

56. Gerhard O. Forde, *Theology Is for Proclamation* (Minneapolis: Fortress, 1990), 149–50, italics added.
57. Bartow, *God's Human Speech*, 3.
58. Scherer, *The Word God Sent*, 5.
59. Lischer, *A Theology of Preaching*, 43–44.

A strong preaching habit is needed in order to meet this theological convention. Those learning to preach often struggle to get it right. "At least half the sermons I hear," says Lischer, "are moralistic. These sermons usually preach Jesus-our-example and think that by mentioning his good behavior they have preached the gospel."[60] The task of the preacher in training is to acquire the theological habit of knowing the inevitable shape of grace. Like music that ends on the tonic, or home tone, preachers need to learn that sermons must find their end in the home tone of God's love. (One might even say that grace is the "tonic" for sin.) The task of the practicing preacher is to exercise regularly the habits of announcing inevitable grace. During the period of preparation, the preacher knows, anticipates, that the message wants to give way to the gravitational pull of the good news. When it does not, it can create terror, or confusion, or moralism, or sentimentalism, or any number of substitutions for the message that God's people anticipate they will hear from the pulpit.

What does the listener anticipate the sermon will be? "People listen to preaching only when they are convinced that it is the Word of God," says Lischer.[61] The listener anticipates the inevitable shape of God's story. The good news is to be expected when the law has been articulated. The more clearly a preacher describes the fallen state of the audience's world, the more intently the listeners wait for and need to hear the corresponding announcement of God's love. The old fire-and-brimstone message may have its place, but it creates a strong anticipation of theological resolution. When it does not resolve according to theological convention, it merely confuses people and may even scare the hell out of them.

In addition to the sense of inevitability and anticipation in theological convention that guides the shaping of a sermon, these qualities also come into play during the performance of the sermon. What comes next in the "now" of the delivery? Like musicians, preachers learn habits that guide them as they bring static words on paper to life in the hearing of the church.

A state of readiness and preparedness, what Wells calls relaxed awareness, is achieved by preachers who have learned the habits of performance and who have worked, reworked, and rehearsed their messages. At this stage, they achieve an internalization of the sermon which allows for it to be outered in a lively way.[62]

As in performing music, there are various kinds of memory involved in the internalization of a sermon. They include, as noted above, aural, visual,

60. Ibid., 45.
61. Ibid., 48.
62. For the development of a "lively" kind of preaching, see Jana Childers, "Toward a Lively Homiletic," in *Performing the Word*, 15–35.

and kinesthetic memory. In preparing to deliver a sermon, the preacher hears the sound of his or her voice, learns how to pace the rhythms, how to shape inflections, where to place pauses, how to articulate phrases, and so forth. Just as there is no substitute for learning a piece of music without externalizing it through singing or playing, so the preacher needs to speak the sermon aloud in practice to work out its oral expression and attach it to one's aural memory.

The visual memory of performing music is also critical for preachers. One expects not merely to read aloud from the sermon manuscript or notes. To do more requires that the eye acquire the habit of seeing more. When a person reads aloud, the eye follows the text at the pace of speech. The eye is prepared to move more quickly, but is slowed by the habit of staying with the pace of the oral presentation. A better habit for preachers is to practice using the eye to scan blocks of material. Repeated practice will allow for entire portions of prepared material to come to mind from a mere glance. Another key to the use of visual memory can be learned from the performance of music. Musicians usually mark their scores with cues indicating their rehearsal decisions. Play more boldly here, breathe at the end of this phrase, wait for the conductor there, and so forth. Having worked such matters out in rehearsal, it would be ridiculous for musicians to take clean copies of the score into the performance. They rely on the marked copy so that at a glance the eye can see both the notes to be played and the cues as to their articulation. Likewise, the preacher is advised to bring the rehearsal copy of the sermon notes or text into the pulpit. By the time of performance, the manuscript may be well marked with cues as to pace, gesture, pause, inflection, and changes in wording. If the preacher gives in to the temptation to type all rehearsal revisions into a clean copy of the sermon, pagination will change and blocks of material will shift from one place on a page to another. To preach from a clean copy is to neutralize one of the preacher's chief tools for knowing what comes next in the performance: visual memory.

Likewise, kinesthetic memory is critical for the preacher who internalizes the sermon. Part of the performance of preaching comes in blocking one's body movements. Again, the preacher does not stand and read statically, but hopes to do a number of things with the body. Practice will determine where one looks (at the audience, at the pulpit notes, or at some other point in space to cast a thought or an image). It will also help the preacher work out matters concerning whether and when to walk about, where and how to gesture, how to negotiate the space of the chancel or the pulpit, and so on. The kinesthetic memory will be brought into play only when the sermon has been well prepared through bringing it physically and aurally to life. Reading through the manuscript in one's study is a good practice, but it is not the final practice for preachers who have internalized their message. Standing and speaking the sermon aloud is the only way to find certain kinds of problems with the text, to test the sound of the written language and adjust it for spoken communication, and to exercise the development of kinesthetic memory.

There is an additional kind of memory that preachers rely on. This is similar to the memory that a composer can rely on when the composer is the performer of his or her own work. The very practice of weighing musical ideas and making selections from among them creates a memory that informs the performance of the music. The preacher, in nearly all cases, is composing a work that he or she personally expects to bring to life. The preacher's knowledge of what comes next in the delivery of the sermon is aided by having carefully determined what comes next in the study.

Conclusion

What comes next? It is a critical question in musical performance and in preaching. We have seen how an understanding of what comes next in music is both instructive for those who preach and a source for deriving a theological and homiletical principle: preaching exists only when it is brought to life in the aural world. While many will argue that to discuss performance in relation to preaching is to reduce homiletics to the study of theatrics and entertainment, we have attempted to demonstrate the power of interdisciplinary research for uncovering new ways to understand the power of proclamation and the means by which to bring it to life. Performance studies generally, and particularly our study of musical performance here, have demonstrated that issues relating to the embodiment of the Word are not beside the point of preaching, but critical to its fulfillment. If preaching does not exist until it is externalized, then it is imperative that preachers learn to know and exercise what other performers know. Without acquisition of performance techniques, preaching is flat, dull, and in the worse case, stillborn, if it fails utterly to come to aural life.

Insights for the Practice of Preaching

1. Practice what you preach. This is not meant to be a recitation of an ethical principle. It is, rather, advice for bringing a sermon to life. While many preachers consider their sermon preparation complete when they have crafted an outline, a set of sermon notes, or a manuscript, those who practice the sermon aloud and rehearse physical movements learn that

practicing what you intend to preach is critical to bringing the sermon alive in its most vibrant sense. It allows for the preacher to test the language, hear how the message will sound in the delivery space, learn best how to use electronic amplification equipment, coordinate with artists or technicians in providing illustrative material, become familiar with the pulpit or chancel, choreograph the gestures and movements of the sermon, and so forth.

2. Use the rehearsal copy of your pulpit materials when you preach. It contains visual cues that will guide your delivery. A well-marked copy of a manuscript contains innumerable visual clues to guide the memory and enable an internalized presentation.

3. In preparing each sermon, seek in the biblical text an answer to the question, What is the good news in this pericope? As the sermon develops, ask again, What is the good news in this sermon? If it does not contain some aspect of God's promise, keep praying for guidance, return to the text for insight, and keep writing. Deliver the sermon only when you have found the inevitable grace that proceeds from any announcement of human sin.

4. Whenever possible, discuss performance issues with musicians, actors, broadcasters, speech makers, teachers, mimes, oral interpreters, and other public performers. They can teach preachers things that will improve their writing and delivery of sermons. Practice what they teach. Add to your homiletical technique those things that advance your ability to bring your written words to life. Test your performance of new techniques with the artists in order to learn how to gauge their effect as you employ them in preaching.

11

The Musicality of Black Preaching

Performing the Word

W I L L I A M   C .   T U R N E R   J R .

African American preachers of a previous generation often described preaching by saying you start low, go slow, climb higher, strike fire, then sit down in the storm. The beginning was indeed slow, almost to the point of being torturous. Pauses and silences punctuated the measured cadence. Words were forced into a metric pattern the preacher established to suit his or her person. When done effectively, the effort was authentic and closed the discursive distance between the preacher and the congregation. Often this occurred through the expansion of syllables. In this case there could be several tones corresponding to one syllable, as the preacher pressed to feel the motions of words that transmit the vitality and life of the communication.

The language and cadence of the sermon connected with the congregation. By means of picturesque exegesis, attention to detail, alliteration, illustration, and sometimes storytelling, the congregation was gripped and held in rapt suspense. The inner cultural codes evoked sounds and gestures that amounted to a call-and-response. The congregation became far more than an audience: they were participants in an unfolding drama.

The emotions shared between the congregation and the preacher enabled him or her to "climb higher." Climbing higher amounted to full release of the preacher into the "kairos moment," where preaching becomes a manifestation of power that is sacramental in nature.

As the preacher "climbs higher and strikes fire," the empathy between the preacher and the congregation often brings forth exclamations such as "Yes . . . yes, Lord . . . amen . . . go ahead . . . keep going . . . glory . . . hallelujah," or other, nonverbal responses. The cadence of the preacher's words leaves space for such insertions, which may include "huh" or "ha," sometimes called "hacking." At the same time, it is the congregation's responses that keep the preacher going till the fire strikes.

Striking fire is the moment in which the preacher behaves as if in ecstasy— outside of self, an instrument of the divine. This transformation is typically marked by the intensity of the rhythm and musical tones of the preacher's and the congregation's words. Cadences are clear, meter is explicit. In this moment, preaching breathes in the ether of image, illustration, telling the story, and alliteration. It is nothing less than poetry, laced with images well known from the Scriptures and the experiences of the people. It may even be compared to the chanting of the Psalter, or traditions in which "jubilation" is practiced as an act of worship.

For communities that cherish this way of delivering the Word, this is the moment beyond all others in which preaching is worship—with the mind, spirit, soul, and body. It is embodied worship; it is drama. It is the word "dancing forth" with motions that are not void. This is performance of the Word.

Historically, detractors of black preaching have misunderstood the dynamics and devalued the form as being overly emotional and devoid of reason and theological value. Yet a careful and deep appreciation of black preaching's inherent musical and performative qualities suggests quite the opposite is true and that black preaching is keenly attuned to what is true and reflects Christ, the Word, among us. Six characteristics of preaching in the African American context flesh out this idea: black preaching as music and performance, the pervasive use of music in black preaching, musicality as surplus of meaning in African American preaching, the African tradition of music in African American rhetoric, African American preaching as manifestation of power or *kratophany*, and the relationship between musical preaching in the black community and the fundamental motions of life.

Black Preaching as Music and Performance

In his classic study of "old-time Negro preaching," entitled *Say Amen, Brother*, William Pipes includes a preface by Richard Wright, who describes a preaching moment in the following way:

> The preacher's voice is sweet to us, caressing and lashing, conveying to us a heightening of consciousness that the Lords of the Land would rather keep from us, filling us with a sense of hope that is treasonable to the rule of Queen Cotton. As the sermon progresses, the preacher's voice increases in emotional intensity, and we, in tune and sympathy with his sweeping story, sway in our seats until we have lost all notion of time and have begun to float on a tide of passion. The preacher begins to punctuate his words with sharp rhythms, and we are lifted far beyond the boundaries of our daily lives, and upward and outward, until drunk with our enchanted vision, our senses lifted to the burning skies, we do not know who we are, what we are, or where we are.[1]

Wright's accent here—or at least Pipes's point in highlighting the description in this way—is on the preacher as folk artist, whose main mission is to entertain and to lift listeners to an emotional high. One gets the clear sense from this study that the preacher's listeners are being led on some excursion into not only the transcendent but perhaps even the exotic. Indeed, Pipes goes on to question whether what is being observed is really preaching at all. He views this "old-time" Negro preaching as essentially emotional in appeal and finds little reason, logic, or theological value in it. His view was derived from cultural theorists, especially Franz Boas and Frederick Davenport, who saw black preaching as deriving from primitive (and therefore apparently implicitly inferior!) resources. Boas says, for example, "Lack of logical connections, lack of control of will, are apparently two of [the mind's] fundamental characteristics in primitive society. In the formation of opinions belief takes the place of logical demonstration. The emotional value of opinions is great and consequently they quickly lead to actions."[2] What these ethnographers failed to grasp is that emotion can inspire the intellect, and deep passions can produce associations of permanent value.

A later researcher, Gerald Davis, was critical of the work of Pipes, Boas, and Davenport and drew particular attention to the performance values of black

1. Richard Wright, preface to *Say Amen, Brother! Old-Time Negro Preaching: A Study in American Frustration,* by William Pipes (New York: William-Frederick, 1951), i.
2. Pipes is quoting here from Franz Boas, *The Mind of Primitive Man* (New York: Macmillan, 1938), 98–99; and Frederick M. Davenport, *Primitive Traits in Religious Revivals* (New York: Macmillan, 1905), 14ff.

preaching. Davis invokes the category of the *nommo*, taken from West African culture, to indicate that the spoken word in West African practice is not static. By its very nature, it performs. What is invoked with this image of *nommo* is an oscillating pair that is given as a primordial principle of movement and vitality in the very ordering of the world.[3] By opening his view through the lens of vitality and motion, he was not limited to seeing static propositions alone. Expanding his cultural grid to include an African motif deepened his capacity to comprehend the form he observed.

While an improvement in assessment and analysis over the previous writers, Davis's work ultimately falls short because it fails to take into account the self-understanding of the subjects of his study.[4] What people say of themselves is also empirical data to be taken into consideration for understanding the fullest meaning of performance, and indeed perhaps the primary empirical data. This includes of course also the reflections of the preachers themselves. Whether preaching at a Church of God in Christ, a Missionary Baptist Church, or a Spiritual Temple, what do the preachers consider themselves to be doing? How do they understand the meaning of performance, particularly their performance? For instance, Davis imports the category of fundamentalism to interpret the preaching of the Pentecostal Bishop E. E. Cleveland. He then has to account for preaching that relies on powerful images, rather than on the propositions and arguments of fundamentalist theology. While black Pentecostal preaching is concerned about doctrine, it gives primacy to performing the Word. A similar comment can be made for much of the preaching done in Missionary Baptist churches, which come out of the same spiritual and social soil as the Church of God in Christ. The similarity he observed between preaching in these two settings could have been expected.

It is easy to dismiss image- or performance-based preaching as primitive and less skilled. It is easy, too, to be so caught up in this desire that one forgets, as Davis seems to, that such black preaching performance was taught somewhere by someone. Certainly no performance is done in a vacuum.[5] But how ironic that Davis seems to overlook the fact that the training of "old-time preachers" in the "black belt" was sometimes done by white evangelicals! During the antebellum period, some black Presbyterians had formal mentoring relationships with white pastors to prepare for ordination. Harry Hoosier traveled with Methodist Bishop Francis Asbury, and Andrew Marshall maintained close relations with white Baptists in Georgia. During the postbellum

3. Gerald Davis, *I Got the Word in Me and I Can Sing It, You Know* (Philadelphia: University of Pennsylvania Press, 1985), xii.
4. Ibid., 1.
5. Ibid., 9.

period, black denominational churches established colleges and seminaries for training preachers. Therefore, training should not be regarded as having been absent merely because this kind of preaching was seen primarily as performance. Indeed, there is training in performance through cultural immersion that may require as much time and attention as training in precision of rational discourse.

Davis's outline of the structure of the performed sermon is quite helpful for purposes of analysis.[6] It carries one a long way if the concern is learning the art from a technical standpoint, or if the primary concern is for critique. Still, for all the good he does, his very premises limit what he can say for the purpose of grasping the meaning of preaching as religious act. The ahistorical character of the taxonomy obscures the theological meaning at the very heart of the intention of the Christian preaching he describes. The intention of the preaching he observes is to be "under the anointing of the Spirit." Rhythm, musicality, and deep inner connections between the preacher and fellow worshipers are marks of the pneumatic flow in which preaching is to be done. The flowering of this preaching came during the Civil Rights era, when themes of liberation merged with Southern evangelical spirituality.

Beyond these preliminary views of African American preaching, other research on black preaching has provided much useful insight as to its theological and performance value. Evans Crawford, for example, gives a positive assessment of the quality of rhythm in African American preaching. His location in the African American spiritual tradition makes him intimately familiar with and appreciative of the power and majesty of rhythmic preaching. He understands that strong attention to rhythm is quite normal—and in some settings even normative—for black preachers. But he is careful not to equate attention to rhythm with primitivity or with an absence of logic and reason. Instead, he helpfully introduces the notion of "biformation" to account for the two streams of culture, the African and the American evangelical, that are present within the African American church, and speaks of both as contributing valuable elements.[7]

Crawford particularly values the "talk-back religious heritage" of black preaching that derives from the African movement known as *ntu*.[8] This refers to the force, vitality, and motion that unites and pulses through all of reality. It penetrates all of creation, including all sentient beings, inanimate objects, time, space, even art. Indeed it is the word root to which prefixes are added in

6. Ibid., 7.
7. Evans E. Crawford, *The Hum: Call and Response in African American Preaching* (Nashville: Abingdon, 1995), 19.
8. Ibid., 20.

Bantu culture to designate all categories of reality. There is reciprocal motion in *ntu*, a give-and-take flow of energy, just as there is in black preaching. In a universe dominated by *ntu*, the excision of rhythm or its bifurcation from life is a logical impossibility.

Thanks to the idea of biformation, Crawford is able to avoid the conclusion that use of rhythm and emotion in African American preaching is separated from and inferior to logic and intellectual activity.[9] Biformation suggests that it is utterly consistent to speak of the beauty in both the mind and the eye of the beholder, just as it is utterly consistent to speak of preaching as feeding both the mind and the spirit—the whole person. In the "talk-back" heritage to which Crawford refers, there is a "fusion of sonic and conceptual" things that supplies "resonance for life."[10] The "ether" pulsates with "mystic harmonies." It is this ether that the preacher enters with the people.[11] When the preacher reaches this state with the audience, something more than rhythm is employed. The preacher achieves what Crawford calls a sense of "hum" with the people's vocalizations of different pitches, and their improvisational vocal "riffs" add meaning or contribute or respond to the sermon. The use of wide-ranging vocal pitch and tone is a key element of black preaching's musicality. When combined with riffs, preaching takes on extraordinary vitality.[12]

Crawford likens the preacher's riffs to those of a blues musician. In the blues, riffs are "characterized by improvised free rhythms and idiomatic counterpoint, which make for a style that is difficult to notate since it depends upon the experience, tradition, and sensitivity of the performer." He then adds, "The improvisory and anticipatory aspect of 'riff' can be extended and broadened as a metaphor to illumine several aspects that embrace the call-and-response relationship of laity and preacher in the black tradition."[13]

The "hum" that is achieved by the employment of these musical elements in preaching enables both the preacher and the people to "feel the Spirit." For the preacher, help comes from above and below, from the Spirit of God as well as the resonant spirit of the people.

Henry Mitchell has provided valuable research of a different kind on the history of the musicality of black preaching. One of his key observations is that the values of seminary training have historically attempted to make black preachers "mask," or tone down, the very essence of their spiritual formation (biformation) in order to make their preaching legitimate. Such masking threatened to leave an

9. Ibid., 44.
10. Ibid., 46.
11. Ibid., 51, 53.
12. Ibid., 70, 71.
13. Ibid., 72, 73.

entire generation of preachers without a home in an era when the black church could scarcely recognize these restricted speakers as preachers and the white church would not have them. Quite apart from the outrage of colonizing one people's style with a totally alien one, Mitchell bristled at such "toning down" because it threatened to rob the African American church of a theologically trained clergy and the larger American church of its preaching power.

In their research, Mitchell and Crawford have taken what has been known intuitively for some time within the African American church and made it part of the conscious art of black preaching. In analyzing the use of pitch and tonality, for example, Crawford shows that it communicates more than rational content. Such a holistic understanding assumes unity between theological reflection and the art form. It suggests that there is a space in which the preacher can be "in tune" with the community's mind and heart.

Mitchell and Crawford have re-coupled emotion and theological reflection. Indeed, they would argue that the decoupling of reason and emotion unravels and erodes the very nexus from which the power of black preaching emerges.

The Pervasive Use of Music in Black Preaching

Anyone who observes the black church from within the context of its life as a worshiping community is soon struck by the degree to which the preaching is musical. The features of its musicality include expression (such as loud and sonorous or sweet and melodious delivery), meter, cadence, and rhythm (such as through repetition of key words and phrases), and musical style (such as full-blown chant or song). To those who are a part of this tradition, the musicality of sermon delivery is normative for preaching. Other styles of delivery are seen as mere speech, address, or lecture—but not preaching. Consequently, a preacher who is uninitiated in the customs of the black church may be thanked for his or her "talk" as a courteous intimation that "preaching" per se did not occur! Although few preachers inside or outside the black community and even fewer homileticians would make musical delivery the measure of a sermon's overall effectiveness, it remains a treasured aspect of the African American homiletical experience, as Mitchell, who has been called the "dean" of African American homileticians, suggests in describing the mannerisms and stylistic qualities of black preachers:

> The most common or stereotypical [method] is the use of a musical tone or chant in preaching. Among the initiates it is variously referred to as "moaning,"

"mourning," "whooping," "tuning," "zooning," or any one of several other terms, each with a slightly different shade of meaning. Sustained tone is used in various ways. Some black preachers use it only in climactic utterances, of whatever length. Others, often less well-educated and therefore less inhibited, tend to use some degree of tone throughout the message. Still others use it only in places where the culture of the congregation clearly demands it. The decision will often be made unconsciously, just as a truck driver adjusts his gears to fit the demands of the road. Yet most churches do not demand tone, so that the present significance of this feature is very difficult to assess beyond the fact that it automatically makes some folks "happy" just to hear this aspect of their mother tongue sounded in the pulpit. For people with a certain background, it appears that a moaned message is more deeply spiritual than an unintoned one. While this is not necessarily true, tone does signal a kind of affirmation of black identity which in turn begets a real religious experience.[14]

Yet beyond tone and musicality, though undoubtedly supported by it, the ability of black preaching to speak to the black experience in America with a divinely inspired word is certainly its most distinctive feature. To a situation characterized by bleakness, despair, oppression, and frustration, a word of hope is declared, offering to people the promise of a brighter day and strength to endure the times in which they find themselves. This preaching is not solely "otherworldly" nor simply "protest." Emerging from the depths of a religious consciousness in which God is trusted over against all odds posed by history, black preaching is an affirmation of the will and power of God before it is a protest against or a gesture away from this world. It is toward celebration of this power of God available to us that the preacher leads the congregation using all the musical skills at his or her disposal. Not only does such celebration enhance the understanding and retention of the gospel, it is, as Mitchell asserts, essential to faithful communication of the gospel, without which there would be a "de facto denial of the good news."[15]

This "celebration" is, of course, distinct from what Mitchell calls "cerebration." "Celebration" is more affective and emotional than "cerebration," which is reflective and intellectual. This is not to diminish the significance of the cognitive aspect of black preaching, for celebration does not stand independent of responsible exegesis, careful penetration of the teachings of the church, and sensitive theological insight, but rather builds on and comes from it. The musicality of the African American sermon expresses what is

14. Henry H. Mitchell, *Black Preaching* (Philadelphia: Lippincott, 1970), 163–64.
15. Henry H. Mitchell, *The Recovery of Preaching* (San Francisco: Harper & Row, 1977), 55.

beyond the literal word. It takes rational content and fires the imagination and stirs the heart. Indeed, at the point of celebration, all that has been generated in the cerebral process is offered up in the moment of exultation.

The persistence and pervasiveness of this form of delivery from one generation of black preachers to the next is astounding when one considers the paucity of reflection on the idiom. Among those who appreciate and practice the art, it is almost as though it were a secret of the guild's oral culture. Whereas some academicians ignore or disdain the idiom, disparaging it as a vestige of "folk religion," black preachers not only maintain the tradition but also practice the art with consummate skill. Restricted neither by denomination nor educational status, the musicality of black preaching is employed, it seems, by everyone from Father Andrew Bryan and Andrew Marshall at the beginning of the nineteenth century to Martin Luther King Jr. and Charles Adams in the twentieth century, from the "cornfield preacher" to the "Harvard Whooper," from the "NoD" to the PhD, and "every D in between." It is no surprise, then, that contemporary black preaching resembles descriptions of preaching within the slave communities of long ago.[16]

Yet this skill of musical delivery is not possessed by all black preachers; neither is it a feature unique to black religion. On occasion it is found among white Pentecostals whose worship style is closely aligned to that customarily found in the black church. Among these white preachers has been television evangelist Jimmy Swaggart, who (perhaps because of his style of preaching) in his heyday attracted a substantial black audience. However, the larger American culture, greatly influenced by the Enlightenment and the rise of modern science, offered little support for a style of preaching that even hinted of the mystical.

Any overlap between black and white cultures (between Charles Adams and Jimmy Swaggart, for instance) invariably invites inquiry as to who is mimicking whom. Such questions may be valuable from the standpoint of determining the origin of the practice in North America, yet they do little to describe, interpret, and preserve the form. After all, the concern of this chapter is not to validate musicality in preaching by demonstrating its contagious character for some white preachers. Rather, it is to explore the character and contribution of this musicality in the context of the culture that sustains it as a normal practice, and so it is that we turn now from the use of musicality to its meaning in preaching.

16. See Jon Michael Spencer, *Sacred Symphony: The Chanted Sermon of the Black Preacher*, foreword by William C. Turner Jr. (Westport, CT: Greenwood, 1978), 1–16.

Musicality as Surplus of Meaning in African American Preaching

At the core of the study of Christian preaching is an attempt to account for its transcendence over ordinary speech. Nearly all homileticians address this dimension wherein the preacher is "outside of self" and speaking on behalf of a divine power. Gardner C. Taylor, one of the most influential black preachers of this generation, reminds us of the awesomeness and presumptuousness of the task undertaken by one who supposes to speak for and of God:

> Measured by almost any gauge, preaching is a presumptuous business. If the undertaking does not have some sanction beyond human reckoning, then it is, indeed, rash and audacious for one person to dare to stand up before or among other people and declare that he or she brings from the Eternal God a message for those who listen which involves issues nothing less than those of life and death.[17]

John R. W. Stott, one of the foremost evangelists and preachers of the twentieth century, similarly notes that the preacher can speak only because God has spoken:

> No attempt to understand Christianity can succeed which overlooks or denies the truth that the living God has taken the initiative to reveal himself savingly to fallen humanity; or that his self-revelation has been given by the most straightforward means of communication known to us, namely by a word and words; or that he calls upon those who have heard his Word to speak it to others.[18]

Stott illustrates the implication of this insight with an anecdote from the career of George Whitefield, the eloquent and spellbinding preacher of the eighteenth century. During a preaching campaign in a New Jersey meetinghouse, an old man fell asleep during Whitefield's discourse, provoking him to exhort: "If I had come to speak to you in my own name, you might rest your elbows upon your knees and your heads on your hands, and go to sleep! . . . But I have come to you in the name of the Lord God of hosts, and (he clapped his hands and stamped his foot) I *must* and I *will* be heard."[19]

Indeed, in spite of preaching's often keen and penetrating focus on "this world," preaching through the ages has, as Whitefield suggests, been uttered

17. Gardner C. Taylor, *How Shall They Preach* (Elgin, IL: Progressive Baptist Publishing House, 1977), 24.

18. John R. W. Stott, *Between Two Worlds: The Art of Preaching in the Twentieth Century* (Grand Rapids: Eerdmans, 1982), 15.

19. Ibid., 32–33.

as a word coming from another world. Human beings have typically found it difficult to utter in ordinary speech the extraordinary pronouncements that preaching requires. The ancient prophets often resorted to signs; the apostles of the early church accompanied their words with signs and wonders; the saints were known to retreat into prolonged silent contemplation, only later to emerge with a pronouncement; still others have incorporated the enchanting and mystical powers of music in their delivery. Black preaching follows the latter pattern.

The ancient and primitive view of the arts, including music, is that they were enchanted and were means for evoking and expressing rapture of the soul. To the present day, music has been integral to the cultic life of nearly every culture and almost inseparable from religion. Analysis and reflection by scholars of religion have revealed further that music, celebration, and ecstasy are crucial ingredients that differentiate religion from philosophy. As anthropologist R. R. Marrett concludes, "religion is more danced out than thought out."[20]

Black preaching draws on these two ideas: inspired preaching is a word from another world, and music is a native means by which to express the ineffable. Black preaching employs music in its delivery of meaning from another world. Music bridges the chasm between the world of human beings and God who speaks to them. It helps establish a direct link among the spirit within the preacher, the word being uttered, and the worshiping congregation. The musicality of preaching supplies what might be seen as a surplus of meaning—which is to say that music adds meaning to the performance of the words. Such music typically produces a mystical and enchanting effect on an audience that is waiting to hear what saith the Lord. There can be no denying the potency of this form of preaching in the black community. It has been a source of untold healing and motivation for struggling people.

The African Tradition of Music in African American Rhetoric

To understand the musical aspect of black preaching, one must first look backward and sideward to Africa. In African culture we can clearly observe the place of music in communicating meaning. In traditional African religion, human life is considered to exist in symbiotic relationship with other forms of life and in relation to rhythmic patterns observable in the natural order. These patterns—the coming and going of daylight and darkness, the phases of the moon, the periodic rhythms of rainfall, planting, and harvest—indicate

20. R. R. Marrett, *The Threshold of Religion* (London: Methuen, 1914), xxi, 175.

202   PERFORMANCE IN PREACHING

the essential rhythmic structure of life. Even biological life has a rhythmic fundament—the conception and bearing of children, the process of reaching puberty and adulthood, and the phases of aging and passing on to join the ancestors. From this rhythm of life flow the manifold expressions of culture. It is part of every aspect of indigenous life and every form of cultural communication: language, art, social structures, religion, government, and so forth. So when the very rhythm of life that pulsates through individuals and communities is expressed through dance and music, they in turn become the aesthetic signification of the force of life sustaining the people.

Among the Fon tribe of Dahomey this principle of rhythmic unity was called *Da* and was represented by a serpent coiled under the world. Among the Dogon it was the *nommo,* which signified the power of word and speech. Among the Bantu it is *ntu,* the force that pulsated through all of life. During moments of ecstatic dancing, tribal dancers experienced the sense that the powers of the universe coalesced and surged through their bodies.

When Africans were carried away from their native lands and tribes and forced to serve as slaves in North America, they carried within them these natural and religious rhythms. In their new context of bondage and oppression, Africans made every effort to preserve their primal connection to the spiritual world of tribal deities, ancestors, and spirits. This consciousness preserved within Africans and their descendants an openness to spiritual power. However, the surplus of deep stirrings, intensity, and zeal found within the African spirit—things that were so naturally expressed in African language by means of rhythm, tone, and pitch—found little correspondence in the vocabulary of a new and strange land. African drumming, which in tribal practice was a means by which humans communicated with their deities and with each other, was strictly forbidden to enslaved Africans. But when the slaves began to be evangelized and brought to the Christian faith, the qualities of rhythm and musicality, still natural to the people, were transferred from African religious expression to Christian worship within the slave communities. Naturally, when black believers began to preach, the musical and rhythmic nature of African expression became a part of the experience of black preaching.

The presence of rhythm within the Africans and African Americans was a means by which they gained a sense of spiritual release from the repugnant world of slavery in which they lived. To them, rhythm was essentially numinous: it was the property of the deities, and it moved the community away from present reality into the realm of traditional religion. The same atavistic influence continued to operate on the adherents of Afro-Christian faith: the rhythm and music in preaching that worked beneath the structures of rational and discursive communication moved the listeners away from the moments in history at which terror had been unleashed against them.[21] Only through perpetuating their quarrel with history while simultaneously sidestepping its terror could they forge a positive identity for themselves.[22]

That the direction of black preaching has always been a "gesture away from history" has understandably given rise to the charge that it is otherworldly. However, because there has never been a historical period in which African Americans could fully behold their dreams fulfilled, the rhythm and music that infuse Afro-Christian preaching—elements that add meaning and surplus to the literal content of the spoken word—are affirmations of the world that is not disordered by slavery, oppression, and injustice.

African American Preaching as Manifestation of Power

Within the tradition of the black church, preaching is truly a manifestation of power, or to use the language of Mircea Eliade, a "kratophany."[23] As in a theophany, which is a manifestation of deity, kratophany refers to an object that opens people to an understanding of the transcendent while simultaneously being rooted in the world of tangible, historical reality. A theophany in African traditional religion might refer to a deified object such as a tree or a stone. In preaching, the kratophany is the spoken word itself and its accompanying layers of gesture. Especially within the context of the culture that sustains black preaching, there is no more kratophanic object, none more indicative of the presence of deity, power, and intrusion from another world, than that of the preached word couched in musicality.

As kratophany, there is more to preaching than the spoken word and the claim that it has spiritual power. Preaching is grounded in the historical and social world of the biblical text. But as a new expression of that word and world, it becomes a living and interactive expression of the Word of God. Because the Word is like "a burning fire shut up in my bones" (Jer. 20:9; cf. 23:29; Heb. 4:12), something transformative is supposed to happen in preaching. This is especially apparent in African American preaching. Replete with drama and musicality, its performative power is expected to move people and to cause reaction. Nodding the head, shedding a tear, holy dancing, speaking in

21. Cornell West, *Prophesy Deliverance: An Afro-American Revolutionary Christianity* (Philadelphia: Westminster, 1982), 19; Mircea Eliade, *The Myth of the Eternal Return* (New York: Harper & Row, 1959), 139.

22. West, *Prophesy Deliverance*, 9; Eliade, *Myth of the Eternal Return*, 139.

23. Mircea Eliade, *Patterns in Comparative Religion*, trans. Rosemary Sheed (New York: Meridian Books, 1967), 14.

tongues, singing, humming aloud, and shouting "amen" are typical responses to the power manifested in effective black preaching.[24]

Words thus spoken are akin to those preached in ancient Hebrew tradition in which words were believed to accomplish and perform the action contained in them, especially when spoken on behalf of God. Moreover, the spoken word could by no means be retracted. When, for instance, the Mesopotamian diviner was summoned by the king of Moab to curse the Israelites as they came up from Egypt, Balaam instead blessed Israel, declaring that he could speak no word other than that which the Lord had given him. Once those words were pronounced, Balaam was powerless to retract them (Num. 22:12–18). Similarly, when Jacob cunningly received the blessing that should have gone to his brother Esau, their father Isaac insisted that the blessing that bestowed inheritance, once spoken, could not be reversed (Gen. 27:36–38). The prophets declared too that the word they spoke for the Lord would not return without doing what it was sent to do (Isa. 55:10–11). They declared that the Word was like a "hammer that breaks a rock in pieces" (Jer. 23:29). When black preachers are caught up in the more ecstatic musical phases of proclaiming the Word, they sometimes enter a trancelike state that parallels that of the early Old Testament prophets, who claimed no responsibility for their own speech but spoke only under the conditions caused by the Spirit of the Lord coming upon them. When they declared, "thus saith the Lord," they did so without fear of punishment or death.[25] The black preacher who genuinely enters such an inspired state of proclamation is able to articulate a message that far exceeds what he or she has prepared to deliver.

The music of black preaching is one of the means by which the kratophanic quality of the genre occurs. Just as a good artist is able to touch the human spirit through his or her work, the black preacher uses music to touch the spirit of the listener. The music of black preaching can be understood as sort of a way to "sing praise with the spirit" (1 Cor. 14:15). The surplus expressed in the sermon's music accompanies its rational content, which is expressed in words literally. The rational portion is contained in

24. See William Turner, "Pentecostal Preaching," in *Concise Encyclopedia of Preaching*, ed. William H. Willimon and Richard Lischer (Louisville: Westminster John Knox, 1995), 369–72. See how black preaching may be called "proto-Pentecostal." Note that early Pentecostal preachers including W. J. Seymour, C. H. Mason, and H. L. Fisher understood themselves as preserving a tradition of black spirituality they deemed to be waning in the church. What came to be called Pentecostal in the twentieth century bore many marks of black religion, and much of what is now called charismatic and neo-Pentecostal similarly traces its roots to the African American church preaching tradition.

25. See George T. Montague, *The Holy Spirit: Growth of a Biblical Tradition* (New York: Paulist Press, 1976), 17–33.

the formal structure of the sermon, which represents the homiletical and doctrinal tradition in which the preacher stands. The surplus portion is achieved when the preacher becomes an instrument—a flute through which divine air is blown, a harp whose strings are plucked by God. For the sake of the audience, the preacher becomes an oracle through whom a divinely inspired message flows.

When preaching attains the level at which rhythm and musicality are unrestrained—where the preacher "lets the Lord have his way"—it is customarily said that the preacher is "under the anointing" and is "being used of God." In the vernacular of the culture, we say, "the preacher has come."

Musicality and the Motions of Life

We are reaching now into the space where speech or verbal descriptions scarcely do justice to the subject. How are human emotions a conduit through which the Spirit moves among worshiping people who are caught up in the ecstasy of preaching? Such movement of the Spirit relates to the deepest level of human experience, where knowledge of faith and the sense of inspiration reside. This movement of the Spirit through the depths of human perception is brought alive in black preaching through the musical tones that accompany the preached word. The movement is a deep stirring that joins the worshipers in a perichoretic flow that is nothing less than the koinonia of the Spirit.[26] The movement is both inward and outward. It flourishes in community, and it creates community. It is the fellowship (communion) of the Spirit that enlivens the believing body.

Let me be clear: we are not talking here about stoking raw emotion or creating emotionalism. The manipulation of raw emotion has no *telos* or goal—or if it does, it is one that is ultimately deleterious. Emotionalism results from the use of forms that have no substance, or with a substance that comes under no theological critique.

The motion to which we refer is inward activity brought about through the Spirit of life, who opposes the law of sin and death. Indeed the very

26. The language of perichoresis is taken from trinitarian theology, where the effort is to articulate the mutual indwelling among the divine persons (hypostases). What is described by this term is a circulation of life, an exchange of energy, a divine dance. For further discussion see Catherine LaCugna, *God For Us: The Trinity and Christian Life* (San Francisco: HarperSanFrancisco, 1992); Molly Marshall, *Joining the Dance: A Theology of the Spirit* (Valley Forge, PA: Judson, 2003); Jürgen Moltmann, *Trinity and Kingdom: The Doctrine of God* (San Francisco: Harper & Row, 1981); and Veli-Matti Kärkkäinen, *Pneumatology: The Holy Spirit in Ecumenical, International, and Contextual Perspective* (Grand Rapids: Baker Academic, 2002).

image depicted in the "motions of life" is rooted in the Pauline discussion of the opposing passions (*pathemata*) corresponding to a law. He makes specific reference to "motions of death," to name and describe what the law does through its weakness. Having no power to inspire obedience, it incites passions that lead to disobedience and ultimately death. For him these are like powerful motions. The overarching image here is that of one who is married to the law. The submerged (or subliminal) image is that of an unborn fetus that has already begun to move in ways that can be felt by the expectant mother. In a very limited time frame those prenatal motions blossom fully in the form and life of a person with all the potential for full life.

The movement of the discussion is to declare the triumph given by the Spirit, the giver of life. The Spirit gives more than all else the motions of life in Christ Jesus. This is the law that makes one free from the law of sin and death. It begins with the motions that may be likened to the kicking of a healthy baby, or the quickening of what was dead or dormant. Indeed, insemination and quickening are initial or inceptual motions.

Such spiritual stirrings within remind us of Mary, the expectant mother of Jesus, who goes to share her joy with Elizabeth. When the mother of the incarnate Lord tells how she has conceived by the Spirit, the motions of life within her prompt a corresponding motion within Elizabeth. At that point, Elizabeth is filled with the Spirit, and the baby leaps within her womb (Luke 1:41).

The image for the ecstatic moment in which preaching makes contact, or passes over into the chant, may well be compared to Mary singing the Magnificat and John the Baptist leaping for joy in the presence of his Lord. In that case we have not only the mode that prompts rejoicing within African American worship or that appropriates the idiom of music but also the message of deliverance that causes the soul to "magnify the Lord."

Motions of life understood in this sense of stirrings of the spirit become a root metaphor for how rhythm and music act to accompany and undergird preaching. In the ecstatic moment, the motions of life and joy within the preacher come forth in the charged ether of worship in the form of an invitation to those who hear to be more than an audience, more than simply attentive and receptive. Music in preaching is a summons to participate, to worship, to rejoice, to celebrate, and ultimately to yield to the deepest motions of life.

The motion of life in the musical tone struck in preaching is like the dance in the heart of the preacher, evoking a dance in the heart of the hearer. These motions are described no better than in the words of worshipers who speak of how the Spirit "runs from heart to heart and breast to breast." The moment is no less than mystical participation in the deep, preconscious, atavistic, liminal spaces where spiritual community is formed.[27]

Participation is at a depth of preconscious intersubjectivity that precedes structure. This openness of one subject to another is comparable to a Platonic notion of *sungeneia*, which permits knowing subjects to hold knowledge in common. Shared signs, symbols, patterns, and gestures fill this cultural space. The potency of this charged ether has an effect that does not allow for indifference. One is drawn into it, or there is deliberate resistance. Resistance may result from either disdain or discernment that questions whether the inward motions truly are of God.

A description of such a moment can be seen in Numbers 11:26–29 where Eldad and Medad remain in the camp while the other elders follow God's instruction and go to the Tent of Meeting. The Spirit comes upon those who go to the Tent of Meeting, and they prophesy. A report soon comes from the camp that Eldad and Medad are also prophesying. Joshua asks Moses to stop the two in camp from prophesying, but Moses refuses to interfere with the working of God's Spirit. A similar moment occurs in 1 Samuel 10, where Saul meets prophets coming down from the high place at Gibeon, playing their music, just as Samuel promised he would. Simply as a result of coming into their presence, Saul falls into ecstasy and prophesies, giving rise to the query, "is Saul also among the prophets?" (1 Sam. 10:11). Such scenes inform Luke's account of the giving of the Spirit (Acts 2:2; 8:14; 10:44–48; 19:5–6).

Those immersed in the culture in which mystical musical tone arises and is sustained are quite aware of the evocative moment in which the chant begins. It may arise out of the truth of what is being declared, the witness of the worshiping congregation, the passion of the preacher to "tell it like it is felt," or the prodding of a musician. In one fleeting moment the rhythm is changed, the pattern of speech is modulated, and a subliminal monitor present within the cultural space is triggered. Where *sungeneia* is not present, the preacher retreats from the moment, or the preacher proceeds to become a spectacle. Where *sungeneia* is present, it is comparable to the "talking drum of Africa," and the communication is precise. Often the voice itself becomes percussive.

Communication occurs not only through the meaning denoted by words, but in the surplus that seeps up and through the spaces between the words. It may

27. For a discussion of "communitas," see William Turner, *The United Holy Church of America: A Study in Black Holiness-Pentecostalism* (Piscataway, NJ: Gorgias, 2006), chap. 4 on "Holy Convocation."

occur even in the expansion of a syllable that carries a number of tones—just as is the case in the correspondence between word and note on the musical score. Some words are suited uniquely for such expansion. Indeed, a great anthem of the African American church comes from the preacher Charles H. Mason, whose soul out of love for Jesus cried, "Ye-e-e-s" in countless modulations of tones sung from one word.

Tonal modulation and voice inflection evoke congregational response on many occasions. In other instances the solicitation for a specific response is made. The preacher may ask, "Can I get an 'amen'?" Or the preacher may ask, "Am I right about?" With no command, question, or direct address, the same response can be "called forth" by the cadence, the gesture, a word combination, or some other communicative device encoded in the very patterns of the cultural mix. Such signals are below the threshold of formal syntax and grammar. Yet they are clear as crystal within the cultural matrix in which preaching is a musical moment.

Disdain may enter at the point of cultural clash. Such dissonance may arise from preconceptions about preaching and worship as "proper acts," measured by notions of dignity and decorum that place highest priority on precision and control in delivery and response. Such responses reflect the residue of bias against primitivity and emotion in religion and a notion of evolution of religion into a form of science. Disdain may also result from the equation some make between emotion and emotionalism. Whatever the source, a sufficient measure of disdain effectively brackets out the surplus carried by musicality.

Where theological or doctrinal norms are valued, discernment factors into reception of the sermon, no matter how it is delivered. Only in exceptional cases does the achievement of the musical moment supersede the content. In that moment no attention is paid to what is being said; the only concern is with how it is said—much as a deeply heartfelt "I love you" signifies much more than the literal words. Within serious Christian communities that cherish the musical moment in preaching, there is no separation between the "truth of the word" and the "anointing of the Spirit" that makes it effective. The witness of the Spirit is not separable from attention to sound doctrine and claims about God that resonate with the believing community. The Spirit works in both the rational sphere where precise auditions are required, and in the nonrational sphere where surplus is supplied.

Motions of life, like what a mother feels when the child is moving within, make one alive to God—to the things of God—to worship, to good works, to the ways of compassion. This aliveness to God makes one receive the Word with joy so the seed can bring forth fruit.

Finally

Openings between the emotions and the intellect allow for a quickening and enlivening of the preacher's imagination. This is spiritual space in which the senses join and one is touched by what is heard; one can feel what is seen. Ideas can be grasped as images, and theological content can be perceived as a whole. There is no competition in this spiritual region between the emotions and rigorous exegesis, or attention to historical, systematic, or dogmatic issues. Theological analysis can be a source of excitement, especially when accelerated by liberationist and salvific motifs. In fact, the sanctified imagination is often triggered by such precision. Not the devil, but the doxological moment is in the detail.

The reinsertion of emotion as a crucial ingredient for the homiletical theology that undergirds preaching re-couples learning with burning, fire with focus, sanctification with education, and the keen mind with the clean life. Most of all, it begins and ends with the conviction that emotion and intellect do not run on a collision course. For powerful preaching this is but another manifestation of the unity of the Spirit. It is a performance of the Word.

Cultural elements, like plant slips transferred from hotbeds, were taken from Europe and Africa and joined genetically in the crucible of evangelical revival. They flourished in the spiritual greenhouse known as the African American church in the climate of oppression and triumph. The result is a powerful art form through which the gospel is performed.

12

Performance Study in Service to the Spoken Word in Worship

CHARLES L. BARTOW

Performance studies into human communication and the human condition have been pursued so relentlessly and extensively that virtually no aspect of human intrapersonal or interpersonal reflective or expressive experience can be regarded as exempt from redescription according to the assumptions and procedures of performance studies researchers and practitioners. In a way similar to, yet perhaps more ambitious than theoretical and critical investigations in the "rhetoric is epistemic" movement,[1] performance studies have sought to give a full account of what makes for the human manufacture and acquisition of knowledge whether in art or in science, whether in ecstatic or mundane affairs. There are anthropologies

---

1. See Richard A. Cherwitz and James W. Hikins, "Climbing the Academic Ladder: A Critique of Provincialism in Contemporary Rhetoric," *Quarterly Journal of Speech* 86, no. 4 (November 2000): 375–85. Also see Edward Schiappa, Alan G. Gross, Raymie E. McKerrow, and Robert L. Scott, "Rhetorical Studies as Reduction or Redescription? A Response to Cherwitz and Hikins," *Quarterly Journal of Speech* 88, no. 1 (February 2002): 112–20. To me it would appear that "reduction" vs. "redescription" is a distinction without a difference. To redescribe without remainder is to reduce. On the question of limit on redescription in performance studies, see James W. Chesebro, "Performance Studies as Paradox, Culture and Manifesto," in *The Future of Performance Studies: Visions and Revisions*, ed. Sheron J. Dailey (Annandale, VA: National Communication Association, 1998), 310–19.

of performance.[2] There are cultural performance studies.[3] There are studies of performance as a mode of resistance to socially sanctioned definitions of the self.[4] There are performance studies of the male body,[5] of the female body,[6] and of the "straight" body and the "gay" body as contested sites of meaning-making and valuation.[7] There are performance studies of texts[8] (more about that later), and of persons as texts to be composed and recomposed, figured and refigured through transformational self-narration.[9] There are performance studies of

2. E.g., the substantial body of work of Victor Turner: Victor Turner and Edith L. B. Turner, *Image and Pilgrimage in Christian Culture: Anthropological Perspectives* (New York: PAJ, 1982); Victor Turner, *From Ritual to Theatre: The Human Seriousness of Play* (New York: PAJ, 1982); Victor Turner, *The Anthropology of Performance* (New York: PAJ, 1988).

3. The literature is vast, from cultural performance studies of a historical sort, e.g., Dwight Conguergood, "Literacy and Oral Performance in Anglo-Saxon England: Conflict and Confluence of Traditions," in *Performance of Literature in Historical Perspectives*, ed. David W. Thompson (Lanham, MD: University Press of America, 1983), 107–45; to recent ethnographic studies, e.g., studies reported (2004–2005) in the performance studies journal of the National Communication Association. See Chaim Noy, "Performing Identity: Touristic Narratives of Self-Change," *Text and Performance Quarterly* 24, no. 2 (April 2004): 115–38; Tracy Stephenson Shaffer, "Performing Backpacking: Constructing 'Authenticity' Every Step of the Way," *Text and Performance Quarterly* 24, no. 2 (April 2004): 139–60; Laura Lengel, "Performing In/Outside Islam: Music and Gendered Cultural Politics in the Middle East and North Africa," *Text and Performance Quarterly* 24, no. 3/4 (July/October 2004): 212–32; Bernadette Marie Calafell, "Pro(re-)claiming Loss: A Performance Pilgrimage in Search of Malintzin Tenépal," *Text and Performance Quarterly* 25, no. 1 (January 2005): 43–56.

4. E.g., Teresa Bergman, "Personal Narrative, Dialogism, and the Performance of 'Truth' in Complaints of a Dutiful Daughter," *Text and Performance Quarterly* 24, no. 1 (January 2004): 20–37.

5. E.g., Frederick C. Cory, "Tim Miller's Body (of Work)," *Text and Performance Quarterly* 23, no. 3 (July 2003): 253–70. This happens to be the performance especially of the homosexual male body. Also, Robert Asen, "Appreciation and Desire: The Male Nude in the Photography of Robert Mapplethorpe," *Text and Performance Quarterly* 18, no. 1 (April 1998): 50–62; Judith Hamera, "The Ambivalent, Knowing Male Body in the Pasadena Dance Theatre," *Text and Performance Quarterly* 14, no. 3 (July 1994): 197–209.

6. E.g., the female body under duress: Carole Spitzack, "The Spectacle of Anorexia Nervosa," *Text and Performance Quarterly* 13, no. 1 (January 1993): 1–20; Elizabeth Bell, "Performance Studies as Women's Work: Historical Sights/Cites/Citations from the Margin," *Text and Performance Quarterly* 13, no. 4 (October 1993): 350–74; Elizabeth Grosz, *Volatile Bodies: Towards A Corporeal Feminism* (Bloomington: Indiana University Press, 1994).

7. E.g., Jeffrey A. Bennett, "Love Me Gender: Normative Homosexuality and 'Ex-gay' Performativity in Reparative Therapy Narratives," *Text and Performance Quarterly* 23, no. 4 (October 2003): 331–52; also review essay, John T. Warren, "The Body Politic: Performance, Pedagogy, and the Power of Enfleshment," *Text and Performance Quarterly* 19, no. 3 (July 1999): 257–70.

8. There are, of course, numerous whole volumes devoted to the performance or oral interpretation of literature. However, for a variety of contemporary approaches to engagement with texts as performatory scripts, see *Text and Performance Quarterly* 22, no. 1 (January 2002) in its entirety.

9. E.g., D. Sonyini Madison, "'That Was My Occupation': Oral Narrative, Performance, and Black Feminist Thought," *Text and Performance Quarterly* 13, no. 3 (July 1993): 213–32; Irene

ritual,[10] of religion,[11] of words and the Word—performance studies, that is to say, of the enactment of faith.[12] There are performance studies of media artifacts,[13] of human artifacts of all sorts, and of the museums or galleries in which human artifacts—or other items—are preserved and displayed.[14] There are performance studies that seem to be tongue in cheek—postmodernist-absurdist performance studies, one might label them.[15] Yet, too, there are performance studies so self-

Kacandes, "Are You in the Text? The 'Literary Performative' in Postmodernist Fiction," *Text and Performance Quarterly* 13, no. 2 (April 1993): 139–53; Elyse Lamm Pineau, "A Mirror of Her Own: Anais Nin's Autobiographical Performance," *Text and Performance Quarterly* 12, no. 2 (April 1992): 97–112; John Rodden, "'I am inventing myself all the time': Isabel Allende and the Literary Interview as Public Performance," *Text and Performance Quarterly* 17, no. 1 (January 1997): 1–24.

10. See Richard Schechner, "From Ritual to Theater and Back: The Efficacy-Entertainment Braid," in *Performance Theory* (New York: Routledge, 1988), 106–52; also Margaret Thompson Drewal, *Yaruba Ritual: Performers, Play, Agency* (Bloomington: Indiana University Press, 1992); Randall T. Hill, "The Nakwa Powamu Ceremony as Rehearsal: Authority, Ethics and Ritual Appropriation," *Text and Performance Quarterly* 15, no. 4 (October 1995): 301–20.

11. Debra L. Sequeira, "Gifts of Tongues and Healing: The Performance of Charismatic Renewal," *Text and Performance Quarterly* 14, no. 2 (April 1994): 126–43; Antonio Scuderi, "Subverting Religious Authority: Dario Fo and Folk Laughter," *Text and Performance Quarterly* 16, no. 3 (July 1996): 216–32; Kristin Bervig Valentine, "Yaqui Easter Ceremonies and the Ethics of Intense Spectatorship," *Text and Performance Quarterly* 22, no. 4 (October 2002): 280–96.

12. E.g., John V. Apczynski, *Doers of the Word: Toward a Foundational Theology Based on the Thought of Michael Polanyi*, AARDS 18 (Missoula, MT: Scholars Press, 1997). Apczynski's work is not technically in the field of performance studies, but enactment of faith is at the heart of it. For a discussion in performance modes of thought of divine revelation and human response, see Charles L. Bartow, *God's Human Speech: A Practical Theology of Proclamation* (Grand Rapids: Eerdmans, 1997), esp. 9–57. An enactment of faith as the vocation of the preaching ministry exercised through poetic composition and the controversialist essay is presented by Jameela Lares, *Milton and the Preaching Arts* (Pittsburgh: Duquesne University Press, 2001). For a discussion of oral performance of Christian faith and its influence on medieval English literature, see Catherine A. Regan, "Liturgy and Preaching as Oral Context for Medieval English Literature," in *Performance of Literature in Historical Perspectives*, ed. David W. Thompson (Lanham, MD: University Press of America, 1983), 147–75.

13. E.g., James W. Chesebro, "Text, Narration, and Media," *Text and Performance Quarterly* 9, no. 1 (January 1989): 1–23; Kenneth M. Cameron, "Paul Robeson, Eddie Murphy, and the Film Text of 'Africa,'" *Text and Performance Quarterly* 10, no. 4 (October 1990): 282–93; Hannah Gourgey and Edward B. Smith, "'Consensual Hallucination': Cyberspace and the Creation of an Interpretive Community," *Text and Performance Quarterly* 16, no. 3 (July 1996): 233–47; Helen A. Shugart, "Performing Ambiguity: The Passing of Ellen DeGeneres," *Text and Performance Quarterly* 23, no. 1 (January 2003): 1–29; Robin Roberts, "Gendered Media Rivalry: Television and Film on the London Stage," *Quarterly Journal of Speech* 21, no. 2 (April 2001): 77–94; Angela McRobbie, *Postmodern and Popular Culture* (London: Routledge, 1994).

14. See Shannon Jackson, "Performance at Hall-House: Museum, Microfiche, and Historiography"; and Elizabeth Gray Buck, "The Musée Gustave Moreau," in *Exceptional Spaces: Essays in Performance and History*, ed. Della Pollack (Chapel Hill: University of North Carolina Press, 1998), 261–315.

15. Michael S. Bowman, "Killing Dillinger: A Mystory," *Text and Performance Quarterly* 20, no. 4 (October 2000): 342–74; followed by analysis by Craig Gingrich-Philbrook, "Revenge

consciously serious that the preservation—or even reclamation—of personal psychosomatic integrity appears to be at stake in them.[16]

Far be it from this writer to dismiss peremptorily any item in this vast array of performance thought and practice, constructive and critical investigation as insignificant for, or totally irrelevant to, seminary or divinity school preparation of women and men for the church's ministry of Word and sacrament. Ours is a pluralistic, interdisciplinary moment in academic and professional pursuits if ever there was one. Therefore almost any research project one might come across, however undertaken, conceivably could be reviewed and critically appropriated for purposes not in the purview of the researcher who undertook the project. Scholarly eclecticism in our pluralistic context often may be warranted. But the term *scholarly* immediately suggests a disciplined, focused approach to interdisciplinary borrowing. So, amid the welter of performance studies briefly identified above, we must ask how those who consider themselves to

---

of the Dead Subject: The Contexts of Michael Bowman's 'Killing Dillinger,'" loc. cit., 375–87. My own response to these and other—at least to me—unfathomables was submitted to the totally-outside-the-margins-of-respectability Bad Poets Society of Princeton Theological Seminary. The following item was inspired by my attendance at a meeting of the National Communication Association. Yet more particularly it was inspired—if that's the word—by the two articles mentioned above in this note. Both had to do with the construction and deconstruction of identity and context through performance. The text is all, I guess, and selves too are texts, or collections of intertextual becomings, or comings and goings. The technical/theoretical citations were of Germanic proportions. The point of the articles, I gather, is that there is no "there there" really, or something like that. But this is only a guess; yet even a guess is not the guess of an acting subject but the textual possibility of a context or con-text's performance actuals, etc. So on to one of the "baddest" poems I ever wrote, combining, as it does, passion, with the most delicate, yet clumsy intertextual becoming (or unbecoming) musings. So I give you, though the "I" of the I is under question:

I Never Thought Myself
I never thought myself a learned man
Nor unlearned, never wise nor unwise,
Never easily comprehending all
Nor uneasily missing everything,
Never certain that I was always right,
Nor uncertain that I was often wrong,
Never altogether sure nor unsure;
But now am I absolutely baffled,
More, daunted, to read in learned journals
The play of "Who am I?" and "What is it?"
As mental hide and seek, where no one hides,
And no one seeks, and no one ever finds,
And no one minds that in this darkened glass
Of text I think not, and therefore am not.
    Charles L. Bartow

16. Larry Russell, "A Long Way toward Compassion," *Text and Performance Quarterly* 24, no. 3/4 (July/October 2004): 233–54.

be "in service to the servants of the Word"[17] may get their bearings. To what or to whom are they to regard themselves as ultimately accountable? And, as a consequence of that ultimate accountability, what priorities of research, practice, critical reflection, and theory building are to be set? In what follows, an attempt is made to answer those questions.

First, the matter of ultimate accountability: as G. Robert Jacks noted in his basic speech for ministry text, *Getting the Word Across*, "there is a God and you [and I] are not it."[18] In other words, the Word God sent[19] has a name, and the name of that Word is given in what the church has received as the "unique and authoritative witness"[20] to it, i.e., the Holy Bible. The name of the Word God sent is Jesus, the Christ, who is the incarnation of the eternally begotten Son of the Father, i.e., the *logos* who was "in the beginning . . . with God, and . . . was God," through whom "all things came into being," and without whom "not one thing came into being," in whom "was life," life that was "the light of all people," which light "shines in the darkness, and the darkness did not overcome it" (John 1:1–5). And this Word, this *logos* of light and life, "became flesh" (John 1:14), and was "heard, . . . looked at and touched" (1 John 1:1). This was no gnostic redeemer-myth word, nor was it the word, the *logos* of Stoic philosophy. To the contrary, this Word, this *logos*, was the very *dabâr* of God,[21] from everlasting to everlasting, veritably and not virtually,[22] as Jesus of Nazareth, destined to enter this life of ours to bear the weight of it, forever merciful in judgment, yet just in compassion.[23] Elsewhere I have referred to this Word as *actio divina*,[24] the flesh-and-blood, oral-aural, face-to-face speech event of divine self-disclosure. This Word has all the uniqueness and specificity of utterance indicated by Jerome's use of the Latin *verbum* to translate the New Testament Greek *logos*. It is not just any word, that is to say. It is not a cipher possessing no quantity or quality distinctive to itself. On the other hand, it is not for nothing that, at one point, Erasmus favored

17. Charles L. Bartow, "In Service to the Servants of the Word: Teaching Speech at Princeton Theological Seminary," *Princeton Seminary Bulletin* 13, no. 3 (November 1992), 274–86.
18. G. Robert Jacks, *Getting the Word Across* (Grand Rapids: Eerdmans, 1995), 21.
19. Paul E. Scherer, *The Word God Sent* (New York: Harper & Row, 1965).
20. "The Confession of 1967," in *The Book of Confessions*, Presbyterian Church USA (Louisville: General Assembly, PCUSA, 1996), 9.27, p. 265.
21. Cullen I. K. Story, *The Fourth Gospel: Its Purpose, Pattern and Power* (Shippensburg, PA: Ragged Edge, 1997), 32.
22. G. B. Caird, *New Testament Theology*, completed and ed. by L. D. Hurst (New York: Oxford University Press, 1994), 347.
23. Paul E. Scherer, a prayer, in Charles L. Wallis, ed., *Worship Resources for the Christian Year* (New York: Harper & Bros., 1954), 333.
24. Bartow, *God's Human Speech*, 3, 36–37, 39, 44, 48, 58, 60, 63, 109, 116, 130, 141.

the term *sermo* (conversation) for translation into Latin of the *logos* of the prologue to the Gospel according to John.[25] For the Word God sent is protean in conversation. It is without rhetorical limit. It is infinitely adaptive and copious, yet true to itself always and everywhere. As is stated in *The Letter to the Hebrews*, "Jesus Christ is the same yesterday and today and forever" (Heb. 13:8).

All of this is in and through the gift of the Holy Spirit to the church which is Christ's body (Rom. 12:4–5; 1 Cor. 10:17; 12:12–27; Eph. 4:4–16), of which he is the head (Eph. 4:15; 5:23; Col. 1:18; 2:19). Divine breath, that is to say, by expiration from the Father and the Son[26] and by inspiration of that same breath by the church, stirs in believers an awareness of Christ's personal presence and causes his voice to be heard (John 10:3–5). As J. D. G. Dunn has put it, Christ Jesus himself is present in his church through the indwelling of the Holy Spirit;[27] therefore, "every spirit that confesses that Jesus Christ has come in the flesh is from God, and every spirit that does not confess Jesus is not from God" (1 John 4:2–3). Or, as Matthew's account of the gospel indicates, Jesus, in person and referring to himself, gave his followers this promise: "where two or three are gathered in my name, I am there among them" (Matt. 18:20). Nowhere is this believed to be more the case than when the church gathers to devote itself "to the apostles' teaching and fellowship, to the breaking of bread and the prayers" (Acts 2:42). It is not for nothing that, as worship begins, a prayer of invocation is offered, not to conjure God's presence in Christ,[28] but to beseech God to cause the divine presence to be known even if it must be known through its felt absence.[29] "For it is the God who said, 'Let light shine out of darkness,' who has shone in our hearts to give the light of the knowledge of the glory of God in the face of Jesus Christ" (2 Cor. 4:6). Nor is the prayer for illumination before the reading and hearing of the witness of Scripture and sermon a matter of indifference, for in it pastors and congregants acknowledge their need of holy inspiration if they are to hear Christ himself speaking in the words of prophets, psalmists, apostles, and evangelists. Human

---

25. Stephen H. Webb, *The Divine Voice: Christian Proclamation and the Theology of Sound* (Grand Rapids: Brazos, 2004), 130–37.

26. "The Nicene Creed," in *The Book of Confessions*, Presbyterian Church USA, 1.3, p. 3.

27. James D. G. Dunn, *Romans 1–8*, Word Biblical Commentary 38 (Dallas: Word, 1988), 429.

28. Bartow, *God's Human Speech*, 9.

29. For a brief summary of the history of *deus absconditus*, see Bernard Ramm, *A Handbook of Contemporary Theology* (Grand Rapids: Eerdmans, 1966), 35. For a discussion of the hiddenness or veiling/unveiling of God in Barth's thought regarding the *analogia fidei*, see Bruce L. McCormack, *Karl Barth's Critically Realistic Dialectical Theology: Its Genesis and Development, 1909–1936* (New York: Oxford University Press, 1995), 16–20.

physical, vocal, and verbal gesture[30] will not avail to make him seen and heard if his Spirit is withheld, his presence withdrawn, his voice muted. So too the sacramental *epiclesis* is spoken that baptism may not be an empty sign but a dynamic signification of an act of Christ in the church, and that the breaking and eating of the bread and the pouring and drinking of the cup in the Lord's Supper may be, by the Spirit, a communion in the body and blood of Christ and not mere remembrance of things past.

Having gotten our bearings and fixed the locus of accountability in performance studies in service to the servants of the Word in worship, it remains to identify priorities for research, practice, criticism, and theory building. And we start with this: that the voice and body of the speaker and, by way of empathy, of the congregant-auditor, are to be thought of as sites of resonance for the Word. They are not first and foremost sites of self-definition through performance. Nor are they exclusively means by which to express the secrets that, unexpressed through vocal and physical gesture, must die within us.[31] Nor are they primarily means by which socio-cultural definitions of class, gender, and group affiliation may be portrayed and subjected to critique. Still less are they the means by which the "myth-making instinct" may play itself out to the dawning of "philosophic thought, which is the last reach of genuine religion, its consummation and also its dissolution."[32] Any strong, biblical definition of *logos* will resist the notion that art (including performance art and the art of the spoken word) displaces sacramental practice. It will resist too the notion that theology can be redescribed and terminated in symbolic analyses of the sort promulgated in certain linguistic and aesthetic philosophies.[33] Unbelief toward transcendent reality typically is a presupposition of such analyses and not a reasoned conclusion of them. Likewise so-called postmodern objections to claims regarding transcendent reality (and thus to "metanarratives") themselves presuppose a capacity for self-transcendence that allows for the raising

30. For a discussion of speech as gesture, see Wallace A. Bacon, *The Art of Interpretation* (New York: Holt, Rinehart & Winston, 1972), 3.

31. Ibid.

32. Susanne K. Langer, *Philosophy in a New Key: A Study in the Symbolism of Reason, Rite, and Art* (Cambridge, MA: Harvard University Press, 1951), 170.

33. See Cleanth Brooks, "Christianity, Myth, and the Symbolism of Poetry," in *Christian Faith and the Contemporary Arts*, ed. Finley Eversol (Nashville: Abingdon, 1962), 100–107; Amos N. Wilder, "Poetry and Religion," loc. cit., 108–14. Also Eva Schaper, "Plato and Aristotle on the Arts: From Prelude to Aesthetics," in *Aesthetics: A Critical Anthology*, ed. George Dickie, Richard Sclafani, and Ronald Roblin, 2nd ed. (New York: St. Martin's Press, 1989), 48–63. For the poetic as implying an agonistic relationship of the human being's speech to the speech of God, see George Steiner, *Language and Silence* (New Haven: Yale University Press, 1998), 36–54. For a strong critique of theories of language implying a banished God, see George Steiner, *Real Presences* (Chicago: University of Chicago Press, 1989), 3–134.

of such objections. In fact, is not the claim that there can be no metanarratives itself a metanarrative? One cannot claim that everything is rigorously, even viciously contextual—and that all truths are exclusively contextualized social constructions—if one in fact is entirely mured up in the wall of one's own context. Yet if we are in any measure free, however we may regard ourselves as mured up, is it not because we are *set* free? George Arthur Buttrick, decades ago, commented thus:

> Said Jesus: "If you continue in my word, . . . you will know the truth." There the word "truth" does not mean university information, despite a thousand baccalaureate sermons. The nearest word in our language might be Reality, the Reality in which we and our world are always held. "The truth will make you free." Then the bold equation: "If the Son makes you free, you will be free indeed." The Son as the disclosure of our destiny, as the revelation of that realm from which we view our life, as the mercy to overcome every failure in responsibility.[34]

Note too that the tendency to chaotic idiosyncrasy in pronunciation, articulation, and voice management in the expression of denotation and connotation (text and subtext, intellectual and emotional content) has its unfortunate parallel in the realm of biblical interpretation and theology. So, for instance, there is the beginning seminary student who dismisses out of hand, as in any way instructive for him, the exemplary preaching practice of G. A. Buttrick and Gardner Taylor. The respective theologies implicit in their sermons seem to the student sufficiently contradictory to his own to render their homiletical practice of no value for the development of his practice of preaching. Note that the student's personal theology was assumed by him to be the measure of all things homiletical precisely because it was his own, authentically his own, one might even say peculiarly his own. Yet again there is the elder, at a presbytery meeting, who insists—and no one offers objection—that the Bible, being a "rubber nose" and so capable of being twisted to mean whatever one might wish to make it mean, has no citable bearing in the social, ecclesial, moral issue being debated. These examples of idiosyncrasy are outrageous, granted. But they are not more so than the idiosyncrasies of voice, pronunciation, and articulation earlier noted. Nor are they to be observed as occurring less frequently. To the point of correction in this regard, there are chapters in this volume speaking of truth in preaching and of the significance for scholarly, disciplined, and responsible biblical interpretation of speech performance

34. George Arthur Buttrick, "Footnote on Freedom," in *Sermons Preached in a University Church* (Nashville: Abingdon, 1959), 64.

theory and practice. In speech, clearly, there are distinctive phonemic shifts (the phoneme being the smallest unit of sound in speech that can bear on meaning) that give distinctiveness to cultural, ethnic, and geographic groupings. But it is not these that are fundamentally being called into question here. Instead, what is called into question is the radical personalizing of these shifts that suggests a lack of concern for transcontextual clarity in meaning-making. And it does not seem entirely coincidental that lack of normative coherence in the spoken word not infrequently is coupled with inattention to what makes for normative coherence in the staking of theological claims.

Yet the objections are raised: "I don't want to perform; I don't want to be an actor; I want to be myself; I want to be natural; I want to be comfortable." Is the "natural," however, to be equated with the habitual? What if what feels natural in fact contradicts the true nature of things? W. J. Beeners always insisted on raising that question. And is "being comfortable" the measure of our obligation faithfully to echo, to give resonance to, the Word? It just could be that insistence on being oneself in speaking Scripture, in leading prayer, in preaching and administering the sacraments is actually a quest to preserve not oneself but one's self-image. For the self, as Jesus noted, is kept only as loss of it—loss of life itself—is risked in a kind of forgetfulness of self (Matt. 10:39; 16:25; Mark 8:35; Luke 9:24; 17:33). The point seems to be that the prosperity of the gospel is of greater consequence for oneself than the self-preservation of the self. In any case, an image of the self insisted upon in the face of the call for pastors, priests, and congregants to present themselves, their souls and bodies, as a living sacrifice (Rom. 12:1) at least comes close to idolatry. In their 1916 volume *Fundamentals of Expression*, Leland Powers and Carol Hoyt Powers addressed the folly of romantic "be true to oneself" expressivism in words that yet today ring true:

> [People may have] certain physical habits, certain pet gestures, certain vocal peculiarities which constantly cloud and dim the truth [they] would express. When [they are] corrected for these habits and [are] told that just as [their] audience was getting a bit of the truth, it was brought back to [their] personality by [their] personal gesture or vocal cadence, which had nothing whatever to do with the literature [they were] reading, [they are alarmed]. [They say] "Oh, but that is natural to me! I have always done that! If I lose that I shall not be myself!" How little we know ourselves when we think our individuality depends upon such trivial things.[35]

35. Leland Powers and Carol Hoyt Powers, *Fundamentals of Expression* (Boston: Leland Powers, 1916), 18.

The technical and theoretical literature in voice science, voice and articulation pedagogy, and bodily action (subdisciplines of *pronunciatio* or *actio*, i.e., delivery) from the elocutionists to contemporary approaches to acting, may not have great frequency of citation now in performance studies journals,[36] but such literature still holds the highest value for those teaching speech and performance in service to the spoken word in worship. Nor is that priority status a matter of functional necessity alone. It is, as I have argued above, a matter of theological integrity. Further, the issue of theological integrity in the teaching of speech and performance for worship leadership and preaching has been explored from a number of viewpoints over the last couple of decades. Some of those viewpoints follow the trajectory of theological reflection taken in what I have written here. Others trace a somewhat different trajectory. But all represent coherence with the priority for research, practice, and criticism just articulated.[37]

Preaching, of course, requires a specific hermeneutic decision regarding the manner in which texts illuminate experience (in the case of Holy Scripture, the experience of Jesus Christ and of his gospel). But interpretative reading or reciting of texts, i.e., performance of them, relativizes these hermeneutic decisions by holding them accountable to the texts themselves and to the variety of interpretive judgments that may have been or yet may be rendered concerning them. Thus texts have a distinctive yet plural vocality and embodiment in performance that calls into question preaching practices that simply cite texts in sermons without the texts themselves having been read (or recited) aloud first in their own integrity. Also implied here is a critique of those approaches to speaking or performing literature popularly designated postmodern, i.e., approaches that find in the performance of texts opportunity to recompose

36. One cannot help concluding that the critique of imposed standards in speech (e.g., Dwight Conguergood, "Rethinking Elocution: The Trope of the Talking Book and Other Figures of Speech," *Text and Performance Quarterly* 20, no. 4 [October 2000]: 325–41) has at last resulted in a lack of interest in any articulation of norms for speech. The further result appears to be lack of interest in what used to be thought of as *speech culture* or *vocal hygiene* or simply mastery of technique. Yet technical/literary/vocal texts still can be obtained and used, e.g., Kristin Linklater, *Freeing the Natural Voice* (New York: Drama Publishers, 1976); Kenneth C. Crannell, *Voice and Articulation*, 2nd ed. (Belmont, CA: Wadsworth, 1991); and the detailed and masterful study focusing (though not exclusively) on the singing voice, D. Ralph Appelman, *The Science of Vocal Pedagogy* (Bloomington: Indiana University Press, 1967).

37. Alla Renée Bozarth, *The Word's Body: An Incarnational Aesthetic of Interpretation* (University: University of Alabama Press, 1979); Jana Childers, *Performing the Word: Preaching as Theatre* (Nashville: Abingdon, 1998); Clayton J. Schmit, *Too Deep for Words: A Theology of Liturgical Expression* (Louisville: Westminster John Knox, 2002); Richard F. Ward, *Speaking from the Heart: Preaching with Passion* (Nashville: Abingdon, 1992); Richard F. Ward, *Speaking of the Holy: The Art of Communication in Preaching* (St. Louis: Chalice, 2001).

texts instead of re-present them, approaches that find opportunity, in fact, to undermine the integrity of texts and their capacity to cause us to view human life in certain ways, or even to view human-being-with-God in certain ways.[38] In contrast to such approaches to the speaking of texts, the stance of the traditional oral interpreter or performer of literature—or, in liturgy, the stance of the lector (or preacher or priest as lector)—is, or ought to be, a stance of humility.[39] As elsewhere I have expressed it, in speaking texts (or, in the case of preaching, in speaking *about* them) the speaker assumes the position of a listener who speaks to facilitate other people's listening.[40] The telos of written texts (in worship, the texts of Holy Scripture) is living speech, i.e., performance, undertaken as an act of sacred attentiveness. The performed work, then, *is* the work, the opus, the event cued by what the performer (as listener), through humble attentiveness to the distinctive plural vocality of the text, has been prompted to do.[41] Christian faith holds that when the word of the scriptural text is given an open and would-be-obedient-to-God hearing (the command to hear the Word of God, after all, hearkens back to the ancient *shema*, which is a call to hear and obey), divine reality discloses itself to us.

So far, I have reviewed the scope of contemporary research and teaching in performance studies. I also have sought to determine a focus in such study for speech teachers (i.e., performance studies theorists, practitioners, and critics) in the theological academies of the church. Further, in theological as well as in practical terms, I have attempted to set priorities for research and pedagogy for those in the speech-performance studies disciplines who understand themselves to be in service to the servants of the spoken word in worship. One thing remains to be done, however, and that is to address the challenge to speech instruction in service to the ministry of the Word brought by the contemporary multimedia environment in which the mighty *te deum* of the people of God takes place. I will not enter what has been called "the worship wars," though that language itself, I might suggest, connotes a bit of media hype. I will not be going into whether or how to utilize electronic media in services of worship. Nor will I investigate the suitability of using these media to extend the compass of those services beyond the gathered congregation in the sanctuary or auditorium. I will not explore the implications of "PowerPoint sermons"

38. See the debate between playwright Sam Shepard and director/performance theorist Richard Schechner in Schechner, *Performance Theory*, 76.

39. Charles L. Bartow, "Who Says the Song? Practical Hermeneutics as Humble Performance," *Princeton Seminary Bulletin* 17, no. 2 (July 1996): 143–53.

40. Charles L. Bartow, *The Preaching Moment: A Guide to Sermon Delivery* (Dubuque, IA: Kendall/Hunt, 1995), 13–20.

41. Louise M. Rosenblatt, "Act I, Scene 1: Enter the Reader," *Literature in Performance* 1, no. 2 (April 1981): 13.

for the theology of proclamation either. Others with up-to-date specialized technical and theoretical knowledge have done some of that, and doubtless a good deal more of it will be done in the future.[42] But I will address the matter of multisensory perception and the nature of the spoken word as embodied speech, i.e., performance. A good deal has been said about oral cultures and about secondary orality in the post-Gutenberg epoch.[43] A good deal also has been said about the possible types of impact that information technology has on the way people obtain data about their world, about nature, and about human nature. And more than a little ink has been spilt—apparently electronic media have not replaced print but simply relocated a good deal of it—in learned speculation about the impact of information technologies on how people think about the data to which those technologies have provided access.[44] The matter that needs study at the moment, however, has to do with synesthesia, the play of the senses off each other, the way we use one or more of our senses to interpret what has been received through still another sense.[45]

One concrete example of what strikes this author as inept is the projection on a screen of the Scripture lesson while the lesson is being read aloud in public, corporate worship. I have observed this being done regularly in so-called contemporary services of worship. Not only is this patently uninteresting as a visual—far more interesting, for instance, is the much disparaged "talking head"—it also suggests that the words of Scripture being spoken are in service to the words of Scripture written on a page now projected for all to see. Yet is not the speaking of the written word to be in service to what the written word itself ultimately signifies: namely, the incarnate Word, the Word of God in the form of oral-aural, face-to-face, synesthetic event? Even the quality of the written word itself as inscripted eventfulness, as living literature and not dead letter, appears to be contradicted by this not uncommon practice of Scripture text projection.

Perhaps the reader's patience will permit one more example of technological ineptitude. It has to do with a cell phone call placed to mourners gathered for a

42. E.g., Pierre Babin and Angela Zukowski, *The Gospel in Cyberspace: Nurturing Faith in the Internet Age* (Chicago: Loyola Press, 2002); Jolyon P. Mitchell, *Visually Speaking: Radio and the Renaissance of Preaching* (Edinburgh: T&T Clark, 1999); Quentin J. Schultze, *Habits of the High-Tech Heart: Living Virtuously in the Information Age* (Grand Rapids: Baker Academic, 2002); Quentin J. Schultze, *High-Tech Worship? Using Presentational Technologies Wisely* (Grand Rapids: Baker Books, 2004).

43. E.g., Bruce E. Gronbeck, Thomas J. Farrell, and Paul A. Soukup, *Media, Consciousness, and Culture* (Newbury Park, CA: Sage, 1991).

44. Chesebro, "Text, Narration, and Media," 1–23.

45. See the book-length discussion of synesthesia and its history in religious discourse in David Chidester, *Word and Light: Seeing, Hearing, and Religious Discourse* (Urbana: University of Illinois Press, 1992). Also Webb, *Divine Voice*, 221–39.

graveside committal service. And yes, this really did happen. Before the paying of final respects and the pronouncing of the benediction, one of the grieving party was obliged to relay the happy remembrances of the deceased phoned in by a friend of the deceased not on hand. The liturgical focus shifted from the hope of resurrection and the care of the Lord for his own, even beyond the bounds of vision, to the jovial remarks proffered by an electronic voice and relayed to the mourners by their cell phone-wielding fellow mourner. The actuals—the casket being set in the earth, the mourners' tears, their prayers, being gathered up into the pastor's reading of the prayers of the church catholic, the promises of Scripture, the apostolic blessing—were muted by an intrusive virtual. Of course anything that can be done badly can be done well. Still, what "well" is surely needs theological definition so that worship may be according to Scripture, and so biblically and theologically normed, and not governed merely by some notion of what is vogue. Whatever the result of the "worship wars," therefore, and whatever may be decided here or there about when and how to use electronic media in worship or to extend worship beyond the sanctuary, we still must do theologically accountable speech-performance theory, practice, and criticism in service to the spoken word in worship. For with the spoken word in worship there are real presences to be encountered, and, with those presences, Real Presence. In the human echo of the divine voice, veritably and not virtually, we may expect to hear, through the written word become a spoken word, the incarnate Word of God.

Bibliography

Common Bibliography

Augustine. *On Christian Doctrine*. In *Nicene and Post-Nicene Fathers*, First Series. Edited by Philip Schaff. 1887. Reprint, Peabody, MA: Hendrickson, 1994.

Bacon, Wallace A. *The Art of Interpretation*. 3rd ed. New York: Holt, Rinehart & Winston, 1979.

Barth, Karl. *Church Dogmatics*, I/1. Edinburgh: T&T Clark, 1956.

———. *Homiletics*. Louisville: Westminster John Knox, 1991.

Bartow, Charles L. *Effective Speech Communication in Leading Worship*. Nashville: Abingdon, 1988.

———. *God's Human Speech: A Practical Theology of Proclamation*. Grand Rapids: Eerdmans, 1997.

———. "Heading West on the Jericho Turnpike." In *Lament: Reclaiming Practices in Pulpit, Pew, and Public Square*, edited by Sally A. Brown and Patrick D. Miller. Louisville: Westminster John Knox, 2005.

———. "In Service to the Servants of the Word: Teaching Speech at Princeton Theological Seminary." *Princeton Seminary Bulletin* 13, no. 3 (November 1992): 274–86.

———. *The Preaching Moment: A Guide to Sermon Delivery*. Nashville: Abingdon, 1980.

———. "Sonnet in Remembrance of Pan American Flight 103." In *Lament: Reclaiming Practices in Pulpit, Pew, and Public Square*, edited by Sally A. Brown and Patrick D. Miller. Louisville: Westminster John Knox, 2005.

———. "Who Says the Song? Practical Hermeneutics as Humble Performance." *Princeton Seminary Bulletin* 17, no. 2 (July 1996): 143–53.

Bate, Barbara. "Oral Communication and Preaching." In *Concise Encyclopedia of Preaching*, edited by William H. Willimon and Richard Lischer, 352–54. Louisville: Westminster John Knox, 1995.

Bonhoeffer, Dietrich. *Ethics.* Translated by Neville Horton Smith. New York: Macmillan, 1955.

Brunner, Emil. *The Divine-Human Encounter.* Translated by Amandus William Loos. Philadelphia: Westminster, 1943.

Buber, Martin. *I and Thou.* 2nd ed. New York: Scribner, 1958.

Buttrick, David. "Proclamation." In *Concise Encyclopedia of Preaching*, edited by William H. Willimon and Richard Lischer. Louisville: Westminster John Knox, 1995.

Buttrick, George Arthur. *Sermons Preached in a University Church.* Nashville: Abingdon, 1959.

Charry, Ellen T. *By the Renewing of Your Minds: The Pastoral Function of Christian Doctrine.* New York: Oxford University Press, 1997.

Childers, Jana. *Performing the Word: Preaching as Theatre.* Nashville: Abingdon, 1998.

"The Confession of 1967." In *The Book of Confessions*, Presbyterian Church, USA. Louisville: General Assembly, PCUSA, 1996.

Davis, Donald. *Writing as a Second Language.* Little Rock: August House, 2000.

Fant, Clyde. *Preaching for Today.* New York: Harper & Row, 1975.

Forde, Gerhard O. *Theology Is for Proclamation.* Minneapolis: Fortress, 1990.

Goffman, Erving. *The Presentation of Self in Everyday Life.* Garden City, NY: Doubleday, 1959.

Graff, H. J. *The Legacies of Literacy: Continuities and Contradictions in Western Culture and Society.* Bloomington: Indiana University Press, 1987.

Gunton, Colin E. *The Christian Faith: An Introduction to Christian Doctrine.* Oxford: Blackwell, 2002.

Hogan, Lucy Lind, and Robert Reid. *Connecting with the Congregation: Rhetoric and the Art of Preaching.* Nashville: Abingdon, 1999.

Illingworth, J. R. *Divine Immanence: An Essay on the Spiritual Significance of Matter.* New York: Macmillan, 1898. Reprint, Kessinger, date unknown.

Jacks, G. Robert. *Getting the Word Across.* Grand Rapids: Eerdmans, 1995.

Johnson, Mark. *The Body in the Mind.* Chicago: University of Chicago Press, 1987.

Kerr, Hugh T. *Calvin's Institutes: A New Compend.* Louisville: Westminster John Knox, 1989.

Lischer, Richard. *A Theology of Preaching: The Dynamics of the Gospel.* Eugene, OR: Wipf and Stock, 1992.

———. *Theories of Preaching: Selected Readings in the Homiletical Tradition.* Durham, NC: Labyrinth, 1987.

Locals, Craig. "Rhetoric." In *Concise Encyclopedia of Preaching*, edited by William H. Willimon and Richard Lischer, 409–16. Louisville: Westminster John Knox, 1995.

McCormack, Bruce L. *Karl Barth's Critically Realistic Dialectical Theology: Its Genesis and Development, 1909–1936.* New York: Oxford University Press, 1995.

McRobbie, Angela. *Postmodern and Popular Culture.* London: Routledge, 1994.

McWhorter, John. *Doing Our Own Thing: The Degradation of Language and Music and Why We Should, Like, Care.* New York: Gotham Books, 2003.

Mehrabian, Albert. *Silent Messages: Implicit Communication of Emotions and Attitudes.* 2nd ed. Belmont, CA: Wadsworth, 1981.

Mitchell, Jolyon P. *Visually Speaking: Radio and the Renaissance of Preaching.* Edinburgh: T&T Clark, 1999.

Old, Hughes Oliphant. *Worship: Reformed according to Scripture.* Atlanta: John Knox, 1984.

Ong, Walter J. *Orality and Literacy: The Technologizing of the Word.* London: Methuen, 1982.

————. *The Presence of the Word: Some Prolegomena for Cultural and Religious History.* Minneapolis: University of Minnesota Press, 1981.

Otto, Rudolf, and John Wilfred Harvey. *The Idea of the Holy: An Inquiry into the Non-Rational Factor in the Idea of the Divine and Its Relation to the Rational.* London: Oxford University Press, 1925.

Pelikan, Jaroslav Jan. *Fools for Christ: Essays on the True, the Good, and the Beautiful.* Philadelphia: Muhlenberg, 1955.

Scherer, Paul E. *The Word God Sent.* New York: Harper & Row, 1965.

————. A prayer, in *Worship Resources for the Christian Year*, edited by Charles L. Wallis. New York: Harper & Bros., 1954.

Schmit, Clayton J. *Public Reading of Scripture: A Handbook.* Nashville: Abingdon, 2002.

————. *Too Deep for Words: A Theology of Liturgical Expression.* Louisville: Westminster John Knox, 2002.

Schultze, Quentin J. *Habits of the High-Tech Heart: Living Virtuously in the Information Age.* Grand Rapids: Baker Academic, 2002.

————. *High-Tech Worship? Using Presentational Technologies Wisely.* Grand Rapids: Baker Books, 2004.

Shuster, Marguerite. *The Fall and Sin: What We Have Become as Sinners.* Grand Rapids: Eerdmans, 2004.

Storey, Peter. *With God in the Crucible.* Nashville: Abingdon, 2002.

Tisdale, Leonora Tubbs. *Preaching as Local Theology and Folk Art.* Minneapolis: Fortress, 1997.

Trilling, Lionel. *Sincerity and Authenticity.* Cambridge, MA: Harvard University Press, 1972.

Ward, Richard F. "A New Look at an Ancient Practice: Public Reading in the Plugged-In Church." *Doxology: A Journal of Worship* 18 (2001): 30–48.

————. "A New Look at the Lector's Art." *Liturgy* 8, no. 3 (1990): 8–14.

————. "Pauline Voice and Presence as Strategic Communication." *Semeia* 65 (1994): 95–107.

————. "Performance Turns in Homiletics: Wrong Way or Right On?" *Journal of Communication and Religion* 17 (1994): 1–11.

———. *Speaking from the Heart: Preaching with Passion.* Nashville: Abingdon, 1992.

———. *Speaking of the Holy: The Art of Communication in Preaching.* St. Louis: Chalice, 2001.

———. *Your Ministry of Reading Scripture Aloud.* Nashville: Discipleship Resources, 1989.

Webb, Stephen H. *The Divine Voice: Christian Proclamation and the Theology of Sound.* Grand Rapids: Brazos, 2004.

Willimon, William H., and Richard Lischer. *Concise Encyclopedia of Preaching.* Louisville: Westminster John Knox, 1995.

Performance and Biblical Studies Bibliography

Achtemeier, Paul J. "*Omne verba sonat:* The New Testament and the Oral Environment of Late Western Antiquity." *Journal of Biblical Literature* 109 (1990): 3–27.

Alexander, Loveday. "The Living Voice: Skepticism towards the Written Word in Early Christian and in Greco-Roman Texts." In *The Bible in Three Dimensions*, edited by D. J. Clines, 221–47. Sheffield, UK: JSOT Press, 1990.

Amador, J. David Hester. *Academic Constraints in Rhetorical Criticism of the New Testament: An Introduction to a Rhetoric of Power.* Sheffield, UK: Sheffield Academic Press, 1999.

Aune, David. "Prolegomena to the Study of Oral Tradition in the Hellenistic World." In *Jesus and the Oral Gospel Tradition*, edited by Henry Wansbrough, 59–106. JSNTSup 64. Sheffield, UK: JSOT Press, 1991.

Babin, Pierre, and Angela Zukowski. *The Gospel in Cyberspace: Nurturing Faith in the Internet Age.* Chicago: Loyola Press, 2002.

Bailey, James L., and Lyle Vander Broek. *Literary Forms in the New Testament.* Louisville: Westminster John Knox, 1992.

Bailey, Kenneth E. "Informal Controlled Oral Tradition and the Synoptic Gospels." *Asia Journal of Theology* 4 (1991): 34–54.

———. "Middle Eastern Oral Tradition and the Synoptic Gospels." *The Expository Times* 106 (1995): 363–67.

Balch, David. "The Canon: Adaptable and Stable, Oral and Written: Critical Questions for Kelber and Riesner." *Foundations and Facets Forum* 7 (1993): 183–205.

Bar-Ilan, Meir. "Illiteracy in the Land of Israel in the First Centuries C.E." In *Essays in the Social Science Study of Judaism and Jewish Society*, edited by Simcha Fishbane and Stuart Schoenfeld with Alain Goldshläger, vol. 2. Hoboken, NJ: KTAV, 1992, 46–61.

Barr, David. "The Apocalypse as a Symbolic Transformation of the World: A Literary Analysis." *Interpretation* 38 (1984): 39–59.

———. "The Apocalypse of John as Oral Enactment." *Interpretation* 43 (1986): 243–56.

Bartholomew, Gilbert L. "Feed My Lambs: John 21:15–19 as Oral Gospel." *Semeia* 39 (1987): 69–96.

———. *Human Encounter in the Spiritual Gospel.* Worship Alive. Nashville: Discipleship Resources, 1981.

———. *Pass It On: Telling and Hearing Stories from John.* Cleveland: United Church Press, 1993.

Barton, Stephen C. "New Testament Interpretation as Performance." *Scottish Journal of Theology* 52 (1999): 179–208.

Betz, Hans Dieter. *Galatians: A Commentary on Paul's Letter to the Churches in Galatia.* Hermeneia. Philadelphia: Fortress, 1979.

The Biblical Storyteller. Online journal of Network of Biblical Storytellers. http://www.nobs.org.

Black, C. Clifton. *The Rhetoric of the Gospel: Theological Artistry in the Gospels and Acts.* St. Louis: Chalice, 2001.

Bland, David, and David Fleer, eds. *Performing the Psalms.* St. Louis: Chalice, 2005.

Boomershine, Thomas E. "Jesus of Nazareth and the Watershed of Ancient Orality and Literacy." *Semeia* 65 (1994): 7–26.

———. "Peter's Denial as Polemic or Confession: The Implications of Media Criticism for Biblical Hermeneutics." *Semeia* 39 (1987): 47–68.

———. *Story Journey: An Invitation to the Gospel as Storytelling.* Nashville: Abingdon, 1988.

Botha, P. J. J. "Greco-Roman Literacy as Setting for New Testament Writings." *Neotestamentica* 26 (1992): 195–215.

———. "Letter Writing and Oral Communication in Antiquity: Suggested Implications for the Interpretation of Paul's Letter to the Galatians." *Scriptura* 42 (1992): 17–34.

———. "Living Voice and Lifeless Letters: Reserve towards Writing in the Greco-Roman World." *Hervormde Teologiese Studies* 49 (1993): 742–59.

———. "Mark's Story as Oral Traditional Letter: Rethinking the Transmission of Some Traditions about Jesus." *Hervormde Teologiese Studies* 47 (1991): 304–31.

———. "Mute Manuscripts: Analyzing a Neglected Aspect of Ancient Communication." *Theologica Evangelica* 23 (1990): 35–47.

———. "The Verbal Art of Pauline Letters: Rhetoric, Performance, and Presence." In *Rhetoric and the New Testament: Essays from the 1992 Heidelberg Conference,* edited by Stanley E. Porter and Thomas H. Olbricht, 409–28. Sheffield, UK: Sheffield Academic Press, 1993.

Bowman, Alan K., and Greg Woolf, eds. *Literacy and Power in the Ancient World.* Cambridge: Cambridge University Press, 1994.

Brown, William. *Seeing the Psalms: A Theology of Metaphor.* Louisville: Westminster John Knox, 2003.

Brueggemann, Walter. "Psalms in Narrative Performance." In *Performing the Psalms,* edited by Dave Bland and David Fleer, 9–30. St. Louis: Chalice, 2005.

Bryan, Christopher. "As It Is Written: Notes on the Essentially Oral Characteristics of Mark's Appeal to Scripture." *Sewanee Theological Review* 36 (1992): 78–90.

Bultmann, Rudolf. *The History of the Synoptic Tradition*. Translated by John Marsh. New York: Harper & Row, 1963.

Caird, G. B. *New Testament Theology*. Completed and edited by L. D. Hurst. New York: Oxford University Press, 1994.

Camp, Claudia. "The Female Sage in Ancient Israel and in the Biblical Wisdom Literature." In *The Sage in Israel and the Ancient Near East*, edited by John Gammie and Leo Perdue, 185–204. Winona Lake, IN: Eisenbrauns, 1990.

Cartlidge, David. "Combien d'unités avez-vous de trios à quatre? What Do We Mean by Intertextuality in Early Church Studies." In *Society of Biblical Literature Seminar Abstracts and Seminar Papers*, edited by David Lull, 400–411. Atlanta: Scholar's Press, 1990.

Cole, Susan Guettel. "Could Greek Women Read and Write?" In *Reflections of Women in Antiquity*, edited by Helen P. Foley, 219–45. New York: Gorden and Breach Science Press, 1981.

Craddock, Fred B. "Is There Still Room for Rhetoric?" In *Preaching on the Brink: The Future of Homiletics*, edited by Martha Simmons, 65–76. Nashville: Abingdon, 1996.

Culley, Robert. "Oral Tradition and Biblical Studies." *Oral Tradition* 1 (1985): 30–65.

Davis, Casey Wayne. *Oral Biblical Criticism: The Influence of the Principles of Orality on the Literary Structure of Paul's Epistle to the Philippians*. JSNTSup 172. Sheffield, UK: Sheffield Academic Press, 1999.

Dewey, Arthur. "A Re-Hearing of Romans 10:1–15." *Semeia* 65 (1994): 109–28.

———. *Spirit and Letter in Paul*. Lewiston, NY: Mellen, 1996.

Dewey, Joanna. "From Storytelling to Written Text: The Loss of Early Christian Women's Voices." *Biblical Theology Bulletin* 26 (1996): 71–78.

———. "The Gospel of Mark as an Oral-Aural Event: Implications for Interpretation." In *The New Literary Criticism and the New Testament*, edited by Elizabeth Struthers Malbon and Edgar V. McKnight, 145–63. Sheffield, UK: Sheffield Academic Press, 1994.

———. "Mark as Aural Narrative: Structure as Clues to Understanding." *Sewanee Theological Review* 36 (1992): 45–56.

———. "Oral Methods of Structuring Narrative in Mark." *Interpretation* 43 (1989): 32–44.

———. "Textuality in an Oral Culture: A Survey of the Pauline Traditions." *Semeia* 65 (1994): 37–66.

Dewey, Joanna, and Elizabeth Struthers Malbon, eds. *Orality and Textuality in Early Christian Literature. Semeia* 65 (1994).

Doan, William, and Terry Giles, eds. *Prophets, Performance and Power: Performance Criticism of the Hebrew Bible*. New York and London: T&T Clark, 2005.

Driver, Tom F. "Performance and Biblical Reading: Its Promise and Hazard." In *Body and Bible: Interpreting and Experiencing Biblical Narratives*, edited by Björn Krondorfer, 159–74. Philadelphia: Trinity, 1992.

Dundes, Alan. *Holy Writ as Holy Lit: The Bible as Folklore*. Lanham, MD: Rowman & Littlefield, 1999.

Dunn, James D. G. "Altering the Default Setting: Re-envisaging the Early Transmission of the Jesus Tradition." *New Testament Studies* 49 (2003): 139–75.

———. "Jesus in Oral Memory: The Initial Stages of the Jesus Tradition." In *Society of Biblical Literature Seminar Papers 1993*, 287–326. Atlanta: Society of Biblical Literature, 2000.

———. *Romans 1–8*. Word Biblical Commentary 38. Dallas: Word, 1988.

Elman, Yaakov, and Israel Garson, eds. *Transmitting Jewish Traditions: Orality, Textuality, and Cultural Diffusion*. New Haven: Yale University Press, 2000.

Finnegan, Ruth H. *Oral Poetry: Its Nature, Significance and Social Context*. Cambridge: Cambridge University Press, 1982.

Fontaine, Carole. *Smooth Words: Women, Proverbs, and Performance in Biblical Wisdom*. London: Sheffield Academic Press, 2002.

Fowler, Robert M. "How the Secondary Orality of the Electronic Age Can Awaken Us to the Primary Orality of Antiquity, or What Hypertext Can Teach Us about the Bible." *Interpersonal Computing and Technology: An Electronic Journal for the 21st Century* 2 (1994): 12–46.

Funk, Robert W. *Parables and Presence: Forms of the New Testament Tradition*. Philadelphia: Fortress, 1982.

Gamble, Harry Y. *Books and Readers in the Early Church*. New Haven: Yale University Press, 1995.

Gerhardsson, Birger. *Memory and Manuscript: Oral Tradition and Written Transmission in Rabbinic Judaism and Early Christianity*. Translated by Eric J. Sharpe. 1961. Reprint, Grand Rapids: Eerdmans, 1998.

———. *Tradition and Transmission in Early Christianity*. Translated by Eric J. Sharpe. 1964. Reprint, Grand Rapids: Eerdmans, 1998.

Goody, Jack. *The Interface between the Written and the Oral*. Cambridge: Cambridge University Press, 1987.

Graham, William A. *Beyond the Written Word: Oral Aspects of Scripture in the History of Religion*. Cambridge: Cambridge University Press, 1987.

Greene, W. C. "The Spoken and Written Word." *Harvard Studies in Classical Philology* 60 (1959): 23–59.

Harris, William. *Ancient Literacy*. Cambridge, MA: Harvard University Press, 1989.

Harvey, John D. "Orality and Its Implications for Biblical Studies: Recapturing an Ancient Paradigm." *Journal of the Evangelical Theological Society* (2002): 99–109.

Havelock, Eric. *The Literate Revolution in Greece and Its Cultural Consequences*. Princeton, NJ: Princeton University Press, 1982.

———. *The Muse Learns to Write: Reflections on Orality and Literacy from Antiquity to the Present*. New Haven: Yale University Press, 1986.

———. "Oral Culture in Scriptural Religion: Some Exploratory Studies." *Religious Studies Review* 24 (1998): 223–30.

———. *Preface to Plato*. Cambridge, MA: Harvard University Press, 1963.

Hearon, Holly E. *The Mary Magdalene Tradition: Witness and Counter-Witness in Early Christian Communities*. Collegeville, MN: Liturgical Press, 2004.

Hendrickson, G. L. "Ancient Reading." *Classical Journal* 25 (1929–30): 182–96.

Holtz, Thomas. "Paul and the Oral Gospel Tradition." In *Jesus and the Oral Gospel Tradition*, edited by Henry Wansbrough, 380–93. JSNTSup 64. Sheffield, UK: JSOT Press, 1991.

Horsley, Richard A., and Jonathan A. Draper. *Whoever Hears You Hears Me: Prophets, Performance, and Tradition in Q*. Harrisburg, PA: Trinity, 1999.

Jaffee, Martin S. "How Much 'Orality' in Oral Torah? New Perspectives on the Composition and Transmission of Early Rabbinic Tradition." *Shofar* 10 (1992): 53–72.

Jasper, David. *Rhetoric, Power and Community: An Exercise in Reserve*. Louisville: Westminster John Knox, 1993.

Journal of Biblical Storytelling. Published by Network of Biblical Storytellers. http://www.nobs.org.

Juel, Donald. "The Strange Silence of the Bible." *Interpretation* 51, no. 1 (1997): 5.

Kelber, Werner. "Biblical Hermeneutics and the Ancient Art of Communication: A Response." *Semeia* 39 (1987): 97–107.

———. "In the Beginning Were the Words: The Apotheosis and Narrative Displacement of the Logos." *Journal of the American Academy of Religion* 53 (1990): 69–98.

———. "Language, Memory, and Sense Perception in the Religious and Technological Culture of Antiquity and the Middle Ages." *Oral Tradition* 10 (1995): 409–45.

———. "Modality of Communication, Cognition, and Physiology of Perception: Orality, Rhetoric, and Scribality." *Semeia* 65 (1994): 193–212.

———. "Narrative as Interpretation and Interpretation as Narrative: Hermeneutical Reflections on the Gospels." *Semeia* 39 (1987): 107–34.

———. *The Oral and the Written Gospel: The Hermeneutics of Speaking and Writing in the Synoptic Tradition, Mark, Paul and Q*. New ed. Bloomington: Indiana University Press, 1997.

Kennedy, George. *New Testament Interpretation through Rhetorical Criticism*. Chapel Hill: University of North Carolina Press, 1984.

Klem, Herbert V. *Oral Communication of the Scripture: Insights from African Oral Art*. Pasadena, CA: William Carey Library, 1982.

Knox, Bernard M. W. "Silent Reading in Antiquity." *Greek, Roman and Byzantine Studies* 9 (1968): 421–35.

Lee, Charlotte. *Oral Reading of the Scriptures*. Boston: Houghton-Mifflin, 1974.

Litfin, A. Duane. *St. Paul's Theology of Proclamation: 1 Corinthians 1–4 and Greco-Roman Rhetoric*. Cambridge: Cambridge University Press, 1994.

Lohr, Charles H. "Oral Techniques in the Gospel of Matthew." *Catholic Biblical Quarterly* 23 (1961): 403–35.

Looser, J. A. "Orality and Pauline 'Christology.'" *Scriptura* 47 (1993): 25–51.

Lord, Albert B. "The Gospels as Oral Literature." In *The Relationship among the Gospels: An Interdisciplinary Dialogue,* edited by O. W. Walker Jr., 33–91. San Antonio: Trinity University Press, 1978.

———. *The Singer of Tales.* Cambridge, MA: Harvard University Press, 1960.

Mack, Burton L. *Rhetoric and the New Testament.* Minneapolis: Fortress, 1990.

Meynet, Roland. *Rhetorical Analysis: An Introduction to Biblical Rhetoric.* Sheffield, UK: Sheffield Academic Press, 1998.

Mitchell, Margaret Mary. *Paul and the Rhetoric of Reconciliation: An Exegetical Investigation of the Language and Composition of 1 Corinthians.* Louisville: Westminster John Knox, 1993.

Neusner, Jacob. *The Memorized Torah: The Mnemonic System of the Torah.* Chico, CA: Scholars Press, 1985.

———. *The Oral Torah: The Sacred Books of Judaism.* Chicago: University of Chicago Press, 1986.

———. "Oral Tradition and Oral Torah: Defining the Problematic." In *Studies in Jewish Folklore,* edited by Frank Tallmadge, 251–71. Cambridge, MA: Association for Jewish Studies, 1980.

———. *Oral Tradition in Judaism: The Case of the Mishnah.* New York: Garland, 1987.

Nielsen, Eduard. *Oral Tradition Studies in Biblical Theology.* London: SCM, 1954.

Ong, Walter J. "Text and Interpretation: Mark and After." *Semeia* 39 (1987): 7–26.

Peterson, Brian K. *Eloquence and the Proclamation of the Gospel in Corinth.* Atlanta: Scholars Press, 1998.

Pogoloff, Stephen M. *Logos and Sophia: The Rhetorical Situation of 1 Corinthians.* Atlanta: Scholars Press, 1992.

Porter, Stanley E. *Verbal Aspect in the Greek New Testament with Reference to Tense and Mood.* New York: Peter Lang, 1989.

Porter, Stanley E., and Thomas H. Olbricht, eds. *The Rhetorical Analysis of Scripture: Essays from the 1995 London Conference.* Sheffield, UK: Sheffield Academic Press, 1997.

———. *Rhetoric and the New Testament: Essays from the 1992 Heidelberg Conference.* Sheffield, UK: Sheffield Academic Press, 1993.

Porter, Stanley E., and Dennis L. Stamps, eds. *Rhetorical Criticism and the Bible.* JSNTSup 195. Sheffield, UK: Sheffield Academic Press, 2002.

Rhoads, David. "Performing the Gospel of Mark." In *Body and Bible: Interpreting and Experiencing Biblical Narratives,* edited by Björn Krondorfer, 102–17. Philadelphia: Trinity, 1992.

Robbins, Vernon K. "Oratorical, Literary and Rhetorical Cultures: A Response." *Semeia* 65 (1994): 75–93.

———. "Progymnastic Rhetorical Composition and Pre-Gospel Traditions: A New Approach." In *The Synoptic Gospels: Source Criticism and the New Literary Criticism,* edited by Camille Focant, 111–47. Leuven, Netherlands: Leuven University Press, 1993.

———. "Rhetoric and Culture: Exploring Types of Cultural Rhetoric in a Text." In *Rhetoric and the New Testament: Essays from the 1992 Heidelberg Conference*, edited by Stanley E. Porter and Thomas H. Olbricht, 443–63. Sheffield, UK: Sheffield Academic Press, 1993.

———. "Socio-Rhetorical Criticism: Mary, Elizabeth and the Magnificat as a Test Case." In *The New Literary Criticism and the New Testament*, edited by Elizabeth Struthers Malbon and Edgar V. McKnight, 164–209. Sheffield, UK: Sheffield Academic Press, 1994.

———. *The Tapestry of Early Christian Discourse: Rhetoric, Society and Ideology.* New York: Routledge, 1996.

———. "Writing as a Rhetorical Act in Plutarch and the Gospels." In *Persuasive Artistry: Studies in New Testament Rhetoric in Honor of George A. Kennedy*, edited by Duane F. Watson, 157–86. Sheffield, UK: JSOT Press, 1991.

Scobie, Alex. "Storytellers, Storytelling, and the Novel in Greco-Roman Antiquity." *Rheinisches Museum für Philologie* 122 (1979): 229–59.

Scott, Bernard Brandon, and Margaret Dean. "A Sound Map of the Sermon on the Mount." In *Society of Biblical Literature Seminar Papers 1993*, 672–725. Atlanta: Scholars Press, 1993.

Shields, Bruce E. *From the Housetops: Preaching in the Early Church and Today.* St. Louis: Chalice, 2000.

Shiner, Whitney. *Performing the Gospel: First Century Performance of Mark.* Valley Forge, PA: Trinity, 2003.

Silberman, Lou H., ed. *Orality, Aurality and Biblical Narrative. Semeia* 39 (1987).

Stowers, Stanley K. *A Rereading of Romans: Justice, Jews, and Gentiles.* New Haven: Yale University Press, 1994.

Vansina, Jan. *Oral Tradition as History.* Madison: University of Wisconsin Press, 1985.

Vermes, Geza. "Scripture and Oral Tradition in Judaism: Written and Oral Torah." In *The Written Word: Literacy in Transition*, edited by G. Baumann. Oxford: Oxford University Press, 1986.

Wansbrough, Henry, ed. *Jesus and the Oral Gospel Tradition.* JSNTSup 64. Sheffield, UK: JSOT Press, 1991.

Watson, Duane F. *Invention, Arrangement, and Style: Rhetorical Criticism of Jude and 2 Peter.* Atlanta: Scholars Press, 1988.

———, ed. *Persuasive Artistry: Studies in New Testament Rhetoric in Honor of George A. Kennedy.* Sheffield, UK: JSOT Press, 1991.

Watson, Duane F., and Alan J. Hauser. *Rhetorical Criticism of the Bible: A Comprehensive Bibliography with Notes on History and Method.* Biblical Interpretation Series. Leiden, Netherlands: Brill, 1994.

Watson, Jane, ed. *Speaking Volumes: Orality and Literacy in the Greek and Roman World.* Leiden, Netherlands: Brill, 2001.

Welborn, L. L. *Politics and Rhetoric in the Corinthian Epistles.* Macon, GA: Mercer University Press, 1997.

Westermann, Claus. *Basic Forms of Prophetic Speech.* London: Lutterworth, 1967.

———. *Prophetic Oracles of Salvation in the Old Testament*. Louisville: Westminster John Knox, 1991.

Wilder, Amos. *Early Christian Rhetoric: The Language of the Gospel*. Cambridge, MA: Harvard University Press, 1964.

Wire, Antoinette Clark. *The Corinthian Women Prophets: A Reconstruction through Paul's Rhetoric*. Minneapolis: Fortress, 1990.

———. *Holy Lives, Holy Deaths: A Close Hearing of Early Jewish Storytellers*. Leiden, Netherlands: Brill, 2002.

———. "Performance, Politics, and Power: A Response." *Semeia* 65 (1994): 129–37.

Wray, Judith Hoch. "Consummation and Celebration: The Revelation of John." In *Chalice Introduction to the New Testament*, edited by Dennis Smith, 306–30. St. Louis: Chalice, 2004.

———. "An Exhortation to Faithfulness: Hebrews." In *Chalice Introduction to the New Testament*, edited by Dennis Smith, 281–305. St. Louis: Chalice, 2004.

Wuellner, Wilhelm. "Greek Rhetoric and Pauline Argumentation." In *Early Christian Literature and the Classical Intellectual Tradition*, edited by W. R. Schoedel and R. L. Wilken. Théologie Historique 54, 448–63. Paris: Beauchesene, 1979.

———. "Hermeneutics and Rhetoric: From 'Truth and Method' to 'Truth and Power,'" *Scriptura* 3, special issue (1989): 1–54.

———. "Where Is Rhetorical Criticism Taking Us?" *Catholic Biblical Quarterly* 49 (1987): 448–63.

Zlotnik, Dov. "Memory and the Integrity of the Oral Tradition." *Journal of the Ancient Near Eastern Society* 16 (1984–85): 229–41.

Performance, Music, and the Arts Bibliography

Alperson, Philip, ed. *What Is Music? An Introduction to the Philosophy of Music*. University Park: Pennsylvania State University Press, 1994.

Arieti, Silvano. *Creativity: The Magical Synthesis*. New York: Basic Books, 1976.

Barron, Frank, and David Harrington. "Creativity, Intelligence and Personality." *Annual Review of Psychology* 32 (1981): 439–76.

Barron, Frank, Alfonso Montuori, and Anthea Barron, eds. *Creators on Creating: Awakening and Cultivating the Imaginative Mind*. New York: Putnam 1997.

Begbie, Jeremy S., ed. *Beholding the Glory: Incarnation through the Arts*. Grand Rapids: Baker Academic, 2001.

———. *Musical Theology*. Grand Rapids: Eerdmans, 2007.

———. *Resounding Truth: Christian Wisdom in the World of Music*. Grand Rapids: Baker Academic, 2007.

———. *Theology, Music and Time*. Cambridge: Cambridge University Press, 2000.

———. *Voicing Creation's Praise: Towards a Theology of the Arts*. London: T&T Clark, 1991.

Bergson, Henri. *The Creative Mind*. Translated by Mabelle L. Andison. New York: Philosophical Library, 1946.

Birch, Carol, and Melissa K. Hackler. *Who Says? Essays on Pivotal Issues in Contemporary Storytelling*. Little Rock: August House, 2003.

Cameron, Julia. *The Artist's Way: A Spiritual Path to Higher Creativity*. New York: G. P. Putnam's Sons, 1992.

Csikszentmihalyi, Mihalyi. *Creativity: Flow and the Psychology of Discovery and Invention*. New York: HarperCollins, 1996.

Davis, Gary. *Creativity Is Forever*. Dubuque, IA: Kendall Hunt, 1998.

Dillenberger, John. *A Theology of Artistic Sensibilities: The Visual Arts and the Church*. New York: Crossroad, 1986.

Farley, Todd. *The Mastery of Mimodrame*. Video and book. 3 vols. Colorado Springs: Meriwether, 2000.

———. *Rhythms and Concepts*. Colorado Springs: Meriwether, 2000.

Gardner, Howard. *Creating Minds: An Anatomy of Creativity Seen through the Lives of Freud, Einstein, Picasso, Stravinsky, Eliot, Graham and Gandhi*. New York: Basic Books, 1994.

Graham, Gordon. *Philosophy of the Arts: An Introduction to Aesthetics*. 2nd ed. London: Routledge, 2000.

Graves, Mike. *The Sermon as Symphony: Preaching the Literary Forms of the New Testament*. Valley Forge, PA: Judson, 1997.

Heyl, Bernard C. *New Bearings in Esthetics and Art Criticism: A Study in Semantics and Evaluation*. New Haven: Yale University Press, 1943.

Hospers, John. *Meaning and Truth in the Arts*. Chapel Hill: University of North Carolina Press, 1974.

Jones, Kirk Byron. *The Jazz of Preaching*. Nashville: Abingdon, 2004.

Langer, Susanne K. *Feeling and Form*. New York: Charles Scribner's Sons, 1953.

———. *Philosophy in a New Key: A Study in the Symbolism of Reason, Rite, and Art*. Cambridge, MA: Harvard University Press, 1951.

Maritain, Jacques. *The Responsibility of the Artist*. New York: Scribner, 1960.

May, Rollo. *The Courage to Create*. New York: W. W. Norton, 1975.

Osborn, Alex. *Applied Imagination*. New York: Scribner, 1953.

Rink, John, ed. *Musical Performance: A Guide to Understanding*. Cambridge: Cambridge University Press, 2002.

Runco, Mark A., and Robert S. Albert, eds. *Theories of Creativity*. Newbury Park, CA: Sage, 1990.

Schechner, Richard. *Between Theater and Anthropology*. Philadelphia: University of Pennsylvania Press, 1985.

Schroer, Silvia, Thomas Staubli, and Linda M. Maloney. *Body Symbolism in the Bible*. Collegeville, MN: Liturgical Press, 2001.

Scruton, Roger. *The Aesthetics of Music*. Oxford: Oxford University Press, 1997.

Small, Christopher. *Musicking: The Meanings of Performing and Listening.* Hanover, NH: Wesleyan University Press, 1998.

Sternberg, Robert, ed. *The Nature of Creativity: Contemporary Psychological Perspectives.* Cambridge: Cambridge University Press, 1988.

Sudnow, David. *Ways of the Hand: The Organization of Improvised Conduct.* Cambridge, MA: MIT Press, 1993.

Uzukwu, E. Elochukwu. *Worship as Body Language: Introduction to Christian Worship: An African Orientation.* Collegeville, MN: Liturgical Press, 1997.

Wallas, Graham. *The Art of Thought.* New York: Harcourt Brace, 1926.

Webb-Mitchell, Brett. *Christly Gestures.* Grand Rapids: Eerdmans, 2002.

Wells, Samuel. *Improvisation: The Drama of Christian Ethics.* Grand Rapids: Brazos, 2004.

Performance Studies Bibliography

Apczynski, John V. *Doers of the Word: Toward a Foundational Theology Based on the Thought of Michael Polanyi.* American Academy of Religion Dissertation Series 18. Missoula, MT: Scholars Press, 1997.

Appelman, D. Ralph. *The Science of Vocal Pedagogy.* Bloomington: Indiana University Press, 1967.

Asen, Robert. "Appreciation and Desire: The Male Nude in the Photography of Robert Mapplethorpe." *Text and Performance Quarterly* 18, no. 1 (April 1998): 50–62.

Auden, W. H. "In Memory of W. B. Yeats." In *Selected Poetry of W. H. Auden*, 48–51. New York: Random House, 1958.

Austin, Gilbert. *Chironomia: Or, A Treatise on Rhetorical Delivery.* Edited by Mary Margaret Robb and Lester Thonssen. Carbondale: Southern Illinois University Press, 1966.

Bacon, Wallace A. *The Art of Interpretation.* New York: Holt, Rinehart & Winston, 1972.

Bakker, Egbert, and Ahuvia Kahne. *Written Voices, Spoken Signs.* Cambridge, MA: Harvard University Press, 1977.

Bauman, Richard. *Story, Performance, and Event: Contextual Studies of Oral Narrative.* Cambridge: Cambridge University Press, 1986.

———. *Verbal Art as Performance.* Prospect Heights, IL: Waveland, 1977.

Bell, Elizabeth. "Performance Studies as Women's Work: Historical Sights/Cites/Citations from the Margin." *Text and Performance Quarterly* 13, no. 4 (October 1993): 350–74.

Ben-Amos, Dan, and Kenneth S. Goldstein, eds. *Folklore, Performance, and Communication.* The Hague: Moulton, 1975.

Bennett, Jeffrey A. "Love Me Gender: Normative Homosexuality and 'Ex-gay' Performativity in Reparative Therapy Narratives." *Text and Performance Quarterly* 23, no. 4 (October 2003): 331–52.

Bergman, Teresa. "Personal Narrative, Dialogism, and the Performance of 'Truth' in Complaints of a Dutiful Daughter." *Text and Performance Quarterly* 24, no. 1 (January 2004): 20–37.

Bial, Henry, ed. *The Performance Studies Reader.* London: Routledge, 2004.

Bozarth, Alla Renée. *The Word's Body: An Incarnational Aesthetic of Interpretation.* University: University of Alabama Press, 1979.

Buck, Elizabeth Gray. "The Musée Gustave Moreau." In *Exceptional Spaces: Essays in Performance and History*, edited by Della Pollack, 294–315. Chapel Hill: University of North Carolina Press, 1998.

Calafell, Bernadette Marie. "Pro(re-)claiming Loss: A Performance Pilgrimage in Search of Malintzin Tenépal." *Text and Performance Quarterly* 25, no. 1 (January 2005): 43–56.

Cameron, Kenneth M. "Paul Robeson, Eddie Murphy, and the Film Text of 'Africa.'" *Text and Performance Quarterly* 10, no. 4 (October 1990): 282–93.

Carlson, Marvin. *Performance: A Critical Introduction.* New York: Routledge, 2003.

Cherwitz, Richard A., and James W. Hikins. "Climbing the Academic Ladder: A Critique of Provincialism in Contemporary Rhetoric." *Quarterly Journal of Speech* 86, no. 4 (November 2000): 375–85.

Chesebro, James W. "Performance Studies as Paradox, Culture and Manifesto." In *The Future of Performance Studies: Visions and Revisions,* edited by Sheron J. Dailey, 310–19. Annandale, VA: National Communication Association, 1998.

———. "Text, Narration, and Media." *Text and Performance Quarterly* 9, no. 1 (January 1989): 1–23.

Chidester, David. *Word and Light: Seeing, Hearing, and Religious Discourse.* Urbana: University of Illinois Press, 1992.

Chopp, Rebecca. "Theological Persuasion: Rhetoric, Warrants, and Suffering." In *Worldviews and Warrants: Plurality and Authority in Theology*, edited by William Schweiker, 17–35. Lanham, MD: University Press of America, 1987.

Conguergood, Dwight. "Literacy and Oral Performance in Anglo-Saxon England: Conflict and Confluence of Traditions." In *Performance of Literature in Historical Perspectives*, edited by David W. Thompson, 107–45. Lanham, MD: University Press of America, 1983.

———. "Rethinking Elocution: The Trope of the Talking Book and Other Figures of Speech." *Text and Performance Quarterly* 20, no. 4 (October 2000): 325–41.

Crannell, Kenneth C. *Voice and Articulation.* 2nd ed. Belmont, CA: Wadsworth, 1991.

Cunningham, David S. *Faithful Persuasion: In Aid of a Rhetoric of Christian Theology.* Notre Dame, IN: University of Notre Dame Press, 1990.

Curry, S. S. *Vocal and Literary Interpretation of the Bible.* New York: Macmillan, 1903.

Drewal, Margaret Thompson. *Yaruba Ritual: Performers, Play, Agency.* Bloomington: Indiana University Press, 1992.

Foley, John Miles. *Immanent Art: From Structure to Meaning in Traditional Oral Epic.* Bloomington: Indiana University Press, 1991.

———. *Oral-Formulaic Theory and Research.* New York: Garland, 1985.

———. *The Theory of Oral Composition: History and Methodology.* Bloomington: Indiana University Press, 1988.

———. "Word-Power, Performance, and Tradition." *Journal of American Folklore* 105 (1995): 275–301.

———. "Words in Tradition, Words in Text: A Response." *Semeia* 65 (1994): 169–80.

Frost, Robert. *Robert Frost Reads His Poetry.* Caedmon Records, 1956.

Gingrich-Philbrook, Craig. "Revenge of the Dead Subject: The Contexts of Michael Bowman's 'Killing Dillinger.'" *Text and Performance Quarterly* 20, no. 4 (October 2000): 375–87.

Gourgey, Hannah, and Edward B. Smith. "'Consensual Hallucination': Cyberspace and the Creation of an Interpretive Community." *Text and Performance Quarterly* 16, no. 3 (July 1996): 233–47.

Gronbeck, Bruce E., Thomas J. Farrell, and Paul A. Soukup. *Media, Consciousness, and Culture.* Newbury Park, CA: Sage, 1991.

Grosz, Elizabeth. *Volatile Bodies: Towards a Corporeal Feminism.* Bloomington: Indiana University Press, 1994.

Hamera, Judith. "The Ambivalent, Knowing Male Body in the Pasadena Dance Theatre." *Text and Performance Quarterly* 14, no. 3 (July 1994): 197–209.

Hill, Randall T. "The Nakwa Powamu Ceremony as Rehearsal: Authority, Ethics and Ritual Appropriation." *Text and Performance Quarterly* 15, no. 4 (October 1995): 301–20.

Jackson, Shannon. "Performance at Hall-House: Museum, Microfiche, and Historiography." In *Exceptional Spaces: Essays in Performance and History*, edited by Della Pollack, 261–93. Chapel Hill: University of North Carolina Press, 1998.

Kacandes, Irene. "Are You in the Text? The 'Literary Performative' in Postmodernist Fiction." *Text and Performance Quarterly* 13, no. 2 (April 1993): 139–53.

Kay, James F. *Christus Praesens: A Reconsideration of Rudolf Bultmann's Christology.* Grand Rapids: Eerdmans, 1994.

Lamar, Nedra Newkirk. *How to Speak the Written Word.* New York: Revell, 1949.

Lares, Jameela. *Milton and the Preaching Arts.* Pittsburgh: Duquesne University Press, 2001.

Lengel, Laura. "Performing In/Outside Islam: Music and Gendered Cultural Politics in the Middle East and North Africa." *Text and Performance Quarterly* 24, no. 3/4 (July/October 2004): 212–32.

Linklater, Kristin. *Freeing the Natural Voice.* New York: Drama Publishers, 1976.

Long, Beverly Whitaker, and Mary Frances Hopkins. *Performing Literature: An Introduction to Oral Interpretation.* Englewood Cliffs, NJ: Prentice-Hall, 1982.

Madison, D. Sonyini. "'That Was My Occupation': Oral Narrative, Performance, and Black Feminist Thought." *Text and Performance Quarterly* 13, no. 3 (July 1993): 213–32.

McLean, Margaret Pendergast. *Good American Speech*. New York: Dutton, 1952.

Noy, Chaim. "Performing Identity: Touristic Narratives of Self-Change." *Text and Performance Quarterly* 24, no. 2 (April 2004): 115–38.

Pelias, Ronald J. *Performance Studies: The Interpretation of Aesthetic Texts*. New York: St. Martin's Press, 1992.

Pineau, Elyse Lamm. "A Mirror of Her Own: Anais Nin's Autobiographical Performance." *Text and Performance Quarterly* 12, no. 2 (April 1992): 97–112.

Powers, Leland, and Carol Hoyt Powers. *Fundamentals of Expression*. Boston: Leland Powers, 1916.

Regan, Catherine A. "Liturgy and Preaching as Oral Context for Medieval English Literature." In *Performance of Literature in Historical Perspectives,* edited by David W. Thompson, 147–75. Lanham, MD: University Press of America, 1983.

Roberts, Robin. "Gendered Media Rivalry: Television and Film on the London Stage." *Quarterly Journal of Speech* 21, no. 2 (April 2001): 77–94.

Rodden, John. "'I am inventing myself all the time': Isabel Allende and the Literary Interview as Public Performance." *Text and Performance Quarterly* 17, no. 1 (January 1997): 1–24.

Rosenberg, Bruce. "The Complexity of Oral Tradition." *Oral Tradition* 2 (1987): 73–90.

Rosenblatt, Louise M. "Act I, Scene 1: Enter the Reader." *Literature in Performance* 1, no. 2 (April 1981): 13.

Russel, Larry. "A Long Way toward Compassion." *Text and Performance Quarterly* 24, no. 3/4 (July/October 2004): 233–54.

Schaper, Eva. "Plato and Aristotle on the Arts: From Prelude to Aesthetics." In *Aesthetics: A Critical Anthology,* edited by George Dickie, Richard Sclafani, and Ronald Roblin, 48–57. 2nd ed. New York: St. Martin's Press, 1989.

Schechner, Richard. *Performance Studies: An Introduction*. London and New York: Routledge, 2002.

———. *Performance Theory*. New York: Routledge, 1988.

Schiappa, Edward, Alan G. Gross, Raymie E. McKerrow, and Robert L. Scott. "Rhetorical Studies as Reduction or Redescription? A Response to Cherwitz and Hikins." *Quarterly Journal of Speech* 88, no. 1 (February 2002): 112–20.

Scuderi, Antonio. "Subverting Religious Authority: Dario Fo and Folk Laughter." *Text and Performance Quarterly* 16, no. 3 (July 1996): 216–32.

Sequeira, Debra L. "Gifts of Tongues and Healing: The Performance of Charismatic Renewal." *Text and Performance Quarterly* 14, no. 2 (April 1994): 126–43.

Shaffer, Tracy Stephenson. "Performing Backpacking: Constructing 'Authenticity' Every Step of the Way." *Text and Performance Quarterly* 24, no. 2 (April 2004): 139–60.

Shugart, Helen A. "Performing Ambiguity: The Passing of Ellen DeGeneres." *Text and Performance Quarterly* 23, no. 1 (January 2003): 1–29.

Sloan, Thomas O., ed. *The Oral Study of Literature*. New York: Random House, 1968.

Soukup, Paul. *Communication and Theology: An Introduction and Review of the Literature.* London: WACC, 1983.

Spitzack, Carole. "The Spectacle of Anorexia Nervosa." *Text and Performance Quarterly* 13, no. 1 (January 1993): 1–20.

Steiner, George. *Language and Silence.* New Haven: Yale University Press, 1998.

———. *Real Presences.* Chicago: University of Chicago Press, 1989.

Story, Cullen I. K. *The Fourth Gospel: Its Purpose, Pattern and Power.* Shippensburg, PA: Ragged Edge, 1997.

Text and Performance Quarterly 22, no. 1 (2002).

Turner, Victor. *The Anthropology of Performance.* New York: PAJ, 1988.

———. *From Ritual to Theatre: The Human Seriousness of Play.* New York: PAJ, 1982.

Turner, Victor, and Edith L. B. Turner. *Image and Pilgrimage in Christian Culture: Anthropological Perspectives.* New York: PAJ, 1982.

Valentine, Kristin Bervig. "Yaqui Easter Ceremonies and the Ethics of Intense Spectatorship." *Text and Performance Quarterly* 22, no. 4 (October 2002): 280–96.

Ward, Richard F. "Speaking of God: Performance Pedagogy in the Theological School." In *Teaching Performance Studies,* edited by Nathan Stuckey and Cynthia Swimmer, 55–67. Carbondale: Southern Illinois University Press, 2002.

Ward, Richard F., with Joanne Buchanan Brown. "A Word Emerging: The Promise of Performance Studies for Homiletics." In *Preaching through Holy Days and Holidays.* Sermons that Work 11. Edited by Roger Alling and David Schlafer, 111–22. Harrisburg, PA: Morehouse-Barlow, 2003.

Warren, John T. "The Body Politic: Performance, Pedagogy, and the Power of Enfleshment." *Text and Performance Quarterly* 19, no. 3 (July 1999): 257–70.

Wilder, Amos N. "Poetry and Religion." In *Christian Faith and the Contemporary Arts,* edited by Finley Eversol. Nashville: Abingdon, 1962.

Index

Aaron, 92, 96
ability, 125
Abraham, 50, 97
absolution, 70
accessibility, 143, 146
accountability, 146, 215
Achtemeier, Elizabeth, 52
Achtemeier, Paul, 103
acknowledgment, 48–49, 83
act/action, 122–23, 134–38
acting/actors, 29, 129, 155, 184, 219
actio, 220
actio divinia, 38, 41–42, 47–48, 53–66, 155–56, 186, 215
activities, 157
Acts, 100, 111, 113–14
Adams, Charles, 199
adequacy, 34
adoration, 118
advertising, 28–29
Aesop, 119
aesthetic, 143, 149
Aesthetics of Music, The (Scruton), 178
affect/affection, 118–19
affliction, 93
Africa/African, 192, 194, 201, 203, 206–7, 209
African American
  culture, 195
  experience, 198
  homiletics, 56

preaching, 16, 191, 193–99
  traditions, 192
aggression, 124, 129
aging, 202
alert/alertness, 184
allegory, 112
alliteration, 191–92
ambiguity, 26, 81n45, 83
amen, 182
America/American
  corporate, 149, 160
  culture, 85, 149, 199
  Midwest, 71
  military, 160
  norms, 32
  North, 70, 74, 104, 121
  Roman Catholics, 70–71
Ammons, A. R., 41
amplification, 190
analysis, 194
Andreason, Nancy C., 160
angels, 127
animated/animation, 121
antebellum, 194
anthem, 173
anthropology, 15, 211
anthropomorphism, 176
anticipation, 44–46, 171, 181–89, 196
antics, 117
anxiety, 84–85, 146
apostle, 22, 107–8, 201, 216

The Apostolic Preaching and Its Developments (Dodd), 171
appetite, 124
application, 55
appropriate, 69
aptitude, 184
Aquinas, Thomas, 56
archaeology, 89
archive/archiving, 173–76, 180–81
argument/argumentation, 54
Aristotle, 54–56, 59
arms, 125
arrangement, 55
arrested performance, 117
arrogant/arrogance, 93
articulate/articulation, 24, 37, 57, 141, 176, 185, 218
artifacts, 213
artifice, 20
arts/artists
  challenges of, 169–70
  discipline, 166
  and emotion, 25
  experience, 160
  folk, 193
  form, 181
  material, 89
  medieval, 193
  and morality, 25
  movement, 124, 129
  and muse, 157
  performance, 167, 211

243